THE LAW AND POLITICS OF THE CONSTITUTION

of the United Kingdom

PETER MADGWICK and DIANA WOODHOUSE

Oxford Brookes University

HARVESTER WHEATSHEAF

New York London Toronto Sydney Tokyo Singapore

First published 1995 by
Harvester Wheatsheaf
Campus 400, Maylands Avenue
Hemel Hempstead
Hertfordshire, HP2 7EZ

A division of
Simon & Schuster International Group

Typeset in 10/12pt Times
by Dorwyn Ltd, Rowlands Castle, Hants.
Printed and bound in Great Britain by
Biddles Ltd, Guildford and King's Lynn

British Library Cataloging in Publication Data

A catalogue record for this book is available from
the British Library

ISBN 0 7450 1346 5 (pbk)

1 2 3 4 5 99 98 97 96 95

CONTENTS

LIST OF CASES

(Page numbers are given in italic. See below for explanation of abbreviations.)

Case references and abbreviations

Because law depends on the record of decisions, references to cases are precise, detailed and follow a standard form. The names of the parties concerned are followed by a citation, i.e. details of the law report in which the case can be found. For example, the case of *Laker Airways* v. *Department of Trade* [1977] QB 643 can be found at page 643 in the 1977 volume of the Queen's Bench Division. Abbreviations are used for all the law reports, the main ones being:

AC	Appeal Cases
Ad. & E.	Admiralty and Ecclesiastical Reports
Admin. LR	Administrative Law Reports
All ER	All England Law Reports
CA	Court of Appeal
Ch.	Chancery Division Reports
CLR	Criminal Law Reports
CMLR	Common Market Law Reports
Co. Rep.	Coke's Reports
DLR	Dominion Law Reports
ECR	European Court Reports
H. of L.	House of Lords
IRLR	Inland Revenue Law Reports
KB	King's Bench Division Reports
PC	Privy Council
QB	Queen's Bench Division Reports
R.	Rex or Regina (King or Queen = the Crown)
St. Tr.	State Trials
TLR	*Times* Law Reports (*The Times* newspaper)
WLR	Weekly Law Reports

LIST OF STATUTES

(Page numbers are given in italic.)

PREFACE

This book is concerned with the place of legal and political rules in the constitutional arrangements of the United Kingdom. Rules are broadly interpreted as laws, procedures and the prescriptions of custom, usage and propriety, and the imperatives derived from historical events and circumstances. These are presented in the framework of an account of the whole system of government. The objective of this approach is to contribute towards an integrated understanding of British government in which the topics of the constitutional lawyer are not fenced off as a no-go area or secret garden for the student of politics. Similarly the constitutional lawyer is invited to take an interest in the total context of government to which the law is relevant.

Inevitably, in a relatively short book this account of the constitution is selective, and skewed towards the law by the rules perspective. This volume does not aim to be a comprehensive textbook on British politics or on constitutional law, but is intended to serve the needs of politics students who are unfamiliar with the law, and offer a useful overview for law students who have not studied politics.

The fulfilment of the modest ambition to be useful for students, gratifying though that would be, raises fundamental questions about the role of law in British government and the nature of the constitution itself. It is necessary to follow with due modesty in the steps of the great prophets of the British constitution, Bagehot,

Dicey and Jennings (whom Ferdinand Mount [1992] calls the 'Three Simplifiers'), and, further, to distil some of the learning of the weighty textbooks on constitutional law which serve the conscientious law student.

The task is daunting, and has required us to make choices about what is or is not within the constitution. In the end the selection is determined by the purposes of this book and is in some degree arbitrary. Thus, some matters which are governed by statute (the Police and Criminal Evidence Act, for example) are treated as within the constitution, whereas many other statutes are not so treated. Equally, some matters which are not much bound by law but arguably ought to be (the civil service and the Bank of England, for example) are treated as within the constitution. Further, some matters combine different kinds of rule, including laws, conventions, customs, the promptings of political prudence and individual motivations (the role of Parliament is an obvious example) in the characteristic confusions of the British constitution.

It is not of course the first time the British constitution has been defined by the purposes and pressures of the writing of a book. We should feel some satisfaction if readers of the book came to understand the elusive complexity of the British constitution and the role of law and politics within it, and to appreciate the nature of legal argument in the constitutional context.

The book is not intended to be 'reformist' in its treatment of the constitution. However, the constitution has been changing rapidly in the last two decades (consider the question of national sovereignty and the constitutional position of the civil service, local government and the media), while a more or less vigorous movement has campaigned for 'liberal' constitutional reform. The book takes notice of actual changes and advocated reforms. The authors are convinced that these matters deserve serious study in a country aspiring to democratic rule and good government in the very late twentieth century.

To assist in the demystification of the law a short glossary of legal terms is provided. There is also, as in most law books, a list of cases cited. This is not comprehensive, but is at least one version of a select list of cases the student of politics ought to know about.

The authors offer their thanks to the series editor, John Benyon, and the publisher's Executive Editor, Clare Grist, for support and advice; to the external reviewer for much helpful comment and criticism on the original plan and the first draft of the text; and to Alison Stanford, the Senior Production Editor, the copy-editor and technical staff for the efficient production of the book.

P. J. M., D. P. W.
Oxford, July 1994

He was always to take a lawyer's careful approach to government, seeking shelter within the Constitution. That the Constitution, like the Judeo-Christian Deity, encompassed ambiguities and mysteries – invitations to men to improvise – was not borne in upon him.

(John Updike, writing of James Buchanan, US President 1857–61, in *Memories of the Ford Administration*, 1992, Penguin: Harmondsworth p. 33)

PART I

THE NATURE OF THE CONSTITUTION

1

INTRODUCTION
The Nature of the Constitution

The nature of constitutions

Does Britain have a constitution?

In countries favoured with a written constitution it is easy to define the constitution. It is 'The Constitution', 'The Basic Law', a legal document (or set of documents) to which all enquirers may refer, and which is interpreted and upheld by the courts, and with which all other laws must comply. Britain has no such codified text and students are faced with a problem of definition or description. But the problem is also an opportunity – to escape from the confines of a single document and include in the notion of the constitution a fuller and more realistic account of the fundamental structure of government.

There is of course a danger that breaking out of the confines of a written constitution destroys any special meaning in the term 'constitution', leaving it to embrace the whole of political activity in what students of politics call the political system. Such a dispersal or degradation of meaning would be regrettable for it is evident that the term 'constitution' carries a special weight of meaning. This is indicated in the use of 'constitutional' and 'unconstitutional' as terms of approval and disapproval – especially the latter.

The implication is that a constitution is a higher or more fundamental statement or structure of rules to which action or behaviour should conform, and a written constitutional document provides a kind of higher law of which other (lower) law must take account.

Constitutional law (proper) is thus at the head of a hierarchy of rules, all of which may be regarded as constitutional (extensively understood):

1. *Constitutional law, defined strictly as judicially enforced law.* The fundamental law, the necessary basis of all other law and of government itself. Obedience to the law is obligatory, so breaches have to be repaired, and dishonour (at the least) may fall upon the transgressor.
2. *Law.* Prescribed codes of conduct, laid down in Britain by 'common law' (law made by judges and established by precedent) and statute law (made by Parliament). Obedience to the law is obligatory and is enforced by the courts with sanctions.
3. *Convention.* Informal constitutional rules established by custom and practice, precedent and prescription, and peculiarly important in the British constitution. Conventions vary in their status from the virtually obligatory to the merely persuasive, disobedience bringing embarrassment but not dishonour.
4. *Custom and practice.* Not much more than guidelines, arising from practice, and not strengthened by precedent or formulated as 'constitutional conventions'.

Such a hierarchy of rules is not confined to the business of governing. It is evident in families and social life, and in commerce and sport. Many groups work by a collection of rules and understandings. For example, a footballer is expected to conform to the law of the land, the rules of the game and the rules of the team as well as the customs of team-mates. The player learns what is obligatory ('it's the rule') and what is merely expected ('as a rule . . .').

Britain is unusual in the thinness and looseness of its rules as they affect constitutional matters: constitutionally Britain lives on the lower slopes of the hierarchy of rules. The British constitution rests on one great and simple (not to say primitive) principle, parliamentary sovereignty; on a rule of law sustained by the common law tradition of judicial precedent; and on an avowed and substantial dependence on convention, custom and practice. This does not mean that Britain has no constitution. Rather, British constitutional arrangements are elusive, uncertain and, when identified, often defective. They do not measure up to the strict definition of a constitution. The study of the British constitution requires both an extensive and a creative approach (that is why writers about the constitution, like Dicey, have been so influential). The objective is to discover the rules by which Britain is governed.

This extended understanding, rather than definition, of constitutions applies to some extent in other countries too. Thus the Constitution of the United States, extensively understood, is more than the revered document devised by the Founding Fathers; and the Constitution of the Fifth French Republic, lovingly drafted by distinguished constitutional experts, is notoriously a poor guide to the relations of President and Prime Minister. So the British constitution, which can claim no such parenthood and certificate of birth, may claim to be more than a poor relation of these great constitutional documents.

Description of a constitution

A constitution is about the rules relating to governing, understood here as influencing or controlling the activities of people in a country for the purposes of the state, or, more briefly, exercising the powers of the state. This formulation leaves aside problems of definition, except to say that the state is most easily recognised historically as the monopoly wielder of force to ensure both external and internal security. A constitution is expected to have permanence and solidity, and so normally establishes institutions or structures to do the controlling (and thus begins to embody the state).

Thus a constitution must make the following basic provisions:

1. empowerment;
2. the establishment of institutions, and the allocation of power between them and between the institutions and the people;
3. the limitation of power by providing for checks and balances to power, and the accountability of power;
4. the confirmation of rights and obligations for both governors and governed.

The origins, authority and functions of constitutions

Constitutions are normally made by assemblies or other bodies empowered to make constitutions; but empowered by whom? The answer frequently is: by the victors in a time of upset, disturbance or revolution. This is plainly true of the Instrument of Government of 1653 (drawn up by Cromwell's Army Council) and the Bill of Rights of 1689. The Instrument of Government vanished even before the restoration of the monarchy in 1660, but the Bill of Rights has survived as the basis of the British constitution, though it began life in a *coup d'état*. The Constitution of the United States is also clearly the product of a revolutionary committee; those of France and Germany are the products of disturbance and collapse. The constitution of the European Community arises unusually from the deliberate choice of members to create some new kind of new union, though significantly the original impulse lay in the constitutional collapse occasioned by war.

Thus constitutions draw their authority initially from history, from the resolution of conflict. They reflect the past, confirming the power of the newly powerful, and the gratitude of the people for pacification and stability. However, they are often grounded in what is recognised as the ultimate power of the people. Legitimacy flows from popular sovereignty, and this may be recognised both in declaratory preambles and in procedures for amendment. Constitutions also look to the future, laying down aspirations and ideals, and reflecting culture and ethos. They are always more than technical and legal documents: they embody history, ideals and authority.

Whatever the historical origin, a constitution aims to legitimate power; it must reach for a special authority, precedent to, or higher than, or more fundamental than, the ordinary acts of the institutions established by the constitution. That authority may be created in several ways:

1. The historical circumstances of the making of the constitution may be remembered and celebrated as the source of authority.
2. The document itself, incorporating the constitution, may assert the authority of its origins – most famously in the Preamble to the Constitution of the United States ('We the people . . .')

3. A special and superior court may be charged by the constitution with its interpretation and application.
4. The amendment of the constitution may be made (by the constitution) subject to special and difficult procedures, for example legislation by substantial majority, or by a referendum.
5. In the end, the authority of constitutions lies in the ultimate power of the people, the 'sovereignty of the people', which alone (now that divine right will not play) confers legitimacy.

In that way the constitution must represent a kind of compact between government and governed. The functions of a constitution arise from that compact.

> In the ultimate analysis, the constitution consists of those rules according to which effective goverment enjoys at least the minimum acquiescence of the vast mass of subjects. (Calvert, 1985, p. 33)

Thus, though a constitution consists of rules, and is to do with legality (in the sense of conformity to those rules, whether laws or not), it is also to do with legitimacy, which implies acceptance or consent. A constitution endorses the contractual nature of all government.

However, a contract has two sides: if consent lies on one side, on the other lies power. In the long term a constitution is maintained by a minimum of consent; but in the short and medium terms (a lifetime for most of us) constitutions are shaped by the needs of the powerful to exercise their power, and by the hard knocks and drives of political practice. A constitution in which consent exceeds power is unlikely to last. Who talks of constitutions talks of power.

Constitutions, law and politics

It is evident from the foregoing that a constitution, broadly understood, includes several kinds of rules, and is defined by politics as well as by law. Where there is a constitutional document, the law, and thus constitutional law, plays the most significant part. This does not mean that it is not informed by politics. The interpretation of a constitution by the judges is part of the political process; moreover, there are political arrangements which relate to the constitution but are outside the legal framework. However, as far as a written constitution is concerned, it is constitutional legality which is paramount. In Britain the absence of a constitutional document means there are no legally defined constitutional boundaries and thus no concept of 'constitutional legality'. In this respect countries like the United States and France are quite different from Britain.

It follows that there is a problem in defining the content of constitutional law. The simple answer, 'the law relating to the constitution', is clearly inadequate as there is no definition of the constitution. A broader definition is that constitutional law is

> the framework in which other laws 'live, move, and have their being': the fountain head from which other laws flow and whence they derive validity; more than that, it describes how a state is constituted and functions. (Pollard and Hughes, 1990, p. 1)

This definition would again seem to be applicable where there is a constitutional document, but to be of little help in the British context. First, while the law-making process, which determines how laws are made and thus their legal validity, is considered to be a matter of constitutional law in Britain, the process does not distinguish between an ordinary law and a law of constitutional significance, which elsewhere is afforded a special status and protection. Thus an ordinary law cannot be tested legally as to its constitutional validity, that is whether it accords with the constitution. It can only be tested in the courts to determine whether it has been processed correctly. Secondly, if, when seeking a description of how the British state is 'constituted and functions', only the law were considered, a false picture would be produced. Significant parts of government and the relationships between the institutions of government are either not covered by law, or the legal arrangements are modified by practice or convention.

Thus lawyers tend to move towards looser or less 'legal' definitions of constitutional law than those that apply in other countries. This may be proof, as Professor Ridley (1988, 1991) has claimed, that in fact Britain has no constitution, or it may be a recognition that whilst Britain has no constitutional document, the way in which the state is ordered and governed is a constitutional matter, and thus a concern of constitutional law.

In pursuit of that understanding, Turpin escapes from the narrowness of law, and the pressure of definition, and 'assembles the different elements of which the constitutional order seems to be composed' (1990, pp. 354). Considering the British constitution, he lists as its elements:

1. 'rules, conventions and practices which describe, regulate or qualify the organization and operation of government';
2. institutions and offices (not just 'bundles of rules' but 'loaded with history and tradition');
3. 'ideas, doctrines or organizing principles which have influenced or inspired the rules and practices of the constitution'.

Such a broad definition, indeed more a description than a definition, is attractive since it fits the diffuse reality of the British case, which is a classic example of an extensive constitution, defined by history and politics as much as by law. It includes hard and soft rules, some enforceable in the courts, and others no more than understandings, tacit and elusive. On the one hand, there are the foundation rules of institutions and constitutional rules derived from statute and common law, the prerogative and European law, all recognised by the courts; on the other, there are the implied or conventional foundation rules of institutions, accepted procedures and the prescriptions of custom and usage. The realm of law is to do with command and obligation, enforced by sanctions; the realm of custom is to do with persuasion and morality, the perception of honour and the preservation of self-esteem (which may include the avoidance of embarrassment).

There are gains and losses in this extension of constitutionality to encompass morality (or what for the moment will be called morality) as well as law. Law controls conduct by being precise and enforceable; morality is neither. Law gives precision and bite to the notion of constitutionality and unconstitutionality. But too much should not be made of the distinction. There is no absolute certainty in law (in fact lawyers thrive on its uncertainty), and most of the utility of law is limited to the kind of conduct which can be defined precisely.

The role of law in the British constitution can be illustrated by comparison with other areas of law. Thus, to take an analogy from motoring law, driving through a red light, if the fact can be established, is clearly an offence; the charge of reckless driving, however, is open to dispute about the meaning of, and evidence for, recklessness; and inconsiderate or discourteous driving lies beyond the law (unless it has serious consequences). Similar analogies can be drawn from sport – for example, compare the rules in cricket for 'leg-before-wicket' with those for intimidating bowling, or the practice of 'sledging' (audibly insulting your opponents), and the catch-all sin of 'bringing the game into disrepute'; and beyond there are questions of fair play, and the ethical code of the gentleman (you must be joking). Similarly, in matters of government, there is a good deal of conduct in government which may reasonably be regarded as lying within the scope of a constitution but is beyond the reach of law (and the concept of fair play is not totally absent).

However, there is a significant difference between sport and government. In sport, as in motoring, there are rules, codes of conduct and referees, umpires and governing bodies with the authority to rule and impose sanctions. When the dissident batsman says to the umpire, 'That was never out!', the umpire may cheerfully reply, 'Just you look at tomorrow's paper then!' In the British constitution there are few rules and no referee. But the constitutional morality sustaining the non-law element of constitutionality is not entirely lacking in precision or force. Understandings, customs and practices may acquire hardness and definition over time, come to be recognised as legitimate or even gain a kind of proto-legality. The constitutional morality which sustains custom and practice is based on the potent maxim 'Do as you would be done by'. This combines prudence with morality and is or was the moral propellant of Britain's Westminster model constitution.

Perhaps 'morality' is not quite the most appropriate term for the force sustaining the non-legal end of the constitutional scale – at least in a British context in which morality is to do with religion, charitable works and kindness to animals. The considerations arising might better be described as political, encompassing the prudential as well as the more strictly moral, and accepting a wholesome rather than a cynical understanding of politics. This accords with the basic test of the scope of a constitution, whether the charge of unconstitutionality can be sustained; and the judgment may be delivered by the opinion of the political classes and the people more often than by a court of law, or a bench of bishops.

The British constitution

It is easier to say what the British constitution is not than to say what it is. *The British constitution is not*:

1. a codified set of rules in a single document, possibly revered and certainly accepted as authorititative;
2. a collection of rules handed down by a high authority having recognised constituent power;
3. whatever the government says, does and 'gets away with'.

However, there is a British constitution in the extensive sense described above, that is, rules, customs and understandings empowering and limiting government. Such a constitution is derived from political history and may perhaps best be described as a political and historical constitution. In rejecting the value of the written/unwritten distinction, Vernon Bogdanor characterises the constitution thus:

> The essence of the British constitution is . . . better expressed in the statement that it is a historic constitution whose dominating characteristic is the sovereignty of parliament, than in the statement that Britain has an unwritten constitution. (1988, p. 55)

The historical nature of the British constitution makes it to some extent a mystery to be understood only by the initiated and eliciting a loyalty based on myth rather than substance. Thus Magna Carta or parliamentary sovereignty or the rule of law become slogans in a sentimental constitutional nationalism, rather than statements or concepts of serious constitutional significance. But if the constitution is best appreciated in an historical perspective, its components may still be discovered in laws and in authoritative works and other documents. Further, the constitution relies on the courts accepting and upholding the principle of parliamentary sovereignty, although whether they accept it as a political fact or a legal rule is subject to debate (see Chapter 2).

The sources of the constitution include the following:

1. statute law (made by Parliament);
2. common law (made by judges working by precedent but 'inventing' precedents where necessary in order to accommodate political reality and legal principle);

3. the treaties and laws of the European Community and the judgments of the European Court of Justice;
4. the laws and customs of Parliament (mainly parliamentary procedure) as set out in Erskine May's *Parliamentary Practice* (1988), the authoritative rule-book of Parliament;
5. ministerial statements, the conclusions of commissions of inquiry and other official statements carrying or purporting to carry authority;
6. 'authoritative works' by academics and others, Bagehot (1867/1963) and Dicey (1885/1959) having set a high standard of public influence.

It is evident that a constitution made up in this way is likely to resemble the camel – a horse designed by a committee – but without the camel's fitness for purpose and its visual appeal. Even before going into detail, and drawing on observation of its origins and development, the fundamental defects of the British constitution are evident:

1. uncertainty about its scope and imprecision about its provisions (hence uncertainty about what is within and in conformity with the constitution);
2. the absence of a higher authority, except the government of the day (and perhaps the people as voters and the occasional intervention of the courts), and in consequence some doubt, to say the least, about the enforceability of constitutional rules;
3. inadequacy of the basic institutional provision for the limitation and accountability of power;
4. inadequate procedures for amendment, no procedure for formal amendment, and no bar to informal modification by practice;
5. no basis for and no encouragement to the development of a vigorous element in the public philosophy or political culture (apart from a now diminishing respect for ancient institutions, Parliament and the monarchy).

Against this catalogue of constitutional defects there can be set two substantial arguments.

1. Under the fundamental principle and political fact of parliamentary sovereignty, power resides effectively in the House

of Commons; and, since the House is subject to periodic election by universal suffrage, power rests ultimately with the people. No doubt the government of the day has many means at its disposal to enlarge and extend its power, but in the end that power may be diminished or ended by popular vote.

2. The British historical constitution, for all its faults, is free of the litigiousness and domination by lawyers which is a normal consequence of a proper, written constitution, backed by a constitutional court. But a price has to be paid for this advantage.

Historical development of the constitution

The fundamental character of the constitution was laid down in the struggles between Parliament and the monarchy in the seventeenth century. In that century of revolution, counter-revolution, royal tyranny, Cromwellian dictatorship and finally aristocratic *coup d'état*, Parliament gained a substantial and irreducible share in power. By the end of the century government lay in the hands of the 'Crown-in-Parliament'; and though the balance of power within that constitutional construction was to vary, the essential principle holds.

The constitutional conflicts of the seventeenth century produced a basis for the sharing of the power of the Crown with Parliament, but they did not produce a constitution, except for Cromwell's short-lived Instrument of Government of 1653. However, the political struggle itself laid down certain constitutional 'markers' – not laws, nor principles, but happenings of historical resonance and political significance.

One, certainly, was the capture, trial and execution of King Charles I (1649), a rupture in the body politic not to be fully repaired by the restoration of the monarchy in 1660. The second was the driving of James II into exile in 1688, and his replacement, at the invitation of a revolutionary assembly, by William and Mary. The succession to the throne was further regulated in the Act of Settlement of 1701. Even without any other provision for the limitation of royal power, these brutal intrusions into divine right and hereditary powers amounted to radical constitution-making.

Moreover, the philosopher John Locke was on hand (actually travelling in the same ship as Mary, on her way to join William) to strengthen the foundation of the constitutional revolution by laying down a theory of government as a contract with the governed. The American colonists and the French revolutionaries were to make more of this a century later, but the English Whigs had at least an ethos if not a complete text for their new constitution.

Thus events and a new political doctrine contributed to a fundamental shift in the balance of power between Parliament and Crown. At the same time statutes and judgments in the courts shaped in more detail the limits of royal power. For example, in the *Case of Proclamations* (1611) two Chief Justices had resolved that 'the King hath no prerogative but that which the law of the land allows him'; and 'the King by his proclamation cannot create an offence which was not an offence before'; and further, 'the law of England is divided into three parts, common law, statute law, and custom; but the King's proclamation is none of them'. Subsequently the courts joined with Parliament in limiting the power of the Crown by recognising the supremacy of Acts of Parliament (statute law) over the common law.

The Bill of Rights of 1689 is justly celebrated as the foundation of the modern constitution. Its significance lies in its confirmation of the power of Parliament by regulating the succession; declaring unlawful the suspension of or dispensing with the law, as practised under James II, as well as the keeping of a standing army in peacetime and the raising of taxes without consent of Parliament. A few years later the Triennial Act 1694 provided for election of a new Parliament after no more than three years (the King's need for money to fight overseas wars already ensured that Parliaments met every year). The Act of Settlement 1701 included provisions 'for better securing the rights and liberties of the subject'. By the Act of Union 1707 England and Scotland, united for a century in the person of the monarch, were united under a single parliament of Great Britain. Thus the settlement which followed the 'Glorious Revolution' became the foundation of a British constitution.

All of this extraordinary political activity contributed to the wresting of arbitrary power from the Crown, the strengthening of Parliament's claim to a share in governing power, and within limits the enlargement of the liberties of 'the people'. However, most of this constitutional settlement was (of course) a seventeenth-century solution to seventeenth-century problems. The balance of power was modified, but there was no provision for its limitation, for checking or accountability, and 'the people' on whose behalf the revolution was made were inevitably a tiny minority.

Even so the achievements of these aristocratic revolutionaries was impressive. They unwittingly opened the way for the emergence over the next two centuries of parliamentary government. They resolved some contemporary grievances in a radical way, but they did not progress very far in the construction of what we should understand as a modern constitution. We could hardly expect that they would; but in our gratitude we should not forget that they were not in the business of making a democratic constitution.

The 'Glorious Revolution' did not, then, invent modern parliamentary government, but rather established a mixed or balanced structure of the 'Crown-in-Parliament'. The place of Parliament in the system was now confirmed and continuous. By the mid-eighteenth century,

> no government could survive which did not possess three pillars: the support of the king, ability to manage a government party by all the arts of patronage and flattery, and – not least important – the power to set forth a case in parliament which would at best arouse support because it was patriotic and moderate, and would at worst neutralize that latent opposition spirit upon which factious men out of place sought to play. (Watson, 1960, p. 66)

The three-pillared structure does not imply that either the monarch or Parliament actually governed in a hands-on, day-to-day sense. That was not practicable for a numerous and ill-organised assembly or for kings concerned for kingship but without the taste or capacity for serious and continuing political work. Government lay in the hands of the managers of kings and parliaments; and the requirements of continuous management forced the development of a more coherent 'management team' led by a chairman known by 1740, somewhat slightingly, as a 'prime minister'.

Thus governed, Britain survived the eighteenth century, engaging with some success in wars and conquest around the world, but losing the American colonies to rebels who regarded British government as an arbitrary tyranny. By the beginning of the nineteenth century Britain faced revolutionary ideas, many of them British in origin, about democracy and the nature of government, and serious financial, structural and ideological challenges to the effectiveness of government in sustaining long and expensive wars and dealing with industrialisation and urbanisation.

The old constitutional balance was transformed in the course of the nineteenth century.

1. A series of Parliamentary Reform Acts (1832, 1867, 1884–5) extended the vote to about one-fifth of adult males in 1833 and three-fifths by the end of the century, and redrew constituencies in a more equitable way. After 1832 it was no longer possible for the Crown with or without the government of the day to gain a parliamentary majority by bribery and corruption. Thus, imperceptibly at first, power slipped from the Crown and the government towards the electorate, and the management of the voters by political means replaced the long purse of the Treasury Patronage Secretary who had looked after the buying of seats and votes.
2. Political parties developed to facilitate the task of political management in both Parliament and country. Compared with the Westminster factions of the eighteenth century, the new political parties were coherent and disciplined, based loosely on principles, a programme and established leaders, and tightly organised both in Parliament and in the country.
3. The government ceased to be simply a collection of gentlemen sitting in Cabinet or addressing Parliament. Government was increasingly based on departments of state, staffed by civil servants and headed by ministers (see Chapter 8). The business of government was increasingly massive, complex in structure and bureaucratic. The 'high politics' of foreign policy and the government of empire was surrounded and invaded by the 'low politics' of local administration, drains, water supply, roads and railways.

Thus by the end of the century party and bureaucracy had transformed the constitutional structure. 'The government' had become a major political force in its own right, even without a defined constitutional position. Its power rested on the support of Parliament and the majority party. Those two pillars of the eighteenth-century constitution remained. The third, the monarchy, still stood, but was, in Bagehot's (1963, p. 61) phrase, more 'dignified' than 'efficient'; in architectural terms the monarchy was no longer load-bearing and essential to the stability of the whole structure. In its place loomed the massive buttress of 'the people', including both the electorate and the major organs of opinion, now known as the media.

The twentieth-century constitution is largely the Victorian constitution in an expanded form. By the ruthless and effective management of party and popular opinion the government was able for long periods to concentrate all executive and legislative power in its own hands, absorbing much of what was implied by the 'Crown-in-Parliament'. At the same time the unitary nature of the constitutional structure was strengthened by the defection of the rebellious Irish and the incorporation of loyalist Northern Ireland. Scotland and Wales remained firmly if not happily within the Union, and local government, though rapidly expanding, was not allowed to develop beyond its subject status.

Radical constitutional change finally arrived from without. The accession of the United Kingdom to the European Community, confirmed in 1975 and followed by the Single European Act 1986, brought about a fundamental shift of power away from 'the government' to parallel institutions and arenas which lay beyond its capabilities of political management and control. In addition, membership of the European Community, and now European Union, has provided the judges with a constitutional authority previously denied them and encouraged them to adopt a constitutional perspective more in line with the rest of Europe, which views Britain's constitutional arrangements as legally unsupportable. The British constitution has acquired an alien pillar, designed for a different structure, and radically affecting the way it works.

The sustaining theory of the constitution

Government needs the consent of the governed, and that consent has to include a general acceptance of the constitutional framework from which the government draws its power. The constitution must be understood and approved as fair, responsive, democratic. In Britain the historic institutions of Parliament and the Crown are deeply embedded in the culture, and they still elicit a substantial loyalty (though recently with some reservation in detail). The constitution itself has not been salient in political dispute (again until recently) and has been usually regarded with some patriotic complacency as a marvel of English constitutional sagacity.

Popular perceptions have been underpinned by the widespread acceptance among the political élite of a sustaining theory of the constitution. This draws on the 'Glorious Revolution' of 1688 (commemorated 'in tablets and obelisks . . . in English parks and market-places' according to the historian G. N. Clark [1934, p. 142]), the Whig tradition of the eighteenth century and the notion of a 'balanced constitution' as expounded by Blackstone in the 1760s. The radical changes of the nineteenth century, including the extension of the franchise, seemed to upset the balance, but were incorporated in the liberal constitution described by Dicey. His great work, *The Law of the Constitution*, was first published in 1885, and the tenth edition (1959) is still in print and still read today.

Dicey has been much criticised, not least by Sir Ivor Jennings, who published *The Law and the Constitution* in 1933 (see Jennings, 1959). These two, together with Walter Bagehot, journalist and editor of *The Economist* and author of *The English Constitution* (1867, see Bagehot, 1963), are the three founding fathers of the modern theory of the British constitution. We owe much of our understanding of the constitution to their exposition, though they (like all other writers on the constitution) misperceived, over-simplified, and were unduly influenced by their own political anxieties and the concerns of the times. Even so, we are all in their debt, and an exposition of the theory of the contemporary constitution is necessarily based on their efforts to impose a pattern on a constitution which was never invented or designed but just grew, so that political facts became constitutional rules.

2

THE THEORY OF THE CONSTITUTION
Law and Politics

The institutions and principles of the British constitution

The British constitution incorporates the following institutional arrangements:

1. A partial separation of powers such that whilst the legislature and executive are 'fused', the judiciary is more or less separate and independent, in the sense that judicial appointments are not overtly political.
2. A constitutional monarchy, whose role is dignified rather than efficient, but in which legal, but not actual, power for much of the business of government still resides. Hence the business of government is still conducted in the name of the monarch, and 'the Crown' signifies governing or executive power, and 'the government'.
3. A bicameral Parliament with the lower House (Commons) composed by some form of popular election and the upper House (Lords) hereditary and now in part appointed.
4. Parliamentary government, in the sense that the government is responsible to the House of Commons and bound by that responsibility.

5. A unitary and centralised state with power residing in the London government (the geography is not without constitutional significance).
6. Limited government, in the specific sense of dependence on, and responsibility to, Parliament, and in a more elusive sense of a rule of law and an historic resistance to arbitrary government.

These are all important characteristics of the British constitution. However, for Dicey (1959), expounding Britain's constitutional arrangements in the nineteenth century, there were three key elements in the British constitution which determined the way in which it worked:

1. parliamentary sovereignty;
2. the rule of law;
3. conventions of the constitution.

Dicey's constitutional theory was coherent and easily understandable, if somewhat naïve and idealised. It was also reassuring, suggesting balance, harmony and above all stability. At a time of apparent constitutional instability, notably the threat of universal suffrage, Dicey sought to demonstrate that even the most radical government would be constrained by the supremacy of Parliament and the rule of law. Dicey's constitutional perceptions were affected by his own political concerns (not an unfamiliar condition), but over a century later his work still offers a useful starting-point for an understanding of the contemporary constitution.

Parliamentary sovereignty

The term 'parliamentary sovereignty' has both political and legal connotations. Politically the electorate is ultimately sovereign but between elections this sovereignty is held 'on trust' by Parliament. Sovereignty in this context therefore resides only with the elected chamber, the House of Commons. Dicey was concerned to distinguish such political sovereignty from legal sovereignty, which encompasses the 'triumvirate' of Parliament (Queen, Lords and Commons), usually referred to as the 'Crown-in-Parliament'. The threefold nature of legal sovereignty is demonstrated by the words of enactment at the beginning of a statute:

> Be it enacted by the Queen's most Excellent Majesty, by and with the advice and consent of the Lords Spiritual and Temporal, and Commons, in this present Parliament assembled, and by the authority of the same . . .

Parliamentary sovereignty can justifiably be called, in Dicey's words, the 'very keystone' of the British constitution, for without it the constitution would collapse.

The nature of parliamentary sovereignty

The legislative sovereignty of Parliament came about during the seventeenth century by a growing alliance between Parliament and the judges to curb the powers of the King to rule by prerogative power. This was confirmed by the Revolution of 1688. The Revolution brought about a breach in legal continuity (court business was suspended, the throne was vacant, and new judges were appointed). This enabled or impelled the judges to recognise a change in the legal and constitutional order, which confirmed the sovereignty of Parliament.

Thus parliamentary sovereignty can be seen as 'at once historical reality, theory of the constitution, and a fundamental principle of the common law' (Turpin, 1990, p. 24). This description demonstrates the relationship between the political situation and judicial attitudes, and is born out by a number of more recent examples (Pakistan, Uganda, Rhodesia), where judges 'seem to have proceeded on the assumption that they have to accept a successful revolution as a law-constitutive fact if they remain in office' (de Smith and Brazier 1989, p. 68).

Dicey laid down a definition of parliamentary sovereignty which derived authority from both his magisterial prose and his eminence in the field of constitutional law:

> The principle of Parliamentary sovereignty means neither more nor less than this, namely, that Parliament thus defined has, under the English constitution, the right to make or unmake any law whatever; and, further, that no person or body is recognised by the law of England as having a right to override or set aside the legislation of Parliament. (Dicey, 1959, p. 39)

Thus Parliament is the supreme law-making body and statute law overrides the common law, including the prerogative. Moreover, Parliament's legislative power is unlimited and the laws that it passes cannot be questioned by the courts. The unreviewable nature of legislation was emphasised in *Cheney* v. *Conn* [1968] 1 All ER 779;

> What statute itself enacts cannot be unlawful, because what the statute says and provides is itself the law, and the highest form of law that is known in this country. It is the law that prevails over every other form of law, and it is not for the court to say that a parliamentary enactment, the highest law in this country, is illegal.

Parliamentary sovereignty thus limits the jurisdiction of the courts and determines the relationship between the legislature and the judges. Judges are confined to interpreting and upholding Acts of Parliament. This position is confirmed by the absence of any constitutional document which in other countries provides the courts with the grounds to strike down legislation as unconstitutional. However, this historic principle of the British constitution is now diminished, even undermined, by membership of the European Union. This has conferred on the courts the authority to overrule national law if it conflicts with Community legislation; the implications of this radical change are discussed below.

Legislation cannot be entrenched

The role of the courts in relation to legislation is further reduced by the absence in Britain of any procedural protection or 'entrenchment' of legislation of a constitutional nature. Such entrenchment is inadmissible under the traditional theory of parliamentary sovereignty, for, it is argued, entrenchment would limit the freedom of action, and therefore the omnicompetence, of Parliament. Thus no one Parliament can bind itself or future Parliaments to the retention of a particular statute and, as a result, there is no difference in Britain between constitutional laws and ordinary laws. Any law can be repealed or amended at any time through the ordinary parliamentary procedures. This position is used as a practical argument against the enactment in Britain of a written constitution or a Bill of Rights in Britain (establishing protected or guaranteed civil rights).

The belief that Parliament cannot bind itself has been supported by the courts, who, in the case of conflict between two Acts of

Parliament, will recognise the later act as valid law, holding the earlier statute to have been repealed by implication (implied repeal). This doctrine of implied repeal was confirmed in the case of *Ellen Street Estates Limited* v. *Minister of Health* [1934] 1 KB 590. The case revolved around the Acquisition of Land (Assessment of Compensation) Act 1919 which seemed to suggest that any future legislation had to be consistent with the Act. A judge in the Court of Appeal set out the constitutional position:

> The Legislature cannot, according to our constitution, bind itself as to the form of subsequent legislation, and it is impossible for Parliament to enact that in a subsequent statute dealing with the same subject matter there can be no implied repeal.

The validity of legislation cannot be questioned

Thus the courts will not pronounce on the constitutionality of legislation nor will they apply legislation which seeks to prevent the operation of implied repeal. In addition, they will not look behind the formal words of enactment to determine whether a Bill has passed through the necessary procedures and is therefore valid. This position was confirmed in the *Pickin* and *Manuel* cases.

The *Pickin* case

In *British Railways Board* v. *Pickin* [1974] AC 765 the House of Lords was asked to rule that a private act was invalid because it had not complied with the Standing Orders of each House. These required that notice should be given to persons likely to be affected by a private Act. Pickin maintained that in the case of the British Railways Act 1968 this notice had not been given but that Parliament had been misled into thinking it had. None of the judges in the House of Lords was prepared to look behind the Act to the way in which it had been passed. Moreover, they gave strong support to the view that an Act of Parliament, whether private or public, cannot be invalid: 'When an enactment is passed there is finality unless and until it is amended or repealed by Parliament.'

The *Manuel* case

In *Manuel* v. *Attorney-General* [1983] Ch. 77 the Court of Appeal refused to hold the Canada Act of 1982 to be *ultra vires*. The case raised the question of whether Parliament could bind itself as to the form or procedure to be followed, and, if it could do so, whether the court would look behind the Act to determine whether the form had been followed. It also raised questions concerning the status of conventions (see below). Manuel sought to challenge the legality of the Act on the basis that it was inconsistent with the Statute of Westminster of 1931, section 4 of which provides:

> No Act of Parliament of the United Kingdom passed after the commencement of this Act shall extend, or be deemed to extend, to a Dominion unless it expressly declared in that Act that that Dominion has requested and consented to the enactment thereof.

The Canada Act, which amended the Canadian Constitution, had been passed at the request of both Houses of the Canadian Parliament and with the consent of nine out of ten of the provinces. Manuel argued that to comply with the Statute of Westminster the consent was required of all the provinces and the Indian peoples. Both the Divisional Court and the Court of Appeal rejected Manuel's arguments.

The Court of Appeal considered that as the Act contained the declaration required by section 4, it was unnecessary to decide whether the absence of a declaration would have affected its validity. Thus a classic problem about parliamentary sovereignty (can a Parliament bind its successor?) was ducked. Some judicial comments (dicta) indicated support for the view that section 4 was binding; judges are often most expansive in interpretation or the development of legal theory when their ruminations are deemed not to affect the case before them. In the event the case was decided on the strict interpretation of section 4 of the Statute of Westminster, which the court said required only that an Act 'expressly declared . . . that that Dominion had requested, and consented to, the enactment thereof'. The Act did so declare, and it was not for the court to look behind the Act to see what consent had actually been obtained.

Thus the *Manuel* case supported *Pickin*. Providing an Act had passed through both Houses and received the Royal Assent, and was correct on its face – in this case giving the required declaration – the courts would not look further to see if procedures or conditions had been complied with; this was for Parliament to determine.

The *Manuel* case also gave rise to broader comments from the judges on the sovereignty of Parliament and whether the English courts would recognise legislation purporting to apply to a territory to which independence had previously been granted and to which, it could be argued, sovereignty had been transferred. In the Divisional Court Megarry stated:

> I have grave doubts about the theory of the transfer of sovereignty as affecting the competence of Parliament. In my view, it is

> a fundamental of the English constitution that Parliament is supreme. As a matter of law the courts of England recognise Parliament as being omnipotent in all save the power to destroy its own omnipotence. Under the authority of Parliament the courts of a territory may be released from their legal duty to obey Parliament, but that does not trench on the acceptance by the English courts of all Parliament does. Nor must validity in law be confused with practical enforceability.

Thus the judges will uphold legislation enacted by the British Parliament, regardless of its legal status in the country to which it purports to apply. In pursuit of this principle Sir Ivor Jennings (1959, p. 70) had argued that Parliament could make it an offence in English law for Frenchmen to smoke in the streets of Paris. Of course, the law could not be enforced, but the concern here is with the theory of the constitution; in practice even a French law of that kind might prove unenforceable!

The judges will also uphold legislation which is contrary to international agreements and treaties to which Britain is a signatory. Parliamentary sovereignty makes it inevitable that the 'dualist' approach to law operates. Thus international law and national law are seen as quite separate, and international treaties cannot be applied by the courts unless they have been enacted into national law by Parliament. This contrasts with the 'monist' approach taken by countries such as Germany and the Netherlands which consider national and international law to be part of the same legal structure, and thus applicable by the national courts.

However, the British courts will endeavour to interpret national legislation to comply with external obligations on the ground that Parliament would not intend to contravene such agreements. Further, they have no problem giving European Community law the required priority over national law because this obligation has been given legal effect through the European Communities Act 1972.

The 'new' view of parliamentary sovereignty

Whilst the traditional doctrine of parliamentary sovereignty holds that Parliament cannot bind itself, a so-called 'new' view contests this position. This alternative formulation of parliamentary sovereignty recognises that Parliament cannot bind itself as to the substance of legislation. However, it is argued that Parliament can bind itself procedurally, thereby providing a degree of protection to certain legislation (for example, a Bill of Rights). The new view rests on a different interpretation of the status of the rule of judicial obedience, which, it suggests, can be changed by Parliament.

For the traditionalists, the acceptance by the courts of statutory limitations as to the form of subsequent legislation would contravene the rule that requires them to recognise that 'whatever the Queen-in-Parliament enacts is law'. This is taken to mean 'whatever the Queen-in-Parliament enacted last is law', thereby upholding the principle of continuing sovereignty upon which no limits can be placed. According to Professor Wade:

> The rule of judicial obedience is in one sense a rule of common law, but in another sense – which applies to no other rule of common law – it is the ultimate *political* fact upon which the whole system of legislation hangs. (1955, p. 172)

Thus Wade argues that the only way in which the rule can be changed is by a new political fact – indeed, a revolution. This does not necessarily mean a repeat of 1688 (the revolution which brought the rule into existence). A break in 'legal continuity' through the shift of 'sovereign legislative power' would be sufficient (Wade, 1980, p. 37). The requirement is for the judiciary to recognise the existence of a new rule brought about because of changed political circumstances.

However, the alternative or 'new' view believes the rule of judicial obedience to be a legal rule with its roots in the common law, hence capable of being superseded by statute. Thus there is nothing to prevent Parliament passing legislation which stipulates the 'manner and form' necessary for a particular statute to be passed, amended or repealed; for instance, by requiring the consent of the people (by a referendum) or, say, a two-thirds majority in both Houses of Parliament, perhaps meeting together. Proponents of the 'new' view argue that in effect what Parliament is doing is 'redefining' itself for a particular purpose, and the courts will recognise this redefinition.

Indeed, supporters of this view suggest that the passing of the Parliament Acts of 1911 and 1949 already constitute such a redefinition. These Acts limit the power of the House of Lords to one of delay only, allowing the House of Commons to bypass the

Lords and send a Bill directly for the Royal Assent if the Lords fail to pass it (see Chapter 9). The procedure has been used four times altogether.

It is not universally agreed that the Parliament Acts constitute a redefinition of Parliament. The Acts may be seen rather as to do with internal procedures which make it easier for Parliament to function as a legislature; and the 1949 Act, which was itself approved using the bypass procedure, may be regarded as a form of delegated legislation. In any case, it is argued, even if the Acts can be seen as redefining Parliament, they increase Parliament's power to legislate rather than limiting it, and thus do not provide a model for self-limitation by Parliament.

The Northern Ireland Constitutional Act 1973 may provide a better example of a legislative limitation through 'redefinition'. The Constitutional Act provides that Northern Ireland shall not cease to be part of the United Kingdom without the consent of the people of Northern Ireland expressed in a poll. However, the Act itself is not procedurally protected and could be repealed in the normal way. This is in fact what happened to its predecessor, the Ireland Act 1949, which made the consent of the Northern Ireland Parliament necessary in the same situation. Thus if Parliament wished to pass legislation which removed Northern Ireland from the United Kingdom, it could simply repeal the Northern Ireland Constitutional Act and with it the requirement for the consent of the people.

There are Commonwealth cases which support the 'new' view, and Parliaments in Australia, South Africa and Ceylon have been held to be limited by manner and form. However, in all the cases the Parliaments concerned had been created by the same Act that provided the limitation. This is a different situation to that existing in Britain, and there are no British examples to complement the Commonwealth ones. Rather the courts seem committed to the doctrine of implied repeal; at least they were until Britain joined the European Community.

Membership of the European Community

Britain's membership of the European Community has required some adjustment to the traditional view of parliamentary sovereignty and may be seen as offering significant support to the 'new view'.

The European Communities Act 1972, section 2 (1) states:

> All such rights, powers, liabilities, obligations and restrictions from time to time created or arising by or under the Treaties, and all such remedies and procedures from time to time provided for by or under the Treaties as in accordance with the Treaties, are without further enactment to be given legal effect or used in the United Kingdom shall be recognised as available in law, and be enforced, allowed and followed accordingly: and the expression 'enforceable Community right' and similar expressions shall be read as referring to one to which this subsection applies.

Thus the courts are required to give effect to European Community law. Moreover, section 2 (4) requires that any legislation passed by the Westminster Parliament 'shall be construed and have effect subject to the foregoing provisions of this section'. This has been seen as an attempt to 'entrench' section 2 (1) above, by providing that subsequent national legislation cannot override EC law. In areas of Community competence, EC law is therefore supreme, and it follows that the doctrine of implied repeal would not operate if a conflict arose between EC law and subsequent national legislation. This view has been upheld by the courts. They are usually able to achieve compatibility through interpretation; wherever possible interpreting a British statute in such a way that it accords with Community law. However, in *Macarthys Ltd* v. *Smith* [1981] QB 199, a case concerning equal pay, Lord Denning indicated the position if such interpretation proved impossible:

> It must be made plain – that the provisions of Article 119 of the EEC Treaty [these concerned equal pay] take priority over anything in our English statute on equal pay which is inconsistent with Article 119. That priority is given by our own law. It is given by the European Communities Act 1972 itself. Community law is now part of our law: and, whenever there is any inconsistency, Community law has priority. It is not supplanting English law. It is part of our law which overrides any other part that is inconsistent with it.

Lord Denning was careful not to suggest an undermining of parliamentary sovereignty, noting that priority was only given to EC law because Parliament wished this to be so; thus the courts continued to carry out the intentions of Parliament. More recently, in *Pick-*

stone v. *Freemans plc* [1989] AC 66, the House of Lords took the unprecedented step of referring to *Hansard* (the Parliamentary Report) to determine what these intentions were. The case again concerned equal pay, this time the Equal Pay (Amendment) Regulations 1983, which were introduced by the government to bring national law in line with Community law and approved by Parliament on that basis. The court found the Regulations as they stood to be inconsistent with Community law. However, having consulted *Hansard* and examined the terms in which the minister had presented the draft, they adopted a 'purposive construction' (looking at intention not words), and implied additional words in the text to ensure the compliance with Community law which, they concluded, was the intention of Parliament.

This use of a 'purposive' rather than a 'literal' construction by the House of Lords is an indication that senior judges are adopting the methods of their continental counterparts and the European Court of Justice. European judges are used to interpeting according to the 'spirit' of legislation rather than confining themselves to a strict interpretation of the actual words. This is particularly evident with the European Court of Justice, which has moved to fill the gaps in the treaties according to what it believes the purpose of the treaties to be. British judges may be increasingly attracted by a legal tradition which is not limited by parliamentary sovereignty and confers substantial powers on (or attributes substantial powers to) the courts.

The *Factortame* case (1990–1) proved more difficult to accommodate with parliamentary sovereignty.

The *Factortame* case

R. v. *Secretary of State for Transport, ex parte Factortame Ltd* [1990] 2 AC 85 and (No. 2) [1991] 1 AC 603. A group of Spanish fishermen claimed that the Merchant Shipping Act 1988 (and the regulations made under it) deprived them of rights under Community Law because it imposed nationality restrictions. The case was referred to the European Court of Justice and a ruling was also sought on whether the House of Lords had authority under Community Law to grant an interim injunction (temporary stop) restraining the enforcement of the Act. Lord Bridge was certain that under national law the courts had no such authority, for the effect of the interim relief would be to confer rights on the fishermen 'directly contrary to Parliament's sovereign will'. (The position in relation to injunctions against the Crown is discussed in Chapter 5.)

The European Court ruled that where the only obstacle to the granting of interim relief was a rule of national law, then that national rule should be set aside by the national court. Thus the House of Lords 'disapplied' the relevant sections of the Merchant Shipping Act. However, Lord Bridge refuted suggestions that this was a 'novel and dangerous invasion by a Community institution of the sovereignty of the United Kingdom'. He continued:

> Whatever limitation of its sovereignty Parliament accepted when it enacted the European Communities Act 1972 was entirely voluntary. Under the terms of the 1972 Act it has always been clear that it was the duty of a United Kingdom court, when delivering final judgment, to override any rule of national law found to be in conflict with any directly enforceable rule of Community law.

This would seem to be a recognition that parliamentary sovereignty is limited by membership of the European Community, albeit limited only because Parliament wishes it. The effect of the limitation is that the doctrine of implied repeal no longer operates, and the courts can review the legality, in terms of compatibility, of national legislation which falls within the legal competence of the Community. In *Factortame* the House of Lords sought a ruling from the European Court of Justice as to its authority under Community Law to 'disapply' part of an Act of Parliament.

In a subsequent case, brought by the Equal Opportunities Commission (*R.* v. *Secretary of State for Employment, ex parte Equal Opportunities Commission*, [1994] 2 WLR 409) the House of Lords moved confidently on its own to declare that aspects of the Employment Protection (Consolidation) Act 1978 were incompatible with European Community law and thus should not stand. The Act differentiated between full-time and part-time workers, making it more difficult for the latter to acquire rights to redundancy payments and compensation for unfair dismissal. The Equal Opportunities Commission claimed that, as most part-time workers were women, the act was discriminatory and thus contrary to EC legislation, a claim upheld by the House of Lords.

The decision was viewed by *The Times* as evidence that 'Britain may now have, for the first time in history, a constitutional court', for 'in effect, [the House of Lords] struck down as 'unconstitutional' an Act of Parliament' (*The Times*, 5 March 1994). However, there are indications from judges that if Parliament should expressly state its intent to legislate contrary to EC law, the courts would uphold this legislation, despite the European Communities Act.

Moreover, there is also recognition that if Parliament should choose to repeal the European Communities Act, then, according to the legal doctrine of parliamentary sovereignty, it is free to do so. It is not entrenched, and thus can be repealed as easily as any other law. The restraining factors are political and economic not constitutional; and these are likely to be sufficient to prevent repeal.

The attitude of the judges to the European Communities Act shows how the courts could apply a Bill of Rights as a source and standard of interpretation. The question remains whether Parliament can effectively entrench legislation so as to limit its future competence. The support of some senior judges for a Bill of Rights suggests that they would also be prepared to recognise procedural restraints within the Bill itself which protect it from repeal or amendment. Such a recognition of entrenched legislation would clearly alter the nature of parliamentary sovereignty, increasing the role of the judges and diminishing the legislative omnicompetence of Parliament. Thus the historic alliance of the courts and Parliament against royal tyranny would be transformed as the courts took up more vigorously a role of resistance to an over-mighty Parliament.

The rule of law

The second pillar of the constitution, as far as Dicey was concerned, was the rule of law, which really meant the rule of common (or judge-made) law. Dicey saw the common law embodying principles and values which protect important liberties and impose standards of fairness and justice, making a written constitution unnecessary; in a 'fundamental sense . . . Britain has a common law constitution' (Allan, 1993, p. 4). The rule of law also enables the judges to claim a constitutional role in upholding 'constitutional' values and in reviewing the legality of executive action.

Dicey's formulation of the rule of law contained three elements which related to the exercise of executive power. First, executive power should never be exercised in an arbitrary manner. Dicey distrusted the granting of wide discretionary powers to ministers, for he feared that these might be used arbitrarily (and he distrusted the new social welfare legislation which conferred such powers on the government).

Secondly, Dicey's rule of law meant equality before the law, in the sense that those who wielded public power should be subject to the 'regular' or ordinary law in the same way as private individuals. Dicey's concern here was to distinguish the situation in Britain from that in France, where a separate system of administrative courts had developed to police the exercise of public power by government officials. Dicey seems to have believed mistakenly that this gave officials special legal privileges, thus reducing the extent to which they were subject to the law.

Thirdly, for Dicey the rule of law meant that Britain did not need a constitutional document to protect rights or impose limitations upon the exercise of powers. The courts provided the necessary protection. In any case, Parliament could be relied upon never to pass legislation which was morally repugnant, partly because it was an assembly of 'gentlemen', but also because of the internal checks of what he saw as a tripartite structure of Crown, Lords and Commons.

Thus for Dicey the rule of law complemented parliamentary sovereignty. Both acted as a check upon the executive – Parliament because the government needed its support to acquire the legal powers to act, and the courts because they ensured that these powers were not exceeded. It is evident that Dicey's exposition of the constitution was driven in part by his concern that any claim to power of the newly enfranchised lower classes should be checked (just as constitutional reformers of the 1980s were to some extent at least motivated by antipathy to the prospect of permanent Conservative government – and in the 1970s by hostility to a Labour government).

It also needs to be remembered that at the time Dicey was writing statute law formed a less significant part of the body of law than it does today. Thus his concentration upon the common law was appropriate. In any case the common law values supported by the courts are applied by the judges in their interpretation of legislation and therefore are still relevant to a discussion of the constitution.

Dicey confined his exposition of the rule of law to a narrow legalistic meaning. However, the rule of law can be understood to include broader constitutional principles:

1. *Legal principles.*
   (a) The law should be certain and clear; hence legislation should not be retroactive.

   (b) There should be equality of all persons before the law, and the legal process should accord with the rules of natural justice, including fairness and openness.
   (c) There should be legal redress for damage sustained.
2. *Political values*. Governments should behave 'legitimately' as well as legally; thus they should seek popular support for their policies, exercise self-restraint, respect the role of Parliament, accept competing seats of power (i.e. local government) and the rights of opposition parties, protect the rights of minority groups, and so on.

The legal principles are upheld by the courts; the political values are generally accepted as aspiration, although politicians may use the term to support 'law and order' and repel challenges to government power. Altogether the 'rule of law' is an impressive if somewhat indeterminate package of principles and values. It is open to criticism on the grounds that it is either universal and unquestioned in democracies (the exercise of power must be based on law), or vague and lacking in authority and mere aspiration (the 'political values'), or specifically mistaken in some respects (the law is uncertain, and governments and the wealthy enjoy substantial advantages before the law).

There are grounds for such scepticism, as for much of the extensive British constitution; yet the rule of law is asserted, if not always understood, by political leaders, accepted in popular rhetoric (even perhaps rooted in political culture), and (more important) respected and applied by the courts. The importance of the rule of law in constitutional terms lies in the values it encompasses and the basis it offers for an element of separation of powers and specifically a check on executive power. It provides the courts with a foundation for the control of executive power, control which extends beyond legality to the application of the rules of natural justice, fairness and reasonableness.

Indeed, following the principle of the rule of law, the courts have been ready to extend the applicability of natural justice, and more recently the duty to act fairly, and to regard it as an important ground for judicial review. Interestingly, the concept of natural justice has also been drawn upon by the European Court of Justice in determining the general principles under which it operates. The judges seem likely to remind the politicians from time to time of the practical import of their rhetoric about the rule of law.

Conventions

In a constitution lacking a basic foundation document, custom and practice play a larger role than is the case in a well-founded constitution. This was recognised by Dicey, who considered 'those constitutional understandings which necessarily engross the attention of historians or of statesmen' (1959, p. 417) as crucial to Britain's constitutional arrangements. He referred to these non-legal rules as the 'conventions of the constitution' or 'constitutional morality' (p. 23), and acknowledged that some conventions were more important in constitutional terms than the law.

The following rules, amongst others, are regarded as conventions:

1. The Queen assents to all laws duly passed by both Houses of Parliament;
2. The Queen acts only on the advice of ministers, and ministers exercise the prerogative of the Crown (it was this group of conventions which Dicey particularly noted, because they transferred legal power);
3. Ministers are responsible to Parliament;
4. Members of the Cabinet (or now government) are collectively responsible to Parliament;
5. The Prime Minister cannot be a member of the House of Lords.

These examples illustrate the imprecision and uncertainty of standing of conventions. The first appears to be firm enough since the monarch has not refused assent to a Bill since 1708 (though George V was pressed to refuse assent to the Home Rule Bill of 1914, Dicey being among those who urged him to dismiss the Prime Minister!). The second does not work in the case of a 'hung Parliament' (see Chapter 4). Both conventions dealing with responsibility to Parliament are open to dispute as to meaning and practical consequences (Chapters 7 and 8). The fifth convention appears to be confirmed by recent precedents (1923, 1940, 1963), and is a good example of the development of a conventional rule to reflect changed perceptions of what is proper in the constitution of a modern parliamentary democracy.

Thus the imprecision of constitutional conventions does not argue against their existence, still less their utility. Imprecision allows adjustment to practicality and constitutional development without the controversy which would arise by attempting formal enactment. However, there is the grave disadvantage that a convention, as a rule grounded in politics, falls if political practice ceases, while disobedience to a law does not damage the law, but may damage the disobedient. The imprecision, flexibility and absence of sanctions work to the advantage of those in positions of power, for it becomes difficult to determine, and thus appeal to, the constitutional position and constitutional limitations.

Distinguishing characteristics

Conventions are not 'lesser laws' or laws in the making; they become law only if they are enacted as such. A convention has certain characteristics which distinguish it from law on the one hand and mere practice on the other. These include the following:

1. A convention relates to a customary practice for which there is by definition some kind of precedent.
2. A convention is recognised as forming a rule which imposes an obligation on those acting within the constitution.
3. A convention serves the purpose of mediation in the application of the law and the regulation of discretion.
4. A convention is not enforceable in the courts though recognised by them and used as an aid to interpretation.
5. A convention serves a political purpose; otherwise it will not be sustained.

The attitude of the courts to conventions

The recognition of conventions by the courts and the way in which they are used to aid interpretation was demonstrated in *Attorney-General* v. *Jonathan Cape Ltd* [1976] QB 752. The case also served to emphasise the non-enforceability, in the legal sense, of conventions.

The *Crossman Diaries* case

The case concerned the publication of an ex-minister's diaries. Richard Crossman had kept a record of his time as a Cabinet minister, which it had been his intention to publish after he had left office. He died but his literary executors decided to publish his diaries as a book. This was to be serialised in *The Sunday Times*. The Attorney-General sought an injunction to stop publication on the grounds that publication would be against the public interest. He argued that the doctrine of collective responsibility would be harmed by the disclosure of Cabinet discussions; disclosure might limit the scope of advice given by civil servants, and damage the careers of individual civil servants. The Attorney-General reinforced his argument with reference to the developing law of confidence, the principle of which is that a man or woman should not profit from the wrongful publication of information received by him or her in confidence.

Lord Widgery recognised the importance of the convention of collective responsibility and its requirement for confidentiality, using this to uphold the Attorney-General's claim that publication of discussions which had taken place within the confines of the convention could be a breach of confidentiality, and thus of the law of confidence.

> [T]he doctrine [of collective responsibility] is an established feature of the English form of government, and it follows that some matters leading up to a Cabinet decision may be regarded as confidential . . . In my judgment, the Attorney-General has made out his claim that the expression of individual opinions by Cabinet Ministers in the course of a Cabinet discussion are matters of confidence, the publication of which can be restrained by the court when this is clearly in the public interest.
>
> The maintenance of the doctrine of joint responsibility within the Cabinet is in the public interest, and the application of that doctrine might be prejudiced by premature disclosure of the views of individual ministers.

However, Lord Widgery did not consider that publication of the Diaries would be prejudicial to, or a breach of, confidentiality, as the material contained within them was nearly ten years old. He then considered whether the publication of advice given by civil servants and opinions concerning the capabilities of individual senior civil servants would be a breach of confidentiality.

> I see no ground in law which entitles the court to restrain publication on these matters. A Minister is, no doubt, responsible for his department and accountable for its errors even though the individual fault is to be found in his subordinates. In these circumstances, to disclose the fault of the subordinate may amount to cowardice or bad taste, but I can find no ground for saying that either the Crown or the individual civil servant has an enforceable right to have the advice which he gives treated as confidential for all time.

Lord Widgery concluded:

> For these reasons, I do not think that the court should interfere with the publication of volume one of the Diaries, and I propose, therefore, to refuse the injunction sought.

Lord Widgery was careful to distinguish between law and convention and to stress the inability of the courts to enforce conventions. Thus conventions may be seen, in the perspective of the courts, as similar to the preamble of a statute – an aid to interpretation but not part of the law.

The nature of conventions and their distinction from law was discussed at length by the judges in the Supreme Court of Canada in *Reference re Amendment of the Constitution of Canada* (1982) 125 DLR (3d) 1.

The case of the *Canadian Constitution*

The Canadian government wished to patriate the Canadian Constitution by altering the legal position which required that constitutional amendments still had to be made by the British Parliament. It also wanted to introduce a new Charter of Rights which would be binding on both federal and provincial legislatures. Eight of the ten provinces opposed these proposals and three of them took the matter to the Supreme Court. They claimed there was a convention that required the federal authorities to obtain the agreement of the provinces before asking the British Parliament to legislate on matters which affected the constitutional arrangements within Canada, and that the federal authorities would be acting unconstitutionally if they failed to comply with the conventional requirements. Moreover, they claimed that although the rule requiring agreement was in origin a political rule, it had over time crystallised into law.

The Supreme Court found that in law there was nothing to prevent the federal authorities requesting the British Parliament to patriate the Canadian Constitution. It then turned its attention to the conventional requirement and whether a convention could become law.

> The conventional rules of the Constitution present one striking peculiarity. In contradistinction to the laws of the Constitution, they are not enforced by the Courts. One reason for this situation is that, unlike common law rules, conventions are not judge-made rules. They are not based on judicial precedents but on precedents established by the institutions of government themselves. . . .
>
> Perhaps the main reason why constitutional rules cannot be enforced by the Courts is that they are generally in conflict with the legal rules which they postulate and the Courts are bound to enforce

> the legal rules. The conflict is not of a type which would entail the commission of any illegality. It results from the fact that legal rules create wide powers, discretions and rights which conventions prescribe should be exercised only in a certain limited manner, if at all. . . .
>
> It should be borne in mind, however, that, while they are not laws, some conventions may be more important than some laws. Their importance depends on that of the value or principle which they are meant to safeguard. Also they form an integral part of the Constitution and of the constitutional system. . . .

The Supreme Court considered that there was a convention which required the agreement of the provinces before the federal authorities could request the British Parliament to legislate and therefore concluded that acting without this agreement 'would be unconstitutional in the conventional sense'. The Court made a clear distinction between legal 'unconstitutionality', which would amount to illegality and thus could be dealt with by the courts, and conventional 'unconstitutionality', the penalty for which was political and not legal. Moreover, it stressed that conventions were different from laws and, regardless of their importance and usage, could not crystallise into law.

Thus the Canadian Supreme Court had usefully recognised the importance of conventions in the constitution as substitutes for, or additions to, law.

Why are conventions obeyed?

The question remains: why should politicians, often under pressure and in a hurry, feel obliged to conform to constitutional conventions? The answer is similar to questions about general obedience to rules. Considerations include, shall I be found out? Can I bear the shame and the pain of punishment? Most politicians and governments can sustain some political embarrassment; evident dishonour may be more difficult to bear; and loss of office in the next election is equivalent to capital punishment. In that way the system of responsibility to Parliament and indirectly to the electorate helps to ensure good behaviour.

Further, the ethic of 'do as you would be done by' comes into play. The condition of playing an adversarial team game is that you obey the rules (at least within very broad limits, as can be observed in a football stadium most Saturday afternoons); otherwise the game collapses. If a government accepts that it may not always be in power, then it has a strong incentive to observe the rules and eschew an excessive exploitation of its temporary hold on power. Problems arise when a government is in office for a long time and challenges to it are ineffectual, for it may come to see conventions and the 'rules of the game' as irrelevant or insubstantial.

The nature of the binding or obligatory force of non-legal rules is not a trivial matter: it goes to the heart of the constitutional morality which underlies the legitimacy and stability of a political system. Jennings wrote that conventions were obeyed 'because of the political difficulties which follow if they are not' (1959, p. 134). However, more is at issue than embarrassment of the government and damage to its dominance. The ultimate sanction for conformity to constitutional conventions resides in the maintenance of the constitution itself.

> [T]he crucial questions must always be whether or not a particular class of action is likely to destroy respect for the established distribution of authority and whether or not it is likely to maintain respect for the constitutional system of changing or (sustaining) the distribution of authority. (Marshall and Moodie, 1971, p. 32)

A more sceptical view of conventions is that their authority depends on 'what you can get away with', and that the normal political security of party-supported governments and ministers enables them to get away with deception, corruption, injustice, even murder . . . And, once got away with, the convention itself is weakened. So it is important that conventions still flourish in the textbooks!

Dicey's constitution unbalanced

For Dicey and others, writing at the end of the nineteenth century, Britain's constitutional arrangements, which centred on parliamentary sovereignty, the rule of law and conventions, provided a model of balance and harmony, far superior to that provided by written constitutions. Dicey's 'ideal' theory of the constitution suggested a system of automatic checks which made a written constitution seem unnecessary and indeed an inadequate substitute.

Parliament was legally supreme, unchecked by any external authority but checked in the substance of what became law by its triumviral nature, the need for a Bill to be approved by the two Houses and be given the Royal Assent, and by the consciences of individual Members. The executive was held in check by Parliament and the courts. Parliament held ministers to account and scrutinised legislative proposals. The courts upheld the intentions of Parliament, reviewed the actions of the executive to ensure their legal authority and protected the rights of the individual from the arbitrary use of power. Further, convention allowed the 'peaceful' transfer of power to ministers and Parliament and the limitation of the role of the monarch without political controversy.

Dicey's theory of the constitution was readily accepted because it seemed to accord with a political ideal of a balanced constitution and with political practice. In fact political developments were already taking place which distanced the practice from the theory and meant that the constitutional checks within the system no longer operated or operated ineffectually.

1. The triumviral nature of Parliament rarely acts as a check on legislation. The House of Commons is dominant, while the role of the House of Lords is much reduced by the Parliament Acts, 1911 and 1949, and the political environment. The Royal Assent no longer acts as a check on legislation, since the Queen by established convention acts on the advice of ministers in approving legislation. (This was already the accepted position when Dicey was writing.)
2. The independent judgment and individual representative function of Members of Parliament has been transformed by party solidarity and discipline, so that the House of Commons normally supports the executive (except in the unusual condition of government by minority or insecure majority).
3. The accountability of government is seriously weakened, despite the convention of ministerial responsibility, by the solidarity of the majority party, and by the size, complexity and bureaucratic capacity of government. The government may exercise self-limitation, but that is not a check by Dicey's constitutional criteria.
4. The role of the courts has been confused and no theory of administrative law has been developed to support a role for them in an expanded state. This may be blamed on Dicey's exposition of the rule of law, but is in fact a consequence of

> the nineteenth-century development of the administrative functions of government under the umbrella of departments rather than independent boards. The establishment of ministerial responsibility to Parliament has inhibited the courts from taking up a role which seemed constitutionally to lie with Parliament.

Thus the government is dominant in both legislative and executive functions, both because of its control of the House of Commons and because of the transfer of powers from the sovereign to ministers. The limited role of the courts arises from, and is justified by, the doctrine and practice of parliamentary sovereignty. Thus, Dicey's exposition was not only overtaken by history, but was perhaps oversimplified (though not misconceived) to start with. It has provided an attractive façade for executive dominance, and is plainly an insecure basis for a modern constitution. So far it has survived the massive expansion of the state in the twentieth century, but may be undermined by the impact of membership of the European Community and the European Union on the constitution and the law of the United Kingdom.

3

THE EUROPEAN COMMUNITY
The Parallel Constitution

Britain became a member of the European Economic Community (and the Communities for Coal and Steel and Atomic Energy) in January 1973, and at that point the body of Community law became effective within Britain. Since then, Britain has enjoyed (if that is the word) dual constitutional arrangements, as an independent state and as a member of the European Community. The constitution of the Community is contained within the founding treaties, notably, the Treaty of Rome 1958 (EEC Treaty), and in amendments made in the Single European Act 1986, and the Treaty of European Union (Maastricht) 1993, collectively referred to as 'the Treaties'. This European constitution runs in parallel with national constitutional arrangements.

In Britain the dual constitution raises problems for the judges, who have a constitutional role with regard to legislation under Community law that is not available to them for domestic legislation under the doctrine of parliamentary sovereignty. It seems likely that the courts will move towards the harmonisation of the two systems of law, wherever possible applying the principles of European Community law to national law. Thus the legal framework of the European Community will pervade the judicial approach to law, and thereby come to influence Britain's constitutional arrangements. Such a change will take place incrementally and without reference to an overall ideal or objective, but there is evidence to suggest that it is under way.

The effect of the dual constitution on the structure and processes of government is more obscure. Every institution of British government is changed to some extent by British membership of the European Community and European Union. Yet much of the change lies in the private processes of decision-making. The public processes of politics – the national theatre of politics – are little changed except by summit conferences, the now forgotten referendum of 1975, and the recent marathon ratification of the Maastricht Treaty. We notice a Prime Minister in Brussels for the day, but not scores of senior civil servants permanently posted to Brussels. This kind of change in the structure and process of British government, in effect constitutional change, has already taken place.

The development of the European Community

The European Community had its origins in the aftermath of the Second World War and the political and economic needs and aspirations of that time. The main concerns were to rebuild Europe's economy and political structure, to tie Germany into a wider economic and political interest, thus discouraging nationalism and military aggression, and to protect the smaller countries of Europe. There was also a less specific aspiration towards European unity and political integration. For some this meant a formally unified federal Europe; for others a form of free trade area, and at most a loose confederation. These differences are unresolved. Moreover, although the EC was not a military organisation, it gained some purpose and definition from the Cold War, the end of which has left it uncertain of its stance towards the countries of Eastern Europe.

There were a number of co-operative ventures prior to the establishment of the European Communities, including those fostered by the Marshall Plan for American aid (1947). The first of the new 'Communities', the European Coal and Steel Community (ECSC), was created by the Treaty of Paris 1951, signed by France, Germany, Italy, Belgium, Netherlands and Luxembourg. The motivation was both economic and political – economic recovery and development, but not dominated by Germany.

Two more Communities were established in 1958 under the first and second Treaties of Rome. These were Euratom and the European Economic Community, both of which had the same signatories as the Treaty establishing the ECSC. The Communities have doubled in size since then, Britain, Ireland and Denmark joining in 1972, Greece in 1981, and Spain and Portugal in 1985. It is, however, the EEC which has been by far the most significant community because of its wider scope.

Its founding treaty, the Treaty of Rome, was substantially amended by the Single European Act 1986, which provided for the establishment of a Single European Market and laid the basis for co-operation in foreign policy. The Maastricht Treaty (1993) renamed the EEC the European Community and established a European Union based on the three 'pillars' of economic co-operation, foreign and security policy, and interior and justice policies. It took as its goal the creation of 'an ever closer union among the peoples of Europe', and set itself the following objectives:

1. economic and monetary union, including a single currency;
2. a common foreign and security policy;
3. co-operation on justice and home affairs;
4. European citizenship.

Until recently the main thrust of the Community was towards the regulation of economic relations. This aroused little controversy since all Member States broadly accepted the objective of free trade. There were skirmishes, particularly over the Common Agricultural Policy and the budgetary contributions of Member States, but the overall direction of the Community was seldom questioned. However, the creation of the 'single market' under the Act of 1986 (operative from 1993) enlarged the scope of Community activity and strengthened the hands of those within the Community who sought a more thorough-going political and economic union.

Thus there was a spill-over of concern from the regulation of trade to the economic and social environment, including such matters as the health and safety of workers, education and training, culture, public health and consumer protection. 'Harmonisation' in economic and social affairs (the achievement of 'the level playing field') ranged from the regulation of the fat content of chocolate or the design of electric plugs, to a concern for, and so potential intervention in, macro-economic matters such as the level of inflation or the value of the currency.

This extension of the competence of the Community was taken further in the Maastricht Treaty. Britain specifically opted out of the 'Social Chapter', which provided for regulation and improvement of conditions of employment. The device of the opt-out clearly raises problems about the integrity of the European Community, the harmonisation of economic conditions, the procedures for policy-making, and the wider aspirations of the European Union towards economic and monetary union and a common foreign and security policy. Not surprisingly, the forward drive inscribed in the Maastricht Treaty revealed sharp differences in approach to membership of the Community.

Institutions of the Community

The Maastricht negotiations raised deeper political and constitutional questions concerning the relationship between the Community and the Member States, and the allocation of, and accountability for, power within the Community. These problems have their basis in the institutional structure as contained within the Treaties and in the way in which the institutions have developed. The institutions of the European Union have become part of Britain's institutions of government and must be understood as such. A brief account of them is necessary, and is convenient at this point. This early treatment may serve as a forceful reminder of the relevance of the European Union to any consideration of the contemporary British constitution.

The European Community is unique because its institutions are supra-national, that is, separate from, and, within limits, superior to, national governments. The function, membership and mode of operation of each institution is constitutionally prescribed by the treaty, and 'each institution shall act within the limits of the powers conferred upon it by this Treaty' (i.e. Treaty of Rome or EEC Treaty; Art. 4 EEC). The actions of the political/administrative institutions, the European Parliament, the Commission and the Council of Ministers, can be challenged in the European Court of Justice, the fourth institution listed in the Treaty of Rome. There is also a Court of Auditors, which after Maastricht counts as an institution; as well as two advisory bodies (not counting as institutions of the European Community), the Economic and Social Committee and, again since Maastricht, a Committee of the Regions.

The European Council

The European Council is not an institution of the Community, and thus is neither limited nor obligated by Community law, nor can it be challenged in the European Court. It comprises the heads of state or government and the foreign secretaries together with the President of the Commission. Unusually there are no officials present at the formal meetings of the twice-yearly Councils. The European Council is the driving force of the Community. It makes the broad policy decisions setting out the direction and development of the Community and puts these into legislative form through the signing of treaties (which constitute the primary legislation of the Community).

All reference to the supra-national power of the European Community or European Union is subject to the reservation that the European Council is the directing power. But within the Council each nation has only the power to persuade and negotiate. Formal collaborative arrangements of this kind permit neither the retention of national power, nor the creation of an alternative (supra-national) sovereignty

The Commission

The Commission consists of seventeen members, who 'shall be chosen on the grounds of their general competence and whose independence is beyond doubt'. The Commission must contain at least one national of each Member State and not more than two. In practice this has meant that the five largest Member States – Germany, France, Italy, Britain and Spain – have had two Commissioners and the smaller countries have had one.

Prior to Maastricht, the Commissioners and the President of the Commission were appointed by 'common accord' of the governments of the Member States for a four-year term of office which was renewable. Maastricht extended the term of office to five years and required that the European Parliament be consulted on nominations for the President and then give its vote of approval on the proposed composition of the Commission before all members were appointed by the Member States.

The involvement of the European Parliament in the appointment of the Commission may give the Commission, or certainly its President, greater political authority. Hitherto it has lacked an independent political base; it cannot appeal over the heads of the national governments to the Parliament, still less to 'the people'. At the same time the Commission has derived some freedom from its lack of accountability to the Parliament.

Commissioners are required to forgo national interests and act only in the interests of the Community.

> In the performance of their duties, they shall neither seek nor take instructions from any government or from any other body. They shall refrain from any action incompatible with their duties. (Art. 157 EEC)

The Commission is collectively responsible for its actions, but, unlike members of a national government, individual Commissioners are not personally responsible for their portfolios.

The Commission has three main duties:

(1) It acts as the guardian of the Treaties and in this capacity brings enforcement actions against Member States who fail to fulfil their treaty obligations.

(2) It is the initiator and co-ordinator of Community policies. In doing so it acts on the instructions of the European Council and the Council of Ministers. However, it also acts on its own initiative to further the objectives of the EEC Treaty, from which the Member States might be diverted by their national interests. In this way the Commission is again the keeper of the Communities.

In formulating policy the Commission consults with interested parties, representative groups, and experts in the field. The EEC Treaty requires consultation with the Economic and Social Committee in many areas, and the duty to consult is extended by Maastricht to include the Committee of the Regions. The Commission then puts forward its policy proposals to the Council of Ministers. When the broad lines of policy have been agreed, the

Commission drafts the details of implementation, again in consultation with interested and knowledgeable parties, for approval by the Council.

(3) The Treaty gives the Commission executive and legislative powers to implement the Community objectives which are detailed within it. For example, the Commission is given specific power to make regulations concerning the conditions under which workers have a right to live in a Member State in which they are employed (Art. 48 EEC). The Commission also has legislative power delegated to it by the Council to ensure the implementation of Council decisions. One major area of such delegation is the Common Agricultural Policy, which has accounted for more than half of the budget and most of the two thousand or so regulations and decisions made by the Commission. The Commission also administers the funds of the Community and is responsible for drawing up the budget. In addition, it represents the Community in negotiations with non-Member States and international organisations, for instance the GATT.

Thus the Commission can be seen in many ways to be the 'government' of the Community. However, it still lacks both the full authority and the discretionary power and the accountability of such a body. The Maastricht reforms, which require the European Parliament's approval of the composition of the Commission, may increase political authority but do little to strengthen democratic accountability.

The Council of Ministers

The Council of Ministers is the Community institution in which political authority resides (subject to the European Council). The Council consists of one ministerial representative from each Member State. This is the Foreign Secretary when matters of external policy or general Community concern are under discussion. Otherwise, the responsible minister attends; thus if fishing or agriculture policy is on the agenda, then the representatives will be the agriculture ministers. The Presidency of the Council rotates, with a Member State holding it for six months. The Council is the least supra-national institution of the Community, its individual members inevitably being concerned to protect and foster their country's interests within the Community.

The Council of Ministers is empowered under EEC Article 145 to take decisions. Generally, however, it can only act on a proposal from the Commission. Thus, in simple terms, the Commission proposes and the Council disposes. The Council can accept or reject a proposal from the Commission, or send it back for reconsideration. However, it cannot amend a proposal except by a unanimous vote. There is therefore a need for Council and Commission to work together; without their accord it is unlikely that legislation can be passed. In the legislative process the European Parliament also has a role which has been enhanced by the Single European Act and the Maastricht Treaty (see below). This reform may be seen as increasing either the democratic pluralism or the bureaucratic complexity of the Community's legislative process.

The extent to which all members of the Council need to be in agreement depends on the matter before it. Unanimous voting is exceptionally required, otherwise voting is by a simple or 'qualified' majority. The exercise of most legislative powers requires a qualified majority, based on weighted voting; this is designed to prevent the dominance of the larger countries whilst allowing them a voice related to their size. Thus, it is intended, the vote represents a broad consensus across the Member States rather than the interests of one group of nations whether large or small.

The voting system provides Germany, France, Italy and Britain with ten votes each, Spain with eight votes, Belgium, Greece, Netherlands and Portugal with five, Denmark and Ireland with three, and Luxembourg with two. In proportion to population the smaller countries are heavily overrepresented: at the extreme Germany has 10 votes for 80 million people, Luxembourg 2 for 400,000. Of the 76 votes available the requirement is for 54 votes to be cast in favour of proposals from the Commission; this means that even if the five biggest countries vote together they will not secure enough votes and will require support from at least two other countries. On the other hand, two large and one small country can block proposals (with 23 votes), and it is impossible for the smaller countries to push legislation through without support from three of the big five. (Under the projected enlargement of the European Union to include Norway, Finland, Austria and Sweden, 14 votes altogether, the blocking total will rise from 23 to 27 – over Britain's strenuous objections.)

A fundamental problem posed by the Council is its lack of accountability. Within the Community it is accountable to no one. The individual members of the Council are of course accountable to their national Parliaments. In Britain, and indeed elsewhere, such accountability is difficult to extract, partly because of the volume and nature of Community law and partly because of the inherent weakness in the process of accountability itself. There is also the problem that with simple and qualified majority voting, the representative of a Member State may actually have opposed a measure which the Council as a body has passed. Further, there is a tendency, perhaps understandable, for ministers to blame unpopular measures on the Commission, which initiated them, rather than on the Council, which approved them. The actual responsibility of ministers for their part in the process tends to get overlooked in a joint condemnation of the Commission, frequently portrayed as an interfering bureaucracy.

Committee of Permanent Representatives

The Council of Ministers is not a permanent fixture but assembles and reassembles when required and in the form that is appropriate. There is therefore a need for a permanent organisation to carry out administrative tasks and prepare the groundwork for meetings of the Council. This group is the Committee of Permanent Representatives (COREPER), whose members are of ambassadorial status. The Committee is not a deputising committee, and in practice does a great deal of work on its own account. It has forged a unique role for itself, working to smooth and foster the relationships of the Member States, both with each other and with the institutions of the Community, and to negotiate solutions that will satisfy all participants.

The European Parliament

The European Parliament has been the least influential of the Community institutions; indeed, until recently the role of the democratically elected assembly has been minimal. It consists 'of representatives of the peoples of the States brought together in the Community' (Art. 137 EEC). The allocation of seats in the Parliament broadly reflects the populations of the Member

States, although it favours the smaller states whose influence in terms of representatives is larger than their size warrants. There are 567 MEPs (1994): Germany has 99 (increased following reunification), Britain, France and Italy 87 members each, Spain 64, the Netherlands 31, Belgium, Greece and Portugal 25 each, Denmark 16, Ireland 15 and Luxembourg 6.

Members are directly elected for five years, at present according to the national electoral system, although the European Parliament has been instructed to 'draw up proposals for elections . . . in accordance with a uniform procedure in all Member States' (Art. 137, as amended by Maastricht). These are likely to provide for some form of proportional representation.

A major difference between the European Parliament and national Parliaments is that the European Parliament does not support or oppose a government, nor divide into government and opposition or majority and minority parties. However, there are party groupings within the Parliament and the Maastricht Treaty recognised the importance of these for the health of the Community in a declaratory flourish:

> Political parties at European level are important as a factor for integration within the Union. They contribute to forming a European awareness and to expressing the political will of the citizens of the Union. (Art. 138a)

However, there is still a problem of geographical and psychological remoteness of the European Parliament from most European citizens. There is very little of the political conflict and drama characteristic of national assemblies, little reporting by the media (for that reason), so some difficulty for the citizens of the European Union to take an interest in, still less to identify with, the European Parliament.

Functions and powers of the European Parliament

(1) The Parliament was conceived as a representative assembly rather than as a legislature, although there has always been a requirement that it should be consulted by the Commission or the Council, as appropriate, over major policy proposals. Failure by these institutions to consult with the Parliament can result in legislation being declared void by the Court of Justice. In recent times the involvement of the Parliament in the legislative process has increased. The Single European Act and the Maastricht Treaty have introduced new procedures which provide Parliament with the opportunity in specified areas of Community law to amend proposed legislation or to vote against it. In such cases the original legislation can then be passed only by the Council acting unanimously (the co-operation procedure), and in some instances the matter has to go to the Conciliation Committee, a joint committee of Parliament and the Council, for resolution (the co-decision procedure). Clearly it has become necessary for the Commission, Council and Parliament to work more closely together.

(2) The European Parliament has a supervisory role. It has the power to ask questions, both written and oral, of the Commission and the Council. In addition it has the power to censure the Commission, even forcing its resignation. A censure motion has to secure 'a two-thirds majority of the votes cast, representing a majority of the members of the European Parliament' (Art. 144 EEC). No censure motion has so far been carried, but the possibility gives the Parliament a standing in relation to the Commission, which has been strengthened by the provision of the Maastricht Treaty for the Parliament to be involved in the appointment of the Commission.

(3) The European Parliament has significant powers in relation to the Community budget. The budgetary proceedings are complex, requiring consultation, negotiation and agreement between the Council and the Parliament on the proposals of the Commission. Parliament has the last word on non-compulsory expenditure, which mainly concerns the administrative costs of the institutions, and it can propose modifications to compulsory items, which are items of expenditure arising automatically from the implementation of Community policies and rules, most notably the Common Agricultural Policy. Such modifications can be rejected by the Council. However, when the budgetary procedure has been exhausted, the budget has to be formally accepted by the European Parliament. This is not an automatic process, and the budget may be rejected if, in the opinion of a majority of the members and two-thirds of the votes cast, there are 'important reasons' why this should be the case. A new draft budget then has to be submitted.

The draft budget for 1980 was rejected in this way and there was conflict over the 1986 budget, which required the intervention of the European Court.

(4) Under the Maastricht Treaty the Parliament has powers of oversight of the implementation and administration of Community law. The Treaty provides that:

> In the course of its duties, the European Parliament may, at the request of a quarter of its members, set up a temporary Committee of Inquiry to investigate . . . alleged contraventions or maladministration in the implementation of Community law. (Art. 138c)

The Parliament already practises a version of Parliamentary Questions (a British import) addressed to Commissioners and occasionally to ministers from the country of the Presidency, but attendance is poor.

In addition, the Maastricht Treaty provides for Parliament to appoint an Ombudsman

> empowered to receive complaints from any citizen of the Union . . . concerning instances of maladministration in the activities of the Community institutions or bodies, with the exception of the Court of Justice and the Court of First Instance acting in their judicial role. (Art. 138c)

The powers of the Community Ombudsman are greater than those of his British counterpart (see Chapter 16). He can conduct inquiries 'either on his own initiative or on the basis of complaints submitted to him direct or through a member of the European Parliament'. The introduction of an Ombudsman and the provision of powers of inquiry enhance the role of the European Parliament in Community life, and are a response to criticisms about the remoteness of the Parliament from European citizens and the unaccountability of Community bureaucracy.

The European Parliament may well be regarded as an expensive charade; it is also a necessary gesture towards democracy with potential to develop as an effective representative assembly and legislature. But utility, effectiveness and life-giving popular interest depend absolutely on the development of much greater European political vitality and will.

The European Court of Justice

The European Court of Justice (ECJ), assisted by the Court of First Instance, is, like all the institutions of the Community, a creation of the Treaties and can only act within the powers provided by the constitution. It is based on the French Conseil d'État (the highest administrative law court in France), and its French basis is indicated by the fact that the working language of the court is French and its procedure follows that of a civil, rather than common, law system. Its procedures are inquisitorial rather than adversarial, and involve the extensive use of written evidence, the oral hearing playing a much smaller part than in Britain.

There is a difference, too, in the composition of the court.

> The Judges and Advocates-General shall be chosen from persons whose independence is beyond doubt and who possess the qualifications required for appointment to the highest judicial offices in their respective countries or who are jurisconsults of recognized competence. (Art. 167 EEC)

In Britain all senior judges are or have been practising barristers. In other countries this is not always so, and academic lawyers may be appointed to the bench. This is the case in the ECJ. The Court is composed of thirteen judges, appointed for a renewable period of six years. In practice each Member State provides one judge and the additional judge comes from one of the 'big five'. Here, as elsewhere, enlargement of the Community will force revision of this kind of agreed sharing out.

The ECJ is concerned to protect its reputation as being completely independent of national influences and concerns. A feature of the Court's procedures, which emphasises its independence, is that only one judgment is given on a case. The Court thus appears to act as a cohesive unit, and the anonymity of the judgment protects individual judges from accusations of national bias or from the opposite complaint from their Member States that they are acting against their national interests.

The jurisdiction of the Court is laid down in the Treaties and can broadly be categorised as the following:

1. direct actions, where the Court decides the case before it;

2. indirect actions or preliminary references, where the Court gives a ruling on the matter of EC law but does not itself decide on the outcome of the case.

Direct actions can concern the institutions of the Community and the Member States. Those concerning the institutions involve the legality of their actions, that is, whether they have legal authority for what they have done and the way in which they have done it, or whether there has been a failure to act. Actions against the institutions can be brought by Member States, by another institution, or by an individual who has sufficient interest in the matter. The ECJ also hears actions against the Community for damages in tort, appeals against the imposition of fines by the Commission, and disputes between the Community and its employees. Direct actions against Member States are in the form of enforcement actions, which are usually brought by the Commission.

Preliminary references are very different as the ECJ does not decide the case. They concern references made by national courts on points of Community law and its interpretation. The case itself remains to be decided in the national court according to its application of the ECJ's ruling. Preliminary references are fundamental to the effectiveness of EC law in the Member States. They provide for a partnership between the ECJ and the national courts, in effect incorporating the courts of the Member States into the Community's judicial system, and providing them with a distinctive role. Thus the European Court is not an appeal court, but a court working in conjunction with the national courts; it interprets the law, they apply it.

The ECJ is the most supra-national of the institutions of the Community. It takes its prime objective to be the promotion of European integration, which is after all the objective of the Treaties which confer its powers. To this end the Court works to increase the scope and effectiveness of EC law and the strength of the Community institutions, thereby extending uniformity and hence integration.

At times the Court's decisions have been controversial because of its tendency to interpret according to the spirit and not the letter of the Treaties. Certainly its approach is unlike that of the British courts. The Court is based on a different judicial tradition, and it is, amongst other functions, a Constitutional Court in an emerging and changing polity. The Court cannot be abstracted from the political process. It is therefore inevitable that some of its decisions will have more to do with policy and politics than with legal reasoning. It is involved in interpreting a Treaty which concerns not just procedural and administrative detail but aspirations, broad policy objectives and general principles of law.

The relationship between the European Community and the Member States

The powers given to the institutions of the European Community (which is the main part of the European Union) clearly have an impact upon the national institutions of the Member States. Legislatures are required to relinquish some of their power, not to another representative assembly but to the Council of Ministers and the Commission, both of which are unelected. The power of individual governments or executives is also reduced since many policy decisions are made in Brussels or by the European Council. The only national institutions which might be seen as gaining power are the courts, for whilst the European Court of Justice is the final court on matters of EC law, it is the national courts that have responsibility for ensuring the primacy of Community law. For the British courts, which have lacked a constitutional role, this is especially significant.

The institutions of the Community have a duty to work towards the objectives of the Treaties, as amended, and actions can be brought against them in the ECJ if they fail in that duty. But there is some lack of clarity and definition about the actual powers of the Community. On the one hand, the Community has only the power that is delegated or attributed to it by the Member States under the Treaties. On the other hand, such delegations of power are not all explicit. Delegation also arises under Article 235 EEC, which provides for Community legislation on matters relevant to the EC and not expressly dealt with by the Treaty. Thus the Community has substantial legal competence, not all of which is specified.

It was partly in an attempt to limit this non-specific competence that the principle of subsidiarity was given legal form within the Maastricht Treaty. Article 3b stipulates:

> The Community shall act within the limit of the powers conferred upon it by this Treaty and of the objectives assigned to it therein. In areas which do not fall within its exclusive competence, the Community shall take action, in accordance with the principle of subsidiarity, only if and in so far as the objectives of the proposed action cannot be sufficiently achieved by the Member States and can therefore, by reason of the scale or effects of the proposed action, be better achieved by the Community.

There has been considerable debate over the wisdom and practicality of giving legal effect to a broad political concept, and it is not known how the judges will move to enforce it. The wording of the Article suggests that the Community has to justify its actions with regard to subsidiarity, prior to acting. It remains uncertain whether it will be sufficient for the Community to show it has considered the principle (by means of the preamble before the legislative act), or whether the European Court will review the substance of the legislation to determine that the objectives 'cannot be sufficiently achieved by the Member States'.

The Maastricht Treaty also gives effect to the principle of proportionality, a legal concept applied by the ECJ to keep Community law within bounds. The Treaty provides: 'Any action by the Community shall not go beyond what is necessary to achieve the objectives of this Treaty' (Art. 3b). Thus the Community is limited as to the scope of its action by what the Court considers to be appropriate. It is of some significance that senior judges in Britain have indicated that they consider the principle of proportionality to be a useful import into English law (see Chapter 6).

The Treaties lay limitations and obligations upon the Member States as well as the Community. There is a general duty of solidarity, which is provided by Article 7 EEC. This requires Member States to take all appropriate measures to promote, and to refrain from frustrating, the objectives of the Treaty, including establishing the necessary administrative machinery. A legal action can be brought by the Commission if a Member State fails to comply. However, the procedural requirements for such actions (brought under Art. 169) demonstrate a recognition that political persuasion may be a better enforcer than legal action. The Commission must provide opportunities for the Member State to submit its observations and endeavour to resolve the matter, before bringing it before the ECJ.

One of the weaknesses in such actions has been that although Member States are obliged by treaty, and therefore law, to comply with rulings of the Court, there has been no penalty for not doing so. The Maastricht Treaty addressed this problem by providing a mechanism for the Court to impose a fine or penalty payment (Art. 171). There is also a duty of reciprocity or co-operation between Member States. The most significant, although unenforceable, requirement is that the assent of all Member States is required before a country leaves the Community.

Thus the Treaties of the Community provide a constitutional framework for the powers of the Community, the operation of the Community institutions and the duties of Member States. They also lay down constitutional principles on which the law of the Community must operate, and the rules for the relationship between European Community law and national law and the ECJ and the courts of the Member States.

The principle of direct effect

The development of 'direct effect' by the ECJ has proved to be one of the most important integrating factors within the European Community, and has had the greatest impact upon British law and constitutional arrangements.

The principle of direct effect grants individuals rights under Community law which must be upheld by the national courts. It is a means of ensuring the supremacy of Community law over national law, and of providing the national courts with a role in upholding that supremacy. Initially, the principle was applied to Articles of the Treaties and to regulations, which are secondary sources of Community legislation made by the Commission or the Council. Regulations are 'binding in their entirety and directly applicable' (Art. 189 EEC). This means that they do not have to be enacted into national legislation; they apply uniformly across the Community to everyone. Regulations automatically acquire the force of law in all Member States of the Community. It is therefore logical that they should have 'direct effect', giving individuals rights they may claim in their national courts.

The European Court's extension of direct effect to directives has been more controversial. The Treaty of Rome defines directives as 'binding as to the result to be achieved' (Art. 189 EEC). They are therefore not directly applicable but have to be incorporated in national law before they have legal effect. Member States may have some discretion in implementation; the outcome is required to be the same across Member States, but the manner in which it is achieved may vary.

Member States are required to implement directives by the date upon the face of the directive. Failure to do so means the country is in breach of its Community obligations and the Commission can bring an enforcement action. However, such an action takes a long time, and thus works to the advantage of a Member State trying to delay the implementation of a directive. It is in part in response to delay in implementation by Member States that the ECJ has held directives to have direct effect, so that an individual may claim rights from a directive which a Member State has failed to implement. This clearly makes directives more effective and supports the primacy of Community law.

The *Van Duyn* case

The operation of the principle of direct effect was illustrated in *Van Duyn* v. *Home Office* (case 41/74) [1974] ECR 1337. Miss Van Duyn was a Dutch national and a member of the Church of Scientology. She came to England to take up employment with the Church but was refused entry by the Home Office, which considered the cult's activities to be harmful to the public interest. Miss Van Duyn argued that under EC law she was entitled to enter. She relied upon Article 48 of the EEC Treaty, which provides freedom of movement for workers within the Community, and upon Council Directive 64/221. She needed to claim rights from the Directive as well as the Treaty Article because the Treaty allows Member States to restrict entry on 'grounds of public policy, public security or public health'. However, this derogation is modified by Directive 64/221 which states: 'measures taken on grounds of public policy or of public security shall be based exclusively on the personal conduct of the individual concerned'. Miss Van Duyn argued that her membership of the Church of Scientology could not amount to 'personal conduct' and thus she had a right to enter the United Kingdom.

The key matter to be decided by the ECJ was whether the Directive had direct effect and thus provided Miss Van Duyn with a right that she could enforce in the courts of the United Kingdom. If it did not, then 'public policy' did not need to be based upon her 'personal conduct'. The ECJ held that Directive 64/221 did have direct effect and thus limited the United Kingdom's ability to limit entry on the grounds of 'public policy'. It reasoned:

> It would be incompatible with the binding effect attributed to a directive by Article 189 to exclude, in principle, the possibility that the obligation which it imposes may be invoked by those concerned. In particular, where the Community authorities have, by directive, imposed on Member States the obligation to pursue a particular course of conduct, the useful effect of such an act would be weakened if individuals were prevented from taking it into consideration as an element of Community law.

In the event, the Court ruled that Miss Van Duyn's membership of the Church of Scientology could be considered as 'personal conduct' and therefore the United Kingdom was not in breach of Community law. However, the principle established in Van Duyn that directives could have direct effect has been of fundamental importance to the application of Community law.

The principle of direct effect is not without limitation, notably the question against whom a claim can be made. Directives are addressed to Member States and it is only Member States who can implement them. Thus direct effect only applies against the organs of the state and not against individuals or private companies. The question then arises whether direct effect can only be claimed against the state when it is acting as a public authority or whether it can also be claimed when it is acting as an employer.

The *Marshall* case: retirement ages for men and women

This matter was addressed in *Marshall* v. *Southampton Area Health Authority* (Case 152/84) [1986] ECR 723. Mrs Marshall worked for the Area Health Authority which had a policy that the age of retirement should be in line with the state retirement pension, 60 for women and 65 for men. Mrs Marshall was in fact allowed to stay on until she was 62, at which point she was dismissed on the basis that she had passed the retirement age for women.

She brought an action against the Area Health Authority on the ground that she had suffered discrimination on the basis of her sex, contrary to the Equal Treatment Directive (Directive 76/207), which, amongst other things, provided that 'equal treatment with regard to working conditions governing dismissal, means that men and women shall be guaranteed the same conditions without discrimination on grounds of sex.' Mrs Marshall claimed that the directive had direct effect, but her claim was contested by the Area Health Authority on the basis that to allow direct effect against the state, when it was acting as an employer, would advantage those who were employees in the public sector and it would not 'be proper to put persons employed by the state in a better position than those employed by a private employer'.

The European Court held that the dismissal of Mrs Marshall had breached Article 5 (1) of the Directive and that the provisions of the Directive could be relied upon by Mrs Marshall. It made no difference whether the state was acting as a public authority or an employer: 'In either case it is necessary to prevent the state from taking advantage of its own failure to comply with Community law.' Moreover, with regard to the creation of unfairness between public and private employees, the Court noted that the solution lay in the hands of the Member States: '[S]uch a distinction may easily be avoided if the member state concerned has correctly implemented the directive in national law.'

Since the *Marshall* case the ECJ has further developed the principle of direct effect, indicating its determination to ensure that Member States do not benefit from the non-implementation of directives. Thus it has ruled (in the *Marleasing* case) that national law should be interpreted in accordance with the purpose of a directive, even if the directive had not been implemented. It has since opened the way for damages to be claimed against the state for the non-implementation of a directive (*Marleasing SA* v. *LA Commercial International de Alimentacion SA* (Case 196–89) [1992] 1 CMLR 305; *Francovich and Bonifaci* v. *Italy* (Cases 6/90 & 9/90) [1992] IRLR 84.

In these judgments the Court is concerned to see that Community law is implemented and effective. Direct effect is a powerful legal principle: it requires the clear acceptance by the national courts of the primacy of Community law and involves them in its enforcement. Since 1973 the British judges have become increasingly confident in their role in this process.

The constitutional consequences of membership of the European Community and Union

Membership of the European Community and the European Union has profound consequences for Britain's constitutional and political arrangements:

(1) Membership of the European Community incorporates Britain into the constitution of the Community, a largely written constitution of a quasi-federal character, interpreted and enforced by a constitutional court. In the perspective of British constitutional development and traditions this is a radical departure, more radical than most of the early enthusiasts for a common market intended, or knew about.

(2) The sovereignty of Parliament is diminished in practice (at least whilst the European Communities Act and its amendments are on the statute book). Parliament cannot enact, or will be unable to secure implementation of, legislation which conflicts with European Community law. The operation of the doctrine of parliamentary sovereignty has been amended to allow for the primacy of Community law. This has constitutional significance not just in relation to the European Community but also for a written constitution or Bill of Rights for Britain.

(3) The political influence of Parliament is also reduced by the transfer of decision-making in an increasing number of policy areas to the Community and Union. The power of Parliament to hold ministers to account is also reduced; and the House of Commons has not developed procedures sharp enough to check what ministers do on its behalf in Brussels (for the good reason that the detail of what ministers do in London is equally beyond their grasp). Thus the convention of ministerial responsibility is further weakened.

(4) The government (the executive) exchanges the constraints of the Westminster Parliament for the less manageable, more 'tentacular' constraints of Brussels. The autonomous power of the national government is decreased by the competing powers of the Community, the growing integration of the economic structure and policy-making, and aspirations, declared and determined, towards a European Central Bank, a single currency and the concertation of a European foreign policy. While some of the more ambitious proposals for a federal union may be deferred or abandoned, it may be difficult in practice to retreat from the already extensive scope of inter-governmental and supra-national arrangements.

(5) The Departments of State and the civil service have adapted to the fresh administrative pastures of the European Community, finding the bureaucratic culture to their taste, and relishing opportunities for wielding some influence independent of ministers. The Foreign Office in particular has welcomed a European mission to replace diminished diplomatic opportunities elsewhere, but has to accept that home departments may now also engage in multilingual negotiation in foreign parts. In general, and taking 'bureaucratic' as a neutral descriptive term, membership of the European Community has reinforced the bureaucratic elements in British government.

(6) Britain, lacking a written constitution itself, is now enmeshed in a parallel European constitution, written down in the Treaties and promulgated as such. It is interpreted positively and enforced by the European Court of Justice, a kind of Supreme Court. Consequences of some significance follow. In particular, the British judges have been given a constitutional role which in the 1990s they seem pleased to play. Moreover, comments from senior members of the judiciary suggest that, where appropriate, they will work to apply more widely the principles contained within Community law. Britain may thus acquire a 'legal' constitution through judicial interpretation of the consequences of parliamentary enactment. Such a development is in line with the seventeenth-century remaking of the constitution by a combination of judicial recognition and parliamentary enactment.

One important example of such a development is in the field of human rights. The constitution of the European Community provides that the Community should act in accordance with the principles enshrined in the European Convention of Human Rights. This means that whilst the Convention itself does not have legal force within Britain (as it has not been enacted into British law), the principles contained within it do apply, in so far as they relate to an area of Community legislative competence. Similarly, the principles of proportionality and non-discrimination can be appealed to.

(7) The existence of the Community encourages devolutionary tendencies in Britain. The Community includes small nation-states like Belgium and Luxembourg, large states like Germany, Italy and Spain, which have serious devolutionary structures (federal in the case of Germany), and, after Maastricht, a Committee of the Regions, and significant regional programmes for economic development. The nations of Britain, in particular Scotland and Wales, draw comfort and encouragement from the European connection. It is less plausible to argue against Scottish aspirations to autonomy on the grounds that Scotland could not survive in a world of large and powerful nation-states. Whether this consideration will hasten new devolutionary arrangements for Scotland may be doubted – at least under a Conservative government which believes in subsidiarity between Brussels and London, but not between London and Edinburgh.

(8) Although the political parties appear to be outside the formal constitution, they are essential to its working, and influence the shape and functioning of institutions and institutional relationships. Membership of the Community has divided the parties along new lines. The divisions, particularly within the Labour Party, led to the referendum of 1975, confirming British membership; but the divisions persisted and contributed to the breakaway of the Social Democratic Party from the Labour Party (1981). By the early 1990s sections of both Conservative and Labour parties were still not reconciled to the permanence and pervasiveness of the European Community and, after Maastricht, European Union, and were opposed to its further development.

For all the detail of the European 'constitution', the Community, and the Union of which it is a part, is only half-formed, still under negotiation by Members with differing aspirations and interests. The Community is not a government and may be understood by analogy with international collaborative organisations (like NATO or UNO) or the rather better defined structures of federations (for example, the United States, Germany, Canada).

Of these, federalism is a familiar constitutional device for the sharing of power, including sovereign power. However, the Community and the Union do not yet amount to a federation, even in the weaker form known as confederation. But Europe does seem to be located on the lower slopes of what is plainly a federal formation – and facing upwards. The analysis of the European Community as a weak form of federal government is difficult but of some interest. Such analysis is obscured and complicated by current polemical debate about the Community based on tendentious understandings (not to say misunderstandings) of the nature of federalism.

For its opponents, federalism means the centralisation and bureaucratisation of power at the expense of the nation-states (the Soviet model). For its proponents, federalism is the sharing of power, as appropriate, between different levels of government (the US or German model). The debate has been further confused by the use of the term 'subsidiarity' for polemical purposes. For the British, the principle of subsidiarity is a defence against 'creeping federalisation' (that is, centralisation); for the Germans, subsidiarity was intended to promote a federal Europe on the decentralised German model with power devolved to the regions.

There is much scope for disagreement about the constitutional values and political attractions of the two ideals of Europe, which may be called 'federalist' (without an automatic pejorative implication) and, for the British Conservative view, Gaullist, in the sense of 'L'Europe des patries' (similarly accepting that formulation as a reasonable and not at all ignoble aspiration). But, whatever position you take up, and whether or not the European Community goes further up the federal mountain, or stays where it is, or slips a little, a constitutional revolution has already taken place. For better or for worse, short of a major political uprooting, the British constitution will never be the same again.

PART II

CONSTITUTIONAL GOVERNMENT

4

THE CROWN

The struggle of Parliament and Crown

Britain may be described as a constitutional monarchy. This is not a helpful description since there is no formal constitution, and the monarchy does not rule. In fact the term does no more than acknowledge the victory of Parliament in the historic struggle to limit the powers of the monarchy.

That victory was achieved in stages. In the 1640s the King, Charles I, was defeated in a civil war with parliamentary forces, captured and beheaded (1649). England was governed as a Protectorate or Commonwealth, under Oliver Cromwell, and his son, until the restoration of Charles II in 1660, this republican interregnum being the only break in a thousand years of the English monarchy.

The Restoration proved to be short-lived. In 1688 another king, James II, accused of arbitrary government and Catholic bigotry, was removed by an aristocratic coup. In 1689 the 'Convention Parliament' (in fact, a revolutionary assembly) invited William of Orange and his wife Mary (respectively the deposed King's nephew and daughter) to accept the throne, deemed to be vacant. The succession was then formally declared by the Act of Settlement of 1701 to lie with the heirs of the Electress of Hanover (James I's granddaughter). The Act imposed a religious condition: Catholics, and those married to Catholics, were barred, and the monarch must swear to maintain the Churches of England and Scotland, and be a communicant member of the Church of England. Succession is by 'primogeniture', sons before daughters.

This regulation of the succession was revolutionary in subjecting rights of inheritance to the will of a strictly illegitimate Parliament. The triumph of Parliament was emphasised by the drawing up of a Declaration of Rights, subsequently enacted as the Bill of Rights (1689), which established rights against an arbitrary monarchy, and referred specifically to freedom of elections and frequent Parliaments. The Act of Settlement of 1701 further provided for 'better securing of the rights and liberties of the subjects'. In a new coronation oath the monarch swore to 'govern according to the statutes in Parliament agreed on'.

In fact much of the force of this constitutional revolution springs less from its specific constitutional change than from the political circumstance of a forced change of succession and the 'Whig' interpretation of those events as a limited constitutional revolution. The revolution lay in the eye of the beholder and the interpreter. Thus the constitutional historian D.L. Keir concedes that William and Mary 'were armed on their accession with a panoply of undoubted legal powers as ample as that borne by their two immediate predecessors' (1966, p. 269). On the other hand:

> Sovereignty in 1688 was for practical purposes grasped by the nation. . . . Not for nothing had England been kingless for two months in 1688–9. . . . Thus perished, at the hands of an assembly animated by . . . popular sovereignty in action, the idea of sacred and inalienable governmental powers, inherent in kings possessing a divine, indefensible, hereditary title, which had lain at the basis of the Restoration monarchy. (Keir, 1966, pp. 269–71)

The principle of heredity remained (supported by a hereditary peerage), and the monarch as Head of the Church of England retained some of the aura of religion. But political power waned as the House of Commons became an instrument of a mass electorate. The monarchy declined into a ceremonial Head of State of the United Kingdom; and in a residual imperial role remains the Head of State in some former colonial territories (but represented by a Governor-General) and 'Head of the Commonwealth' – a courtesy title in a very loose association of countries.

The finance of the monarchy

Most of the costs of the monarchy are borne by the state, through what is known as the Civil List, currently over £7.9 million p.a., and the direct expenditure of departments of state, now about £42 million p.a. In addition, the Crown enjoys the income of the Duchies of Lancaster (almost £4 million p.a. surplus), and, for the Prince of Wales, the revenues of the Duchy of Cornwall (investment of about £35 million + 130,000 acres). The Departments of State provide for the upkeep of royal palaces, trains, 'yacht' and aircraft, though significant economies were proposed (1994) and in particular the yacht is to be decommissioned. Given the difficulty of knowing what to include, and formidable secrecy, the value of the Queen's private fortune is not known precisely, and estimates vary from £50 million to between £400 and £500 million – but the higher figure is likely to be nearer the truth. In addition, the Queen enjoys the use of palaces, pictures, furniture and the like worth perhaps as much as £5 billion; but all that is really part of the wealth of the Crown (or what would be called 'the state' in other countries).

A sudden change in the public mood of loyal affection for the monarchy following the breakdown of royal marriages and a change in attitude of some tabloid newspapers (and made apparent after an immediate and ill-judged offer by the then Heritage Secretary of compensation for the fire at Windsor Castle) led to the Queen offering to pay income tax. The deal subsequently arranged, Memorandum of Understanding on Royal Taxation 1993, accepted such payment was voluntary, on the constitutional grounds that the Queen, being above the government or part of the state, cannot tax herself, and, more specifically, that the legislation on taxation does not apply, and, shifting to dubious sociology, that the aura and trappings of wealth were a necessary part of the mystique of monarchy. The deal further excluded the monarchy from inheritance tax, and thus ensured that great wealth will continue to be an essential part of the character of the modern British monarchy.

The agreement was made between the Queen, the Prince of Wales, the Treasury and the Inland Revenue. The right of the Queen or her successors to end the agreement and opt out of taxation at any time after one year is reserved. An accompanying statement signed by the Prime Minister, the Chancellor of the

Exchequer and the Keeper of the Queen's Privy Purse confirms (or asserts) that the Queen is not liable to income, capital gains or inheritance tax, 'because the relevant enactments do not apply to the crown'.

Political functions of the monarch

The monarchy has three major political functions: as national symbol; adviser to government; and in the making of governments. Of these, the last is by far the most significant.

The monarch as national symbol

The power and the value of symbols in politics should not be underrated. Government by consent is not to be achieved by reason alone. Loyalty and obedience rest on confidence and faith; leadership by persuasion must be to some extent a confidence trick. Bagehot was aware of the political value of this function when he drew a distinction between 'dignified' and 'efficient' parts of the constitution (Bagehot, 1963, p. 61). While asserting (a little ahead of the facts) that the political power of the monarchy had vanished, he recognised the utility of the ceremonial function of the monarchy (pp. 82, 86).

The monarchy and its associated pomp played a significant part in selling imperialism to the people. In a diminished post-imperialist Britain the monarchy played on, surviving the transition from Empire to Commonwealth, from religious to secular, from deferential to irreverent, from United Kingdom to multi-national and multi-ethnic fragmentation. The monarchy, along with the Union Jack, the Houses of Parliament and 10 Downing Street, symbolised the nation and Union, that is, the United Kingdom.

The monarchy seemed to represent family values too, but the family grew over-extended, and opening the royal family to television proved a misguided way of humanising the monarchy. The breaking marriages of the fun-loving younger royals turned the royal family into a sensational soap-opera exploited by a popular press tinged with republicanism. It turned out that the mystique of the monarchy depended on the maintenance of mystery; and a wealthy aristocratic monarchy which could not easily convert itself to a popular monarchy had best not let the people in. The continental model of a 'bicycling monarchy' was not suitable for those who by preference rode horses.

The evident decline in the effectiveness of the monarchy as national symbol in the Britain of the 1990s diminishes a source of non-partisan loyalty and integration in a system normally divided by adversarial party politics, and weakens support for the monarch's constitutional role.

The Crown and political advice

Walter Bagehot, writing in the 1860s, famously ascribed to the monarch 'the right to be consulted, the right to encourage, the right to warn' (1963, p. 111). At the time Queen Victoria tried to do a little more than that, certainly encouraging the Conservative Disraeli and warning the Liberal Gladstone. Bagehot, by allocating the Crown to what he called the 'dignified', not the 'efficient', part of the constitution, was saying, in effect, the game is up, you have no political power.

In fact Bagehot was ahead of his time; but his formula for the monarch's residual power was taught by a Cambridge constitutional historian to the prince who became George V (thus is the British constitution written), and George V followed the new rule with conscience and skill during his twenty-five year reign. He encountered a series of awkward constitutional problems: the possible creation of peers to ensure the passing of the Parliament Bill; the possible veto of an Irish Home Rule Bill; the formation and dissolution of the first Labour government of 1923–4; the General Strike of 1926; and the formation of a National Government in 1931.

In the first two instances the King's doubts about his constitutional powers were, fortunately perhaps, not put to the test. But the monarch could not – and still cannot – avoid playing some part in the making of governments in a complex political situation, and there is no doubt that George V carried out his constitutional role in 1924, and was active far beyond strict constitutional duty in the formation of a coalition in 1931. His delicate conduct of negotiations with the parties in 1923–4, when Labour formed its first, minority, government, 'showed a masterly understanding of constitutional monarchy' (Bogdanor, 1983, p. 107).

George V was the last of the true constitutional monarchs. His successors have retreated further from any involvement in politics, partly for personal reasons, and partly because they were further away from the Victorian model, but also because politics has been clearly divided on party lines and few constitutional dilemmas have been presented. The making of governments may still require intervention (see below) but Bagehot's advisory role is, it may be surmised, of little significance. It seems Queen Elizabeth II was stirred to compassion by the rioting and brutality of the Miners' Strike of 1984–5, as her grandfather was by the government's harsh reaction to the General Strike of 1926, and her uncle (Edward VIII) by the 1930s depression in South Wales. But the Queen has been moved to the expression of firm opinion only on the design of postage stamps – one of the few points on which a royal opinion would count.

The Crown and the state

The historical development of the Crown as the basis and form of governing power in Britain takes the place of any concept of 'the state'. In Britain the term is used mostly in an international context; the nation-state is recognised as an entity with status, boundaries and the power to maintain itself at home and abroad. The state hardly occurs in English law, except in legislation concerned with official secrets, the security services and the interception of communications, which include references to the 'interests of the State'. Moreover, allegiance is to the Crown not the state, ministers are 'Ministers of the Crown', the armed forces are 'royal', and the rest of us are 'subjects' not 'citizens'. In common parlance, 'the state' is used (often in a somewhat derogatory way) to distinguish public services such as schools and hospitals from the private sector; 'the state' is the monstrous and powerful Leviathan of the seventeenth-century philosopher Thomas Hobbes.

Most other developed countries have a clearer concept of the state and base upon it their understanding of constitution, government and law. Does it matter that Britain is underprivileged in this respect? It may be that 'the state' is an obscure term and we can make do with 'the government', or 'the nation', 'the country' or 'the people' – all terms having resonance if not precise meaning. It is true, too, that 'the state' has been used, in pre-war Germany for example, to expand and glorify the power of the government and the pride and ambitions of the nationalist state. On the other hand, 'the state' provides an entity superior to the government of the day, and from which the government may be seen to draw its power.

In Britain that 'superior entity' is the Crown. Thus the basis of governing power is lost in an historical, semi-mystical institution, rooted in heredity and royalist sentiment. While executive powers have transferred from Crown to ministers and 'the government', the development of a rational-legal theory of the constitution has been frustrated, and the notion of an authority higher than the government of the day excluded from the constitutional culture.

From time to time the courts have confronted the problem, but inevitably they have had considerable difficulty defining 'state', and determining whether the government constitutes 'the state' or is a servant of it. The matter was particularly important in *Chandler* v. *DPP* [1964] AC 763.

Defining the state

A group of nuclear demonstrators were prosecuted under section 1 of the Official Secrets Act 1911. They had entered an airfield with the intention of immobilizing it and the DPP argued that their actions were 'prejudicial to the safety or interests of the State' (as per the Official Secrets Act). This was rebutted by the demonstrators, who considered their actions to be beneficial to the state, as defined as the inhabitants of a geographical area. The Law Lords did not accept this definition of the state. However, there were variations in the definitions they gave. Lord Reid came closest to the demonstrators' definition, suggesting 'perhaps the country or the realm are as good synonyms as one can find'. He was prepared to accept 'the organised community as coming as near to a definition as one can get.' Lord Devlin held that in its legal context the state meant 'the organs of government of a national community', while Lord Pearce contended that 'the interests of the state' meant 'the interests of the State according to the policies laid down for it by its recognised organs of government and authority'. Thus he concluded that anything which prejudices those policies is within the meaning of the Act 'prejudicial to the interests of the State'.

The House of Lords was concerned with the meanings of 'state' and the 'interests of the state' as a matter of statutory interpretation. It saw those interests as being determined by the government of the day, as the representative body of the state. This is not a view accepted by all civil libertarians – or nuclear protesters. It is, however, preferable to the intepretation used by the judge in the Clive Ponting trial (see Chapter 6), who directed the jury that it meant 'the interests of the government of the day', thereby implying that government and the state are synonymous.

The formation and dissolution of governments

The monarch plays a necessary part in the formation of governments. This means that the Queen appoints the Prime Minister. For this purpose, 'the Queen' is the Queen assisted by her advisers, a formation sometimes known as 'the Palace', in touch with, indeed in consultation with, the Cabinet Secretary and the Prime Minister's Office. The monarchy, like the Prime Ministership, turns out to be a network of officials and advisers.

Nor is the Queen's power of appointment quite what it seems: appointment is an invitation to form a government by commanding or organising a majority in the House. The grant of royal approval is thus conditional, but follows without question if the condition is met. This is a rule of politics and reflects the dependence of the monarch on Parliament, initially to raise taxes, later as an instrument of government, and the dependence of Parliament on majorities based on party organisation of a popular vote.

The moment of truth in the recognition of this rule of modern politics came finally after the 1832 Reform Act, when it became evident that the monarch could no longer secure the Prime Minister of his or her preference, since a general election could no longer be managed by influence and corruption. Few people took William IV seriously when in 1835 he raged: 'The cabinet is my cabinet, they had better take care, or, by God, I will have them impeached!' (Woodward, 1938, p. 96n1). Such royal distaste for democracy, shared to some extent by the young Victoria (for whom the word 'democracy' held a revolutionary and French connotation), could not prevent the development of the modern parliamentary constitution.

The role of the Palace in the formation and dissolution of governments is normally straightforward. If the mind of the Commons is apparent, the Palace registers it by issuing the appropriate invitation. However, it may arise that the 'mind' of the Commons is not clear.

Case 1: The leadership of the majority party is uncertain. This was so in 1957 when Macmillan succeeded Eden, and in 1963 when Lord Home succeeded Macmillan. Neither was thought to be the likely successor, and Lord Home was very unlikely indeed. In 1957 Macmillan seems to have emerged after a rapid informal consultation among Conservative Members of Parliament; but the Queen also received in audience two Conservative elder statesmen (Churchill and Salisbury). The 1963 case was more difficult since Macmillan resigned suddenly on the eve of the Conservative party conference, and there were several potential candidates for the party leadership. Lord Home was an unexpected choice (especially as he had to renounce his peerage under the new Act designed by Tony Benn, formerly Lord Stansgate).

It may be argued that in this difficult situation the Palace acted with undue haste, leaving little time for counter-organisation by Conservatives like Macleod and Powell who were outside the 'magic circle'. On the other hand, to delay was to give time for opposition and thus to undermine the succession. In any case, the House had the power to accept or reject the Queen's invited candidate. This is strictly true, but in practice the House might feel constrained by the Queen's action, and supportive by inertia of a *fait accompli*.

The 1963 case was clearly potentially embarrassing for the Queen. To avert a repetition of such a situation and to meet criticism about selection of the leader by a 'magic circle', the Conservative Party adopted a ballot system for the election of the leader. Other parties already had election systems. Thus the parties followed the rule of politics that the Queen should not be embarrassed by being associated with partisan preference. But political parties cannot always be expected to behave with such consideration and restraint when political power is in or near their grasp.

Case 2: There is no clear majority party. This is the problem of the 'hung' Parliament, which occurred in 1924, 1929 and 1974 and is a possible product of the present workings of the electoral system. The same rule about the avoidance of partisan preference governs behaviour: the Palace awaits the negotiation of a party majority by coalition or other arrangement. Subject to this rule, the party leaders seek party advantage, bounded only by the necessity to arrive at a parliamentary majority. The incumbent Prime Minister (even if his party is not the largest) may play his advantage by 'having first go' and, if he wants, by meeting Parliament to test his arrangement. If he fails, the presumption is that the monarch will send for the leader of the largest or next largest party, though this rule does not please a substantial third party.

That version of the position seems to fit the precedent of 1923–4, when Baldwin did not resign until he had been defeated in Parliament, and various plans (not encouraged by the King) were floated for keeping out Labour. In 1974 Mr Heath attempted to construct a coalition with the Liberals, failed and resigned. But in 1929, Baldwin, leading the second largest party, resigned, though a deal with the Liberals would have provided a majority. This was Baldwin's choice (no coalition with the dreaded Lloyd George), not the King's. The Palace necessarily awaits the Prime Minister's resignation.

That is the public position; but there is a question whether it is entirely fair that the sitting Prime Minister is under no obligation to resign. It seems likely that in this situation private negotiations (communications at least) between the Palace, the Cabinet Office and Downing Street may take place, and the Queen may have to make a difficult and sensitive judgment about who is to be given 'first go' at forming a government. To a sitting Prime Minister facing loss of power the political rule of not embarrassing the Queen may seem less binding than the political and constitutional fact that power is determined not by the Queen but by numbers in the House of Commons. For example, if the Conservatives in 1992 had won 295 seats to Labour's 305, would John Major have been justified in staying in office and bidding for the votes of Northern Ireland MPs and Liberal Democrats? And could the Palace have intervened? The answer lies in the arithmetic, not in the constitution.

Case 3: A Prime Minister with an uncertain majority, or without a majority, may seek the dissolution of Parliament so that he may improve his electoral position. Can the Queen refuse, or insist on, a dissolution?

The normal rules may not apply:

1. The Queen accepts the advice of the Prime Minister. But the issue is to do with the legitimacy of the claim of the Prime Minister to his post: he cannot be the sole judge.

2. The Queen appoints as Prime Minister a person able to win the confidence of the House. But there may be more than one possible candidate (another leader within the Prime Minister's party, or a leader of an actual or possible coalition party).

In both cases arithmetic cannot come to the help of the constitution. In a confused political situation the Queen has to exercise discretion. In doing so she follows a third rule, that she should as far as possible not take any action which could be considered partisan, or 'political', favouring one party, section or candidate. In practice this may be difficult. The accepted rule would seem to be that the Queen might refuse a dissolution on one of the following grounds:

1. In war or any national emergency the Queen should have regard to the national interest. However, there have been changes of government in wartime (1915, 1916, 1940, 1945, 1990) and there was a general election in 1945. Nor do economic crises rule out elections (as in 1931). In any case, economic crises are now endemic, and the possibility of a change of government might have a salutary effect. Altogether this rule about national interest is not of high significance: the sovereign serves the national interest by arranging as speedily as possible for the government to be carried on with the support of the House of Commons.
2. Where the Prime Minister seeks a dissolution against the wishes of his colleagues, a majority of his parliamentary party, or, in a coalition, of his coalition partners.
3. Where the Prime Minister requests a dissolution before other possibilities (alternative Prime Ministers, parties, coalitions) have been explored and tested.
4. When there is not a 'decent interval' between one dissolution and the next, to allow for exploration of other solutions, the transaction of minimal government business (for example, financial or diplomatic), and for the electorate to rest and reflect.

These rules appear to fit the main precedents. The monarch has not attempted to dissolve Parliament against advice since the seventeenth century. In 1918, following the end of the war, the King conceded a dissolution to Lloyd George (though with some reluctance). He was to agree to a dissolution again in 1924, in the case of a minority Labour government; and in 1931, in the case of a National Government, which had promised not to go to the country immediately. The Queen granted a dissolution in 1974, after Wilson's minority government had survived for seven months.

The monarch has not refused a dissolution in the United Kingdom in modern times, but no situations of acute uncertainty have arisen. However, Commonwealth countries with constitutional arrangements derived from Westminster (and Governors-General representing the Crown), provide examples of 'Crown' intervention in government formation and dissolution. In practice, it is not at all certain that the acts of a Governor-General can be taken as equivalent to those of the monarch. The Governor-General, even though 'representing' the Crown, holds only a temporary appointment on the advice of the Commonwealth government. So there is a further element of obscurity about the rules. The acts of a Governor-General may be taken not as precedents but as indicators of constitutional propriety.

The recent history of Canada, Australia and South Africa provide examples of the representative of the Crown refusing a request for a dissolution. For example, in Australia in 1975 the Governor-General refused the request of the Prime Minister, Goff Whitlam, for a dissolution of the Senate (the upper House of Parliament) without a dissolution of the House of Representatives. The Senate refused to pass money bills and thus made it impossible to govern. The Governor-General dismissed the Prime Minister and asked the leader of the Opposition to form a government. Shortly afterwards the Governor-General granted a full dissolution as requested by the new Prime Minister, who went on to win the subsequent general election.

In Canada there have been two instances where dissolution has been refused in situations more in line with those outlined above. In 1926 the Governor-General refused to grant a dissolution of the Canadian Parliament, believing that an alternative government could be formed by the leader of the Conservative Opposition. This proved to be wrong and a subsequent request for a dissolution from the Conservative leader was granted. In 1985 a dissolution of the provincial Parliament of Ontario was also refused by the Governor-General on similar grounds, which this time proved correct. The Governor-General thus escaped the criticism and controversy surrounding the refusal of a dissolution in the other two cases.

Similarly in South Africa in 1939 the Governor-General judged correctly that a dissolution was not necessary since the Opposition leader, Smuts, could form a secure government. Still the sensitivity of the 'Crown' decision is clear: the political strategy of the outgoing Prime Minister, Hertzog, to appeal to the people on a policy of neutrality had been effectively frustrated by the Governor-General's action.

The domestic precedents are more significant. Thus in 1924, as noted above, George V granted a dissolution to the ailing minority Labour government, though he believed he was not obliged to do so, and the formation of an alternative government, minority or coalition, was possible (at least on the arithmetic of seats in Parliament). The catch for the monarch in this situation is that an alternative government, though formed at the instigation of the monarch (so it would appear at least), is certain to be insecure, and so likely in its turn to seek a dissolution. The monarch is then faced with difficult and undoubtedly political choices: to grant to one Prime Minister what was recently refused to his predecessor, or to tell the new Prime Minister he must carry on despite the insecurity of his position, or to go looking for a third Prime Minister.

The lessons for the monarch are as follows:

1. to hope that a Prime Minister will not seek a dissolution in a situation in which it could not reasonably be granted;
2. hence never to refuse a request for a dissolution.

The events of 1974 suggest that condition (1) may be fulfilled. Edward Heath lost his majority in the election of February 1974, and, after vain efforts to build a coalition with the Liberals, did not seek a dissolution. Harold Wilson then formed a minority government and was able to leave a decent interval of seven months before requesting a dissolution.

Thus the constitutional position is fairly clear, advisers are on hand to guide the monarch, and the parties are likely to have engaged in pre-election discussion with 'the Palace', and recognise the importance of sparing the Queen political embarrassment. Nevertheless, when the stakes are high (governing power itself), and political passions aroused (as at the climax of an election), the Queen may need to tread delicately to preserve a balance between parties. In the present electoral system the incumbent Prime

Minister can exploit the advantage of his office, and both major parties enjoy access to the grant of dissolution. Under a system of proportional representation, third parties would hold stronger negotiating positions, and the role of the monarch would be more significant and more difficult.

Altogether it may be concluded that the monarchy has a continuing and essential part in the formation of governments. This may from time to time involve difficult political choices, which may be seen as giving advantage to one or other political party or leader. In carrying out such a delicate duty the monarch is supported by her personal advisers, by the Cabinet Secretary and other non-political and independent advisers; and the difficulties of choice are eased by the custom that politicians avoid any political embarrassment of the Queen. Any reform of the electoral system in the direction of proportional representation is likely to make government formation by negotiation normal and thus make the monarch's invitation to form a government a political act.

It may be argued that, by being evidently 'above politics', a hereditary monarch is best qualified to carry through the process of government formation; or that a directly or indirectly elected 'public person' or a commission of such persons (rather like the Speaker of the House of Commons) would do as well. There are practical (but not insuperable) difficulties in devising an alternative system; but a hereditary monarchy is not self-evidently 'above politics', and no one devising a new structure would look to a hereditary monarchy as a model.

The monarch's major constitutional function lies in the formation and dissolution of governments; but the monarchy is also the source of privileges and prerogatives which are actually held and wielded by the government. This is the monarchy in its constitutional form as the Crown, the historic source of governing authority in Britain. The power to govern is drawn from the Crown, legitimated by Parliament; the British are governed by the 'Crown-in-Parliament'. Government is carried on in the name of the monarch, as in treaties, declarations of war, Orders in Council, prosecutions in 'Her Majesty's' courts, incarceration in HM Prisons; civil and military servants of the state are by status 'On Her Majesty's Service'. Here the monarch personifies the constitutional device of the Crown, but we are dealing with what in other countries would be called executive power. Hence it is appropriate now to move to the consideration of such power.

5

EXECUTIVE POWER
The Prerogative

Executive power

Executive power in Britain is derived historically from the Crown and politically from the House of Commons. Its legitimacy therefore rests on both the historic constitutional authority of the Crown and the electoral mandate of the people. In practice the people elect, the House of Commons selects, the monarch appoints. Of these three procedures, that of the House of Commons is most significant, and the executive power is thus largely shaped by its parliamentary and popular source. But its historic source in the Crown endows the executive with a formidable authority not dependent on Parliament, except by a general test of confidence.

The Crown is the source of executive power in the sense of governing authority conferred by the invitation to a political leader to form a government and assume the office of Prime Minister. The power thus conveyed is non-specific and satisfyingly broad for its recipients. The Crown is further the source of the more specific executive powers which inhere in the privileges and prerogatives of the Crown. These are derived historically from the Crown, and are still disguised as royal prerogatives, exercised by Her Majesty's Government and Ministers of the Crown, part of the executive as the 'Crown-in-Parliament'. These privileges and prerogatives complement the specific executive powers derived from statute laws enacted by Parliament.

The prerogative powers

The prerogative powers are historical powers of the monarch which have not been superseded by statute. They are frequently referred to as 'residual' or 'left-over' powers, and by their nature tend to be ill-defined. Prerogative powers include the power to appoint a Prime Minister and ministers.

In the case of the Prime Minister, the Queen may have to exercise some discretion, as indicated in Chapter 4. However, most prerogative powers are exercised by the Crown only on the advice of ministers. This circumlocution is deceptive, perhaps deliberately so. The prerogative powers are executive powers, exercised by the government. The executive has in practice assumed the Crown, and gains thereby a useful set of privileges, immunities and prerogatives, attractively legitimised by the ancient dignity and aura of the monarchy, and repelling the *lèse-majesté* of accountability.

The main executive powers derived from the Crown prerogative are as follows:

(1) *Appointment of ministers, heads and chairmen of government and non-governmental public bodies, and the granting of life peerages.* The Prime Minister has here a substantial fund of influence based on patronage.

A minor but not insignificant part of such influence lies in the grant of honours, certainly used by most Prime Ministers to reward loyal and long-serving backbench Members of Parliament and political friends. For example, Margaret Thatcher awarded honours to sympathetic newspaper proprietors and editors and businessmen, some of whom had contributed to Conservative Party funds. Lloyd George seems to have traded honours for party contributions on a set tariff.

(2) *The conduct of foreign affairs and defence.* These are matters which are normally subject to prescription in constitutions. For example, the US Constitution makes the President the Commander-in-Chief of the army, allocates to Congress the power to declare war, and divides the treaty-making power between President and Senate. In practice these provisions have made the conduct of US foreign policy difficult and confused at times, certainly for allied powers. Indeed, it may be argued that the requirements of international negotiation and the urgent demands of national security make foreign affairs properly an executive function, subject to accounting to the representative assembly, and to procedures for confirmation in the case of treaties, and majority support in the case of declarations of war.

This is the position broadly achieved in the British disposition of power. In the case of treaties, power is, according to the formula, vested in the executive, acting on behalf of the Crown – which means that it is vested in the executive. Parliament has a formal part in the procedure only when the treaty requires a change in the law of the United Kingdom or the spending of public funds. Governments make many comparatively minor agreements which are not subject to ratification, that is, formal confirmation. Ratification is an executive procedure, but where it is required, it is customary for treaties to be laid before Parliament for a period of twenty-one days. This is the 'Ponsonby rule', named after a Labour Member who campaigned for open diplomacy as a backbencher and later found himself a minister in the Foreign Office. Parliament may then request a debate, and the government responds according to its calculation of support.

Ratifying the Maastricht Treaty

The issue of the precise limits of the treaty-making power arose in the debates (1993) on the ratification of the Maastricht Treaty. The Treaty required approval by Parliament since it confirmed and extended fundamental changes in constitutional arrangements, changes or prospective changes in economic and social law, expenditure of public funds and possible increases in the powers of the European Parliament. Indeed the high significance of the Treaty and serious divisions about it within the Conservative Party compelled the government on political grounds to seek endorsement by Parliament.

This legitimation by Parliament is the saving mechanism of the British disposition of power, and usually presents no problems for a government entrenched by a solid party majority. However, in the case of the Maastricht Treaty, the party majority was not nearly solid enough and the government appeared to be in some danger of defeat on a clause to secure the specially negotiated 'opt-out' from the Social Chapter. The parliamentary politics were somewhat confused since the Labour Party amendment would in effect have removed the whole Social Chapter from the Treaty, although the party actually wanted the Chapter incorporated.

The government's first position, as advised by lawyers in the Foreign Office, was that defeat on the clause would damage the whole ratification process, and thus have serious consequences. After taking alternative legal advice, this time from the Attorney-General, the government reversed its position and declared that the loss of the clause would have no consequences, since there would be no impact on UK legislation. A rejection of the clause by Parliament would be irrelevant.

It was commented at the time that the Foreign Secretary appeared to be embarrassed by this reinterpretation of the law which had the effect of nullifying a rare government defeat in the House of Commons. Moreover, the government's failure to seek the advice of the Attorney-General at an earlier stage suggested that ministers had hoped that Conservative backbenchers would support the government if they believed defeat of the clause would damage ratification. Thus, even though the later legal advice seems to have been correct, the choice of when and where to seek legal advice was politically motivated.

Parliament finally approved the Treaty, but voted in favour of the Social Chapter (by a majority of 1). The vote had no effect upon the Treaty or the British ratification; it was merely an expression of opinion, of no legal consequence. The government proceeded to ratify the Treaty, including the British opt-out of the Social Chapter. Parliament's role was to endorse or applaud, except for this one cry of discontent.

(3) *Immigration and the grant of citizenship*. Citizenship amounts in Britain to the right of abode, the right to welfare benefits (including the free use of the Health Service), the right to vote, and the right to a passport for the purpose of travel outside the territory. Passports are issued under the royal prerogative, but a refusal to grant a passport is subject to judicial review. For the rest, citizenship is a matter of parentage, birth and residence. For immigrants, including the children of immigrants, the rights to citizenship are now governed by statute law, especially the British Nationality Act of 1981. All British citizens have rights throughout the European Community under Community law.

(4) *The regulation of the civil service*. The civil service is largely controlled and regulated by Order in Council made 'under the prerogative'. The use of the prerogative power is normally uncontested, but proved particularly controversial in the banning of trade unions at the government's communications centre (GCHQ) at Cheltenham. The ban was challenged in the courts (*Council of*

Civil Service Unions v. *Minister for Civil Service* [1985] AC 374). The case proved to be of major significance in the judicial clarification of executive power derived from the prerogative. Orders in Council provide the legal instruments for the appointment of civil servants, and their terms and conditions of employment. They also provide for the management of the civil service. This regulation of the civil service by prerogative rather than statute enables the government to institute fundamental reform without parliamentary approval (see Chapter 8).

The *GCHQ* case

In December 1983 the Prime Minister, in her capacity as Minister for the Civil Service, issued an instruction that civil servants working at the government listening (spying) station at Cheltenham (GCHQ) could no longer be members of a trade union. The order was issued under the prerogative power in response to a series of strikes within the civil service, two of which had targeted GCHQ. Parliament was informed of the decision in January 1984. The action was criticised for being heavy-handed; some members of the Cabinet would have preferred a negotiated 'no-strike' agreement with the unions.

Legally it was challenged by the civil service unions on the grounds that the Minister had acted unfairly by failing to honour procedural obligations. The unions argued that in matters relating to terms and conditions of employment there was a long-established practice of consultation at GCHQ. Members therefore had a legitimate expectation that their union representatives would be consulted on any related matter, including the restriction on union membership, prior to any change being made. The failure of the minister to consult thus made the decision void.

The defence of the Minister was, first, that the order was made under a prerogative power and was not reviewable by the courts; so far no prerogative act had been reviewed, although a number of judges had indicated that review was not excluded. Secondly, the Minister argued that the lack of consultation had been necessary in order to forestall strikes in protest and protect national security interests, including Britain's relationship with the United States, which used GCHQ to gather information. Significantly, this national security defence had not been used in the Divisional Court, where the government relied on the non-reviewability of the prerogative power, and was only introduced into the Court of Appeal when it was clear that the case might be lost.

The case went on appeal to the House of Lords where it was held:

1. The prerogative power was reviewable by the courts (that is, subject to examination as to its legality). It was not the source of power (statute or prerogative) that was important, but the suitability of the

subject matter for review. Lord Roskill indicated the prerogative powers which he considered to be non-justiciable:

> Prerogative powers such as those relating to the making of treaties, the defence of the realm, the prerogative of mercy, the grant of honours, the dissolution of Parliament and the appointment of ministers as well as others are not, I think, susceptible to judicial review because their nature and subject matter are such as are not amenable to the judicial process.

The distinction was a little elusive; Lord Roskill did not provide a positive list of reviewable prerogatives, but he did consider that the order in the GCHQ case did not fall into an 'excluded category' and was therefore open to review. The first defence of the government therefore fell.

2. The members of the union at GCHQ did have a legitimate expectation that they would be consulted before a change was made in their terms and conditions of employment, and thus the Minister had acted unfairly in not consulting them. However, this 'duty of fairness' was outweighed by considerations of national security, which were for the government alone to weigh. All that the court required was evidence that the decision was taken on grounds of national security.

> The Government alone has access to the necessary information and in any event the judicial process is unsuitable for reaching decisions on national security.

Thus the government was successful on the second line of defence. However, the decision was seen as a moral victory for the unions, for the Law Lords made it clear that had the government not pleaded national security, the court would have ruled its action to have been unfair, and seemed to accept that civil servants might enjoy implied contractual rights. GCHQ was the first case in which the use of the prerogative had been reviewed, and is a good example of the judges shaping the constitution. At the same time, the House of Lords made it clear that the subject matter of many prerogatives would make them unsuitable for review. On balance the government seems to have won this contest by two goals to one!

(5) *Keeping the peace*. In 1988 the question was raised in the courts whether there was a peace-keeping prerogative (*R*. v. *Secretary of State for Home Department, ex parte Northumbria Police Authority* [1988] 2 WLR 590 CA).

The *Northumbria Police Authority* case

The case centred on the issue by the Home Secretary of a circular which informed Chief Constables and Police Authorities that plastic bullets and CS gas for use in cases of serious public disorder would be available from a central store. A Chief Constable, wishing to purchase such equipment, could do so with the approval of his Police Authority, or, if this approval was not forthcoming, by following a procedure outlined within the circular. The Northumbria Police Authority challenged the authority of the Home Secretary both to maintain such equipment and to issue it without the approval of Police Authorities. The Authority pointed to the provision in the Police Act 1964 authorising Police Authorities to maintain vehicles, apparatus and equipment as required for police purposes.

The Home Secretary maintained that his authority came from two sources: first, from the Police Act, which gave him power to provide and maintain such facilities as forensic science laboratories and such other services as he considered necessary and expedient for promoting the efficiency of the police; secondly, from the prerogative power, or rather duty, to keep the peace. The Police Authority's response was that the provision within the Act was not sufficient, and that the prerogative to keep the peace had been superseded by the powers granted to Police Authorities by the Police Act, except in cases of grave emergency.

The Court of Appeal held that the Police Act did provide the necessary authority for the Home Secretary, but had it not done so, then the prerogative could have been relied upon. It had not been abrogated by the Police Act because the sections in the Act concerning the supply of equipment fell short of 'an express and unequivocal inhibition sufficient to abridge the prerogative powers'. The decision demonstrates that very specific wording is required within a statute before it will replace a prerogative such as 'keeping the peace', which was ill-defined and unsubstantiated by evidence of previous use.

The lack of evidence did not bother the Court of Appeal. Indeed, Lord Justice Nourse concluded that the 'scarcity of references in the books to the prerogative of keeping the peace within the realm does not disprove that it exists. Rather it may point to an unspoken assumption that it does.'

Thus the Home Secretary was confirmed in his possession of a substantial and ill-defined prerogative power.

The prerogative clearly provides the executive with important powers, many of which are necessary for the effective functioning of government. However, most prerogative powers are expressed in broad terms and give ministers wide-ranging discretion beyond the capacity of Parliament or courts to review. Even after the

GCHQ case it is clear that many powers will not be reviewed by the courts. The Prime Minister's patronage power derived from the prerogative may be seen as excessive. Altogether, the scope of the prerogative powers raises doubts about maintaining the Crown as the theoretical source of constitutional authority in a modern democracy.

Most of the prerogatives exercised by ministers could be replaced by statutes and thus be more clearly defined and, if necessary, confined. Statutory arrangements centred on Parliament could be devised in place of the present arrangements for most appointments, except of ministers, and for the formation and dissolution of governments. There are of course advantages in the present system based on prerogative powers, and difficulties in devising alternative procedures. But most of the advantages of the prerogative accrue to the executive, and few would argue that if the prerogative did not exist, it would be necessary to invent it.

The privileges of the Crown

Linked to the prerogative are the privileges of the Crown, which again arose as a protection for the sovereign or as a natural consequence of his or her position. Hence the Queen cannot be prosecuted or sued for a wrongful act, and successive monarchs have claimed a privileged position in relation to income tax (see Chapter 4). However, most privileges or immunities protect the executive or Crown bodies or agents, including ministers and their departments and departmental agencies.

Private law immunities

The Crown Proceedings Act 1947 removed the immunity of Crown bodies from actions in tort (civil wrongs such as negligence), but the Crown is still in a privileged position with regard to contracts. This means that the government can claim executive necessity for its failure to fulfil a contractual obligation, and the other party is not entitled to damages. The legal position of the Crown as an employer is also different. Civil servants hold office 'at the pleasure of the Crown' (that is, at the discretion of the government). They cannot sue for damages for wrongful dismissal, although legislation does now provide for their reinstatement and a right to compensation in the case of unfair dismissal.

Immunity from statute law

A particularly broad protection is afforded by the immunity of the Crown from statute law, unless specifically stated within the relevant Act or implied by the courts as necessary to make the act workable. There are undoubtedly occasions when it is not appropriate for the executive to be subject to the same liabilities as private persons. However, the breadth of the protection at times produces unwarranted immunities, which can only be removed by subsequent legislation expressly including the Crown. It is as a result of such legislation that tenants in Crown property now enjoy the protection of the Rent Acts, Crown servants can no longer exceed the speed limit when on urgent Crown business, and National Health Service hospital kitchens are subject to the appropriate public health rules.

The closing of the A814

The question of immunity arose in a Scottish case, which was appealed to the House of Lords *(Lord Advocate* v. *Dumbarton DC* [1990] 1 All ER 1). The Ministry of Defence, in order to improve the perimeter fence around the Faslane Submarine Base, closed one lane of the A814 which ran alongside the base. The local authority claimed that this was in contravention of legislation which required the consent of the relevant local authority before blocking the highway. The Lord Advocate, acting for the Ministry, argued that the Ministry, as part of the Crown, was not bound by Acts of Parliament, unless the Act so stated. The House of Lords found for the Lord Advocate, confirming that 'the Crown can be bound only by express words or necessary implication'.

Injunctions cannot be granted against the Crown

The Crown Proceedings Act 1947 stipulates that the courts cannot grant an injunction against the Crown (an injunction is a direction to cease a wrongful act). It follows therefore that an interim (temporary or 'meanwhile') injunction can also not be granted. Interim injunctions are used to stop the party to a dispute continuing with the disputed action while the matter is before the court and judgment is awaited. The non-applicability of injunctions to Crown bodies may be detrimental to the individual. However, two recent cases indicate developments in this area: first, with reference to the European Court of Justice, and, secondly, when the authority of the court itself is threatened.

The *Factortame* case

(See also Chapter 2, and for the EU generally Chapter 3.) A group of Spanish fishermen had registered their vessels as British vessels, a practice which the British government had sought to prevent by the Merchant Shipping Act 1988 and the Merchant Shipping Regulations 1988. The government was concerned that British fishermen were disadvantaged by the quotas set under the Common Fisheries Policy. The Spanish fishermen brought an action against the UK government on the grounds that the legislation infringed their rights under EC law, which prohibits discrimination on the grounds of nationality. The Divisional Court decided that a preliminary ruling on the law must be sought from the European Court of Justice, but the question arose as to what should happen while the ruling was awaited. This could take several years and during this time the Spaniards argued that their rights under EC law would continue to be infringed and their livelihood would be affected.

The matter went on appeal to the House of Lords (1991) which ruled that it could not under English law grant an interim injunction which would in this case require the suspension of part of the Merchant Shipping Act. The House of Lords asked for a ruling from the European Court of Justice as to whether the Lords had such authority under EC law. The ECJ held that if, in a case concerning Community law, the sole obstacle to the granting of interim relief is a rule of national law, then the national law must be set aside. So the House of Lords accepted that it had jurisdiction to grant interim relief where a matter of EC law was concerned, and thus held that the sections of the Act which withdrew the rights of registration from the Spanish fishermen were suspended until the action was settled.

The decision in *Factortame* was seen as having considerable constitutional consequence. First, it demonstrated beyond doubt the supremacy of Community law over English law (see Chapter 2). Secondly, it enabled courts to grant interim injunctions against ministers where matters of EC law are concerned, even though it was thought the Crown Proceedings Act did not enable them to do so where domestic law was concerned (a point addressed by Lord Woolf in *M.* v. *Home Office* – see below). Thirdly, the decision reversed the prohibition against the suspension of laws dating from 1689.

The immunity of the Crown was further challenged in a case concerning deportation, which led to the minister being held in contempt.

M. v. *Home Office*

(*M.* v. *Home Office and Another* [1993] 3 All ER 541 (H. of L.) M. was a citizen of Zaïre who arrived in Britain seeking political asylum. His application was rejected by the Home Office, as was his application to the courts for judicial review, and an order was made for his return to Zaïre by 6.30 p.m. on 1 May 1991. A few hours before the deadline, another application for judicial review on different grounds was made to a judge in chambers. So that he had time to consider the application, the judge sought the postponement of M.'s departure. He believed that counsel for the Home Office had given this undertaking, although counsel considered that he had only undertaken to endeavour to prevent the imminent departure. Either way communications between Home Office officials seemed to break down and M.'s departure from Britain was not delayed, nor was he removed from the plane during a stop-over in Paris.

At 11.20 p.m. the judge was informed that M. had been removed from British jurisdiction. At this point he made an order requiring the Home Secretary, Kenneth Baker, to return M. However, after seeking legal advice, the Home Secretary concluded that the judge did not have the power (or jurisdiction) to make the order, and thus he did not have to comply with it. An action for contempt of court was then brought on behalf of M. (now somewhere in Zaïre) against the Home Office and Home Secretary on the grounds that they failed to comply with the original undertaking and the later order from the judge. The defence argued that just as the courts could not grant injunctions against ministers and departments, neither could they enforce undertakings or make orders. Ministers and departments could not therefore be held in contempt of court.

Lord Woolf gave the leading judgment for the House of Lords. He held that the procedure for judicial review, as laid down in the Supreme Court Act 1981, allowed for the granting of a stay (holding the situation as it is or maintaining the status quo) pending the hearing of the application for review. This, he considered, must include authority to grant injunctions, and interim injunctions. It followed therefore that the court could also make an order against a minister. Lord Woolf continued:

> Such orders must be taken not to offend the theory that the Crown can supposedly do no wrong. Equally, if such orders are made and not obeyed, the body against whom the orders are made can be found guilty of contempt without offending that theory, which would be the only justifiable impediment against making a finding of contempt.

Lord Woolf dismissed the argument accepted by the Court of Appeal that a minister could only be found guilty of contempt in his personal capacity because the sanctions available for contempt – a fine or imprisonment – were not appropriate for a minister acting in his public capacity, that is, as head of a department. He did not see the lack of an appropriate punishment as relevant. He stated:

> [T]he ability of the court to make a finding of contempt is of great importance. It would demonstrate that a government department has interfered with the administration of justice. It will then be for Parliament to determine what should be the consequences of that finding. . . . The object of the exercise is not so much to punish an individual as to vindicate the rule of law by a finding of contempt. . . . By making the finding against the minister in his official capacity the court will be indicating that it is the department for which the minister is responsible which has been guilty of contempt. The minister himself may or may not have been personally guilty of contempt.
>
> . . . The conduct complained of in this case which justified the bringing of contempt proceedings was not that of Mr Baker alone and he was acting on advice.

The case of *M.* v. *Home Office* was constitutionally important. It acted, first, as a reminder that ministers and departments are not above the law, and, secondly, as a reassertion of the courts' constitutional authority in interpreting and applying the law. In doing so, the House of Lords removed the difference between cases concerned with European Community Law and those concerned with national law, at least in judicial review actions. Thus, without the repeal of the Crown Proceedings Act, the law has changed. The House of Lords has in effect declared that the Rules of the Supreme Court had by implication repealed the protection previously given to ministers where judicial review is concerned.

Public interest immunity (from disclosure)

Public interest immunity has been the most controversial of the privileges of the Crown. Until 1973 it was called Crown privilege. This, while denoting its origins, belied its use by the executive. It was used by ministers (not of course the Queen) to protect documentation from disclosure to the other party in a court action on the grounds that disclosure would be injurious to the public interest.

The *Cammell Laird* case

(*Duncan* v. *Cammell Laird* [1942] AC 624). The submarine, the *Thetis*, sank during its trials, and relatives of the crew pursued a claim in negligence. The action was against the shipbuilder and so did not directly concern the government. However, the Admiralty instructed Cammell Laird not to disclose certain documents, and the First Lord of the Admiralty swore an affidavit claiming that disclosure would be against the public interest. It was feared that plans of the submarine (which it was later revealed had been fitted with a new type of torpedo tube) might be acquired by the enemy. The House of Lords accepted the affidavit without question and the litigants were unsuccessful in their claim of negligence.

The decision was no doubt right, given the timing of the case. However, the House of Lords also used the opportunity to lay down rules about the use of Crown privilege, which were much criticised for the breadth and generosity of their grant of privilege to the executive. Their lordships declared that Crown privilege could be claimed either because of the content of a particular document or because the document belonged to a class of document that attracted such privilege. Obvious classes were those where disclosure might injure national security or diplomatic relations. But in addition protection was appropriate in the interests of 'the proper functioning of the public service', clearly a very wide category.

The argument put forward then, and still sustained by some today, was that it was necessary for communications between civil servants and between civil servants and their ministers to be protected so that officials could be candid in what they said (the candour argument). If they believed that their communications might at any time be revealed in court, then they would be less forthright and this could be to the detriment of the proper functioning of the public service.

Duncan v. *Cammell Laird* not only developed the idea of protection as of right because a document belonged to a certain class, but it also made ministers the sole arbiters of the public interest. If they considered that the public interest was served by the non-disclosure of documents, then their decision would not be questioned by the court. Any balancing arguments concerning the interests of justice were for them to address.

Thus there was no check on the abuse of the privilege, and inevitably it was abused. Crown privilege was invoked as a matter of routine to prevent disclosure of communications between government departments and between these departments and outside bodies; it seemed that often its use had less to do with protecting the public interest than frustrating civil actions against the government. For example, Crown privilege was invoked to prevent a prisoner on remand from obtaining medical reports on a mentally disturbed patient in the prison hospital who had attacked him – the prisoner needed the reports to pursue a claim for negligence. In another case the reports of a marriage conciliator, required in a soldier's divorce proceedings, were withheld.

Such instances led to considerable disquiet about the unfettered discretion conferred on the executive by Crown privilege. In 1968, in *Conway* v. *Rimmer* [1968] AC 910, the House of Lords moved to change the law, unanimously reversing the principles established in *Duncan* v. *Cammell Laird.*

Conway v. *Rimmer*

The case concerned a probationer police officer who had been prosecuted for the theft of an electric torch. After his acquittal, he brought an action for malicious prosecution, and sought discovery (disclosure) of reports on him written by superior officers. The Home Secretary claimed that the reports belonged to a class of documents which it would be against the public interest to reveal. However, the House of Lords was not prepared to accept that the minister's decision was final. The Law Lords asserted that the broad ministerial discretion allowed in the *Cammell Laird* case was wrong, and that the courts had an inherent power and a duty to balance the public interest in non-disclosure with that of the needs of justice. The courts could therefore inspect documents to determine whether disclosure would be appropriate, even though they might belong to what had been regarded as a privileged class. In this case their lordships inspected the reports and ordered their disclosure.

The *Conway* case thus abandoned the principle that some documents were protected from disclosure, as long as the minister claimed the privilege. Before long the Law Lords declared that the very term 'Crown privilege' was misleading; the non-disclosure of documents was not a privilege in the normal sense of the word but existed to protect the public interest. Moreover, the Law Lords considered that non-disclosure in the public interest might be claimed by persons other than ministers; so the use of 'Crown' was inappropriate too. Thus since the early 1970s the term 'public interest immunity' has been preferred.

Public interest immunity can now be claimed by any party to proceedings, although by its nature most claims are still by ministers. The courts may inspect documents covered by a 'class' claim, although the onus is on the applicant to demonstrate that the documents are likely to give substantial support to his or her case. Some judges have gone as far as to indicate that even Cabinet documents might not be immune from inspection if the case concerns the serious misconduct of a minister. On the other hand, there is a clear reluctance to inspect documents relating to national security or the investigation of crime. Having inspected documents, the court then has to decide whether to allow their disclosure to the other party.

It is at this point that the courts are concerned in weighing the competing public interest in non-disclosure against that of the interests of justice. So far the judges have developed few rules regarding inspection and disclosure, but government departments can no longer rely on claiming non-disclosure in the public interest. This was demonstrated in the *Matrix Churchill* case *R.* v. *Henderson* (1992), which raised a number of important issues and demonstrated the way in which the law may serve a political purpose, and conversely how the courts may resist the pressures of the government.

The *Matrix Churchill* case

In November 1992 the prosecution withdrew its case against three men employed by the engineering company Matrix Churchill and accused of illegally exporting arms to Iraq. Evidence given by Mr Alan Clark, a former minister, indicated that departments of government had been aware (or at least not unaware) of the nature of the equipment destined for Iraq when they issued the necessary export licences. It was further revealed that one of the defendants had for some years provided the security services with information about Iraq.

The revelations caused a political storm, especially when it became known that ministers had signed public interest immunity certificates, in order to protect some departmental documents relating to the affair from the scrutiny of the defence. The court ruled that the documents should be disclosed, and the case against the three collapsed. This did not diminish concern about the use of such certificates in a criminal trial, when the liberty of the defendants was at stake, and there were doubts about the motives of the ministers concerned.

In what was seen as an attempt to take the political heat away from ministers, the Attorney-General spoke in the House and wrote to *The Times* (13 November 1992). His letter stressed the legal nature of public interest immunity and the different responsibilities of ministers and the courts in its exercise. However, several of his claims were open to question. In particular, he asserted that ministers had a legal duty to claim public interest immunity, whether in a civil or a criminal action, if they considered that documents fell into a class that they were advised by their civil servants attracted immunity. This, he said, was a duty that could not be 'waived'. It seems extraordinary to deprive ministers of any discretion in this way, and indeed there is evidence that immunity is not always claimed in criminal cases.

The use of public interest immunity by the executive remains controversial, especially since the extent of the practice is uncertain. After the *Matrix Churchill* case it was revealed that fifteen certificates had been signed by ministers in a six-month period, though no long-term record was kept. The present position is that the executive no longer has absolute discretion. The courts decide whether or not the documents are disclosed. However, the judge does not have to exercise his discretion to inspect, and in some situations is clearly reluctant to do so. Scrutiny of the government's claims to immunity is therefore by no means complete; the defendants in *Matrix Churchill* were perhaps fortunate in appearing before a meticulous and sceptical judge.

Nevertheless, there is scope for some concern on the government's side. It may be argued that it is inappropriate for the judiciary to make decisions concerning the public interest; such matters should be decided by the government, which alone has adequate information, and is answerable to Parliament. This is not entirely convincing. When the executive had absolute discretion, prior to *Conway* v. *Rimmer*, it was abused, and the answerability of ministers to Parliament is not effective, especially when Parliament is not kept informed. There seems to be a case for a judicial check on the abuse of executive power. That, after all, is what constitutions are about.

In that perspective it was ironic that the government's embarrassments in the *Matrix Churchill* case led to the setting up of the Inquiry conducted by Lord Justice Scott into the government's apparent duplicity in the supply of arms to Iraq. The Inquiry went beyond the specific issue of public interest immunity to examine the development of the government's policy on the supply of arms to Iraq, the modification or breach of the guidelines, and the openness of communication between departments, between officials and ministers and between them all and the House of Commons. The evidence uncovered by the Inquiry undermined the government's claims of plain dealing within the executive and between the executive and the legislature.

6

THE EXECUTIVE AND THE COURTS

Separation of powers and judicial independence

The relationship between the courts and the executive and legislative arms of government is never easy. There are inherent conflicts which have not been resolved, but in modern times are avoided by mutual respect, judicial and political restraint and the adherence to both legal and conventional rules. These preserve the separateness of the judiciary whilst recognising the limits of its jurisdiction. Britain's constitutional arrangements do not provide the separation of powers (that is, separate functions and personnel of legislature, executive and judiciary) for which the United States is noted. Such separation, which provides checks and balances to prevent the dominance of one arm of government, is clearly absent in Britain.

Anomalies: imperfect separation

There is, however, a partial separation: whilst the legislature and the executive are fused and have overlapping functions and personnel, the courts are more or less separate. Yet there are anomalies, the most significant of which concern the roles of the Lord Chancellor and the Attorney-General and the position of the Law Lords.

Lord Chancellor

The Lord Chancellor holds a political office. He sits in Cabinet and presides, with the assistance of deputies, over the House of Lords when it sits as a legislature. He also frequently speaks for the government and takes part in debates. Thus, like all members of the Cabinet, he fulfils an executive and a legislative role. In addition, however, the Lord Chancellor heads the judiciary, and in this capacity he presides over the House of Lords sitting as an appellate court. He is also responsible for the appointment of judges (or advising on their appointment), a process which requires that no account be taken of political affiliations.

As a result, the Lord Chancellor has three roles – executive, legislative and judicial – which necessitate his switching between political commitment and judicial neutrality. Conflicts of interest and duty are inherent in the office. The personal integrity of the office-holder may be assumed but does not resolve the conflict. Hence there have been recent incidents of dispute between the Lord Chancellor and the Lord Chief Justice, especially arising from the Lord Chancellor's concern for the cost-effectiveness of the courts and the judiciary's commitment to the quality of justice.

Attorney-General

The role of the Attorney-General may be even more demanding. He is a Member of Parliament and thus represents a constituency and takes the party whip. He is also a government minister bound by the convention of collective responsibility and therefore required to support government policy. He and the other law officers (Solicitor-General and Scottish law officers) give confidential legal advice to the government. In addition to party, constituency and government responsibilities, the Attorney-General may instigate or move to stop criminal proceedings, and may bring civil actions in the public interest. In these matters he is required to dissociate himself from the government as a body, and must not take instructions from other ministers. However, there are some civil actions in which he represents the government; he is then expected to defend the government's interest as best he can.

The distinction between the roles of law officer and minister is set out in the official guide for ministers, *Questions of Procedure*:

> In criminal proceedings the Law Officers act wholly independently of the Government. In civil proceedings a distinction is to be drawn between proceedings in which the Law Officers are involved in a representative capacity on behalf of the Government, and action undertaken by them on behalf of the general community to enforce the law as an end in itself. (para. 26).

The requirement that the Attorney-General separate the government from the public interest may be unrealistic, and there have been occasions when a decision about prosecution has allegedly shown the influence of political consideration. In 1924 senior Conservatives argued that the Attorney-General in the minority Labour government had changed his mind over a prosecution following political pressure from his Cabinet colleagues. The government, without a majority in the House of Commons, was defeated in a censure motion and resigned. This was a most dramatic demonstration of the potential difficulties in the Attorney-General's position.

The *Campbell* case

The incident centred upon an article in the *Worker's Weekly*, a Communist publication, which the Attorney-General considered to be an incitement to mutiny. He instructed the Director of Public Prosecutions to start proceedings against the acting editor of the paper, John Campbell. There were angry protests in the House of Commons from the Labour benches, both at the Attorney-General's interpretation of the article and at the prosecution of Campbell, who had demonstrated his courage and patriotism during the war. Subsequently, after a Cabinet meeting, the Attorney-General announced that the prosecution would be withdrawn.

It would seem that this was the Attorney-General's own decision, endorsed by the Cabinet; but his second thoughts followed conversations with colleagues, including the Prime Minister. It might be thought not unreasonable, and was certainly not unknown, for the question of prosecution in political cases (for example, 'terrorists', strikers) to be discussed among ministers. However, the way in which the decision was presented suggested that the Attorney-General had been given instructions by the Cabinet, and it was with this understanding (and, of course, awareness of the government's vulnerability) that the censure motion was pressed.

More recently there was controversy over the decision to prosecute Clive Ponting (*R.* v. *Ponting* [1985] CLR 318).

The *Ponting* case

Ponting, a civil servant in the Ministry of Defence, was prosecuted under section 2 of the Official Secrets Act 1911 for leaking a document to Tam Dalyell, a Labour Member of Parliament. The document purported to show that Michael Heseltine had misled the House of Commons over the sinking of an Argentine warship, the *General Belgrano*, in the early stages of the Falklands Campaign, while peace negotiations were still proceeding. Michael Heseltine had told the House that the *Belgrano* was steaming towards the British fleet and was thus a danger to the Task Force. The document indicated that the ship had been moving in the opposite direction.

Ponting claimed that his action in leaking the classified document was in the public interest, a defence that was available under the Act, prior to its reform in 1989. The jury acquitted Ponting. This was despite a controversial summing-up by the judge, who equated 'public interest' with 'government interest' – thus sharply increasing concern about the practicality of keeping such considerations separate. However, the Attorney-General was adamant. The decision to prosecute had been made without reference to other ministers and thus without thought for political interests. He told the House:

> I . . . decided that the case fell within my published guidelines and that there should be a prosecution. Neither I nor the Solicitor-General nor any of my officials sought the view of or consulted with any other Minister, nor was the view of any other Minister conveyed to us before the decision was taken. (HC Deb., 12 February 1985, col. 180)

Similar concerns about the Attorney-General's conflict of interests were raised in cases where the Attorney-General sought injunctions to stop publication, notably Peter Wright's revelations of his career in MI5, *Spycatcher* (1987, see Chapter 15), and broadcasts of programmes about Ireland such as the radio series *My Country Right or Wrong*.

In all actions concerning the public interest the Attorney General has complete discretion. Moreover, there is no legal requirement for him to give reasons for a failure to act either directly or by a relator action (an action brought on behalf of an individual or group), nor to explain why he has ordered a prosecution to be halted.

The absolute nature of his discretion was made clear in *Gouriet* v. *Union of Post Office Workers* [1978] AC 435. The case concerned the refusal of the Attorney-General to bring a relator action for an injunction against the Union to prevent it boycotting postal mail from South Africa. Lord Wilberforce held the decisions of the Attorney-General to be 'unassailable'. Any questioning of the Attorney-General's decisions was thus left to Parliament within the confines of the convention of ministerial responsibility.

The concern raised by incidents such as those outlined above suggests that constitutional arrangements governing the administration of justice, which rely on the exercise of self-restraint by the Attorney-General, are inadequate. Hence it has been proposed that a Ministry of Justice be established to take over the government role of the Attorney-General, leaving the public interest role to a separate non-political body.

The Law Lords

The Law Lords also pose a problem in the consideration of 'separateness'. They are not members of the government but they do sit in the House of Lords in its legislative capacity. To overcome this problem convention requires that they do not offer opinions on matters of a political nature, at least until they have retired from the bench. They do speak on matters directly concerning the legal process and the administration of justice, and this may occasionally bring them into conflict with the government, as happened when the Green Papers preceding the Courts and Legal Services Bill were debated in the House of Lords in April 1989. Lords Lane and Donaldson were both highly critical of proposals which they considered gave the government greater control over the legal profession and thus threatened its independence.

In a contentious (possibly injudicious?) speech, Lord Lane, the Lord Chief Justice, declared:

> In some common law jurisdictions in other parts of the world with British-style systems of government, the administration of justice has indeed come under the heel of government. . . . We are told . . . 'Of course it could not happen here.' Could it not? . . . one asks whether we are now seeing tools being fashioned which by some future, perhaps less scrupulous, government may be used to weaken the independent administration of justice and so undermine the rule of law. (505 HL Deb. 1329–32, 7 April 1989)

These sentiments were echoed in equally robust terms by Lord Donaldson, Master of the Rolls:

> All governments enjoy great power; all governments know that they know best; all governments, in seeking to further what they regard as the public interest, are tempted, through no doubt the most impeccable of motives, to ride roughshod over the rights of minorities who disagree with them. (505 HL Deb. 1365–9, 7 April 1989)

These are the traditional – and persuasive – arguments for the administration of justice to be in the hands of an independent judiciary and a legal profession free from government regulation. Only thus, it is contended, can the rule of law, understood as the rule of lawyers in an independent profession, escape compromise. However, some critics considered that, behind the constitutional façade and the portentous language, Lords Lane and Donaldson were simply defending the interests of the legal profession. Others considered that the judges were interfering with the executive function. Either way, the independence which the judges are at pains to preserve may be undermined by their own readiness to defend it in extravagant terms.

Nevertheless, it may be increasingly necessary to guard the independence of the courts as their work attracts Treasury concern for costs and general ministerial oversight. The problem is that the court system is expensive and inefficient, and for the most part financed by the taxpayer. This is a problem governments cannot ignore. For example, the provision of legal aid has been reduced, and proposals (1994) to place the administrators of Magistrates' Courts on fixed-term contracts and performance-related pay (apparently without regard for the quality of justice) were withdrawn only after opposition led by the Law Lords in the House of Lords.

The problem still needs to be put in perspective. There must be a point at which even justice becomes too expensive for the public purse. This means not that there is no justice but that justice may be a little rougher, the trappings of its ceremonial delivery curtailed. Similar dilemmas arise wherever professional practice is supported by public finance, notably in medicine, in defence and, for that matter, in education. In each case there is room for dispute about the priority to be accorded to the professionals' judgment, and so far the judges and the generals are accorded considerable respect.

The judiciary and politics

It is not just the Law Lords sitting in the upper chamber who are conventionally required to stay outside political controversy. All judges are so constrained, the constraints covering the written and the spoken word, including broadcasting. The regulations concerning broadcasting were contained in the Kilmuir Rules of 1955. Strict adherence to these has meant that until recently judges could only speak in public in exceptional circumstances with the permission of the Lord Chancellor.

However, in 1987 the newly appointed Lord Chancellor, Lord Mackay, removed any requirement for such permission to be sought, trusting judges to use their own discretion as to whether a particular broadcast or interview would damage their own reputation or that of the judiciary collectively. Since this time, senior judges have been more open about their role and their relationship with government. In 1993 several judges publicly criticised the government's proposals to 'get tough on crime', especially by building and filling more prisons. Ministers, including the Prime Minister, resented an attack on what had just become a central feature of the government's new programme, and a counter-attack was mounted. This may have seemed a little undignified for both sides, but the complete isolation of the judiciary from a significant debate seems equally damaging.

The independence of the judiciary from the political process is also safeguarded by rules within Parliament which prevent politicians interfering in the administration of justice. Thus matters which are *sub judice* may not be debated within either House, and individual and identifiable judges may not be criticised during debate unless the behaviour of the judge is the subject of a motion. Such motions are rarely debated but provide MPs with the necessary authority to bring the behaviour of a judge to the attention of the House, usually in the form of a Parliamentary Question. The rule relating to criticism is not always kept. There are practical difficulties experienced by the Speaker when criticism is expressed in a supplementary question. Moreover, it seems that it is in order to criticise a particular sentence passed by a particular judge.

An additional protection from political interference is provided by the rules governing the tenure of office of judges of the higher courts. These allow for the removal of such judges on an address presented to the Queen by both Houses of Parliament (Supreme Court Act 1981, s.11). However, although in theory Parliament has the power of dismissal, in practice the obstacles MPs face in utilising the power protect judges from political threats to their careers.

No attempt to remove a judge has been successful in recent times. In 1973 more than 180 Labour MPs signed a motion calling for the dismissal of Sir John Donaldson, President of the Industrial Relations Court, but time was not found in the parliamentary timetable for the motion to be debated.

In 1991 after the 'Birmingham Six' were acquitted, more than a hundred MPs signed a petition calling for the resignation of Lord Lane. The concern of the MPs was that Lord Lane, who presided over the court which set the men free, did not apologise to the Six for the miscarriage of justice they had suffered. However, the MPs were admonished by the Lord Chancellor, Lord Mackay, and the 'grandfather' of the judiciary, Lord Hailsham, for acting unconstitutionally.

Thus legal and conventional rules ensure the 'more-or-less' separation of the judiciary from the other arms of government. This imperfect separation reflects a pragmatic compromise rather than a wicked conspiracy by power-crazed politicians. Law and its administration involves political and social values; there is no 'pure' zone of law to be patrolled by 'pure' lawyers disguised in wigs and gowns. Nevertheless, the government already has massive power over the making of the law, and an entrenched constitutional position deriving from parliamentary sovereignty, privilege and prerogative. So there is still much to be said for separating the administration of the law, and giving scope to the judiciary to act as a check on government. Thus the 'rule of law' may be upheld against the brute power of the fused legislative–executive. In this perspective the rhetoric of Lords Lane and Donaldson may be better understood.

Judicial review of executive action

There is no prescribed constitutional relationship between the courts and the executive, but the judges assert their inherent power, derived from the rule of law, to review executive actions. Such review is discretionary and is concerned not (or at least not overtly) with the merits of a case but with the legal authority for the action and the correctness of purpose and procedure.

Since the 1980s the judges have exercised their discretion more widely to review prerogative as well as statutory powers, and they have become considerably more active in the use of their reviewing authority. According to Sir Thomas Bingham, Master of the Rolls, this activism is in response to 'the increase of the powers claimed by Government', while Lord Woolf more specifically saw it as a response to the governments of Margaret Thatcher. 'She was a very confrontational politician, and she was always pushing the limits of her authority' (*The Observer*, 9 May 1993).

The applications for judicial review have shown a correspondingly dramatic rise from 525 in 1980 to 918 in 1984 and 2,089 in 1991, with the figures still rising. They cover the range of activity undertaken by central government and its agencies. For example, planning decisions have been challenged on the basis that the minister did not take all considerations into account; prisoners have claimed the right to know the basis on which the Home Secretary decides the length of a 'life' sentence; miners have challenged the closure of pits on the grounds that they were not consulted; lawyers have questioned the legality of the Lord Chancellor's restriction of legal aid; local authorities have sought to have rate-capping (and subsequently charge-capping) decisions quashed because of the way in which the decisions were made, and have challenged government policies concerning the sale of council houses and the opting-out of schools.

Some applications for judicial review are sought, often with the support of both parties, to clarify the law and set a precedent. In such cases the decision questioned is often an executive or ministerial decision, to do with policy rather than administration; the applicant may be supported by a trade union or interest group. But most applications are made by individuals aggrieved by a specific administrative action; such cases form the main work of special administrative law courts in other countries.

The grounds for review

The grounds upon which an application for review can be made were rationalised in the GCHQ case by Lord Diplock into three broad headings: illegality, procedural impropriety and irrationality, with the possible addition of proportionality – an import from European Community Law. These form the basis for applications to the High Court both by individuals, (actions are brought by the Crown on behalf of the individual – hence the *ex parte* form), and other public bodies, most notably local authorities, who are themselves also open to review.

Illegality

The principle of legality requires that any exercise of public power be in accordance with a specific legal authority. The necessity for such authority was demonstrated in the leading case of *Entick* v. *Carrington* (1765) 19 St. Tr. 1030. Lord Camden's comments in the case are as apposite today as in 1765; hence Professor Heuston's claim that *Entick* is 'a case to take to a desert island' (1964, p. 35).

Entick v. *Carrington*

Entick was alleged to have written seditious pamphlets and the Secretary of State issued a warrant for the seizure of his books and papers by the King's messengers. The messengers broke into Entick's house and took away his papers, whereupon Entick sued them for trespass to his house and goods. The officials claimed that the warrant provided them with the legal authority for their action. They were unable to find the specific authority, either in common or in statute law, under which the warrant had been issued, but argued that such warrants had frequently been issued in the past and had not been challenged, and that in any case the power of seizure was a state necessity.

Their arguments did not impress Lord Camden, who, in one of the most frequently quoted judgments, declared: 'If it is law, it will be found in our books. If it is not to be found there, it is not law.' He dismissed the suggestion that the warrant was lawful because of past practice, asking 'who ever conceived a notion, that any part of the public law could be buried in the obscure practice of a particular person?' Nor was he impressed by the argument of state necessity, which distinguished between offences against the state and other offences, noting, 'the common law does not understand that kind of reasoning, nor do our books take notice of any such distinctions.'

The warrant was found to be illegal and void and the officers liable for trespass. *Entick* v. *Carrington* made clear that those entrusted with public power cannot use that power to act in an arbitrary way (that is, without reference to the law) even on claims of state necessity. They must have specific authority for their actions. Thus *Entick* v. *Carrington* earns its 'desert island' status by providing substance and potency to the notion of the rule of law and its application to executive action.

The courts therefore determine whether the executive has legal authority for its actions. Today this authority derives mainly from statute law, although the prerogative still acts as a significant source of power (see Chapter 5). However, 'illegality' as a ground for judicial review extends beyond the need for there to be lawful authority. Most notably, challenges can be made on the basis that a power was used for an unauthorised or improper purpose, or that in the exercise of a power irrelevant factors were taken into consideration or relevant factors were ignored.

Both the *Congreve* and *Laker* cases were examples of the minister being challenged on the basis that he had abused his powers by using them for a purpose that was not intended by statute. They also demonstrated that some cases can have an outcome that affects the implementation or effectiveness of government policy. This was the effect of the ruling in *Congreve* v. *Home Office* [1976] QB 629.

Congreve v. *Home Office*

The government announced that from a certain date television licence fees would increase from £12 to £18. Mr Congreve was one of 20,000 people who, to avoid paying the increase, took out new licences before this date, even though their old ones had not expired. The Home Secretary sought to revoke these licences, using his discretion under the Wireless Telegraphy Act 1949, which gave him the power to determine the terms, provisions and limitations of television licences and to revoke a licence if he saw fit. However, the Court of Appeal held this to be an abuse of the power granted under the Act, which was not intended for the collection of money or to be used against licensees who had done nothing wrong.

In another case about the same time, *Laker Airways* v. *Department of Trade* [1977] QB 643, the courts frustrated government intentions.

The *Laker* case

In 1972 Freddie Laker was granted a licence for a cut-price transatlantic airline service (Skytrain) by the Civil Aviation Authority (CAA). Skytrain was to operate on the London–New York route in competition with British Airways, the state-owned airline. Such competition was one of the objectives of the Civil Aviation Act which gave the CAA authority to grant the licence. Skytrain was also named by the British government as a designated carrier for the London–New York route, which under the terms of the Bermuda Treaty, meant that the airline had to be given a permit by the

US authorities to land in New York. However, before the permit had been granted, a Labour government took office in Britain and announced a reversal of aviation policy, whereby British Airways was to be protected from competition. The Secretary of State issued guidance to the CAA requiring them to withdraw Laker's licence, which under the Civil Aviation Act the Authority was obliged to obey. He also stated his intention of withdrawing Skytrain's designation, thus preventing it acquiring landing rights in New York.

Freddie Laker successfully challenged both of these actions in the courts. The Court of Appeal held that the guidance given by the Secretary of State was contrary to the intention of the Civil Aviation Act to give commercial opportunities to independent airlines. It was beyond his powers and therefore illegal. The Court of Appeal also held that the removal of designation was illegal. It recognised that designation was a prerogative act and that the exercise of such an act was not reviewable by the courts (Laker predates GCHQ by seven years – see Chapter 5). However, it held that by necessary implication the Civil Aviation Act prohibited the exercise of the prerogative when its intention was to frustrate the objectives of the Act. The Labour government's change in policy was thereby frustrated by the Court of Appeal. If the government wanted such a change, it would have to amend the Civil Aviation Act in the normal way. Freddie Laker was therefore able to fly the Atlantic (that is, until he was driven from the skies by the dominant market power of British Airways, a power not subject to judicial review).

Just as the courts will not allow an Act to be used for a purpose for which it was not intended, so they will move to prevent its purpose being frustrated by the consideration of an irrelevant factor.

The *Padfield* case

In *Padfield* v. *Minister of Agriculture, Fisheries and Food* [1968] AC 997 a group of milk producers had complained about the price fixed for milk from their region by the Milk Marketing Board. They argued it took no account of their higher transport costs. Under the Milk Marketing Act 1959 the Minister had the power to direct a committee to investigate such complaints. He refused to give such a direction, despite the fact that the Act also gave him the final decision regarding the implementation of the committee's recommendations. It emerged from a departmental letter that one of the Minister's reasons had been his fear that the report might recommend changes in the price structure. This he felt would be politically embarrassing, for he would face awkward questions from different factions in the House whether or not he followed the recommendation of the report. The House of Lords held that the Minister should not have taken such a consideration into account. Lord Upjohn said:

> This fear of parliamentary trouble . . . is alone sufficient to vitiate the Minister's decision, which . . . can never validly turn on purely political considerations; he must be prepared to face the music in Parliament.

In addition, their lordships held that such a consideration frustrated the purpose of the Act, which was to provide producers with a mechanism for grievances.

Padfield is an important authority for the determination that discretion granted to ministers by Acts of Parliament does not give them unfettered powers. The courts will ensure that discretion is not exercised for the wrong purpose or in a way which conflicts with the policy contained within an Act.

Procedural impropriety

An executive action or decision can be challenged on the grounds that procedures within the statute, or provided in delegated legislation, have not been followed. This was the ground for the challenge of Michael Heseltine's decision, announced in October 1992, that thirty-one pits were to close. The miners' union claimed that the Coal Board had failed to comply with consultative procedures, a claim that was upheld by the court which quashed the decision. The government therefore had to delay taking any action until the Coal Board had fulfilled the procedural requirements.

Challenges can also be made on the grounds that the rules of natural justice, which embody the right to a fair hearing, have been infringed. In *R.* v. *Secretary of State for the Environment, ex parte Brent London Borough Council* [1982] QB 593 the decision of the minister to rate-cap Brent LBC was quashed for being unfair, because he had refused to allow the borough to make representations to him against the capping. Similarly, in the GCHQ case, the House of Lords declared that trade unions had a right (legitimate expectation) to be consulted, established by previous practice, though in that case the right was overridden by the government's claim of national security interests.

This has been an area of considerable judicial expansion since the case of *Ridge* v. *Baldwin* [1964] AC 40. In that case it was held that the rules of natural justice have a broad relevance and may even apply when the decision-making body is not under a clear duty to act judicially. Natural justice allows for considerable judicial discretion, since what constitutes 'fair' varies from case to case. Generally, the more 'judicial' the situation, the more stringent the rules that apply. Thus in cases concerning the disciplining of prisoners, often through the loss of remission, the courts have held that natural justice requires a full oral hearing, with the prisoner entitled to call witnesses, to cross-examine and in many cases to have legal representation.

Unreasonableness or irrationality

The third head for review is irrationality. This has its basis in what has become known as 'Wednesbury unreasonableness', from the case of *Associated Provincial Picture Houses* v. *Wednesbury Corporation* [1948] 1 KB 223, in which Lord Greene held that a decision made by an authority would be unreasonable in a narrow sense if it were 'so unreasonable that no reasonable authority could ever have come to it'. In the GCHQ case Lord Diplock preferred the term 'irrationality' and considered that a decision was irrational if it were 'so outrageous in its defiance of logic or of accepted moral standards that no sensible person who had applied his mind to the question to be decided could have arrived at it'. Such definitions indicate the extreme or 'perverse' nature of the decision. It is therefore not surprising that challenges on the grounds of irrationality are seldom upheld by the courts.

The infrequency of a finding of irrationality means that as a ground for review its use is questionable. It is for this reason that the judges are increasingly coming to favour 'proportionality' as an additional or more appropriate ground for review.

Proportionality

Proportionality allows the challenge of a decision on the basis that the decision-maker has used his or her power excessively to achieve the objective required. The test is thus whether the decision is out of balance and requires the courts to look at the substance or merits of the decision not just the way in which it was made. Proportionality is a general principle of law recognised by the European Court of Justice and contained within Article 3b of the Maastricht Treaty: 'Any action by the Community shall not go beyond what is necessary to achieve the objectives of the Treaty.'

As yet there have been few decisions in the British courts which have been based upon proportionality. However, the test has been used as evidence of irrationality, and there are occasions when the judgment reflects the principle. For example, in *R.* v. *Secretary of State for the Home Department, ex parte Leech* (*Independent*, 20 May 1993) the Court of Appeal found that prison rules, which authorised the screening of prisoners' correspondence, did not apply to communications between prisoners and their legal advisers other than to the minimum extent necessary to ensure the correspondence was genuinely legal correspondence. The judgment suggested a recognition by the court that the full screening of letters was out of proportion with the mischief it was intended to prevent – prisoners using their solicitors as a way round the general screening process.

The limitations of judicial review

Most of the cases outlined above are exceptional in that the decisions all affected the implementation of government policy, ministers rather than their officials were directly concerned, and the courts found against the minister. Most judicial review cases are less exciting, concerned rather with administrative detail, but this is not to deny their significance and their effect on the process of governing. Indeed judicial review may be regarded as usefully aiding the development of good administrative practice, encouraging departments to develop codes of practice, which increase their effectiveness and reduce complaints.

The initial reaction of government to the increase in applications for judicial review was the circulation to civil servants of an internal publication, *The Judge Over Your Shoulder*. This was criticised for being defensive, as its title implied. A second edition (1994), under the title *Judge Over Your Shoulder II, Judicial Review: Balancing the Scales*, is more positive. Judicial review is acknowledged to be 'part of the process of good administration'; any attempt to evade the courts' supervision 'would not be in the spirit of good administration that the citizen has the right to expect from us'. Thus judicial review is to be seen no longer as a nuisance to be endured, but a proper encouragement and support to fair procedures and good practice.

Despite increasing judicial activism and an expansion in the areas over which the courts consider they have jurisdiction, there are still limitations on the control the judges exert over government action.

Excluded matters

The most important limitations are those that the judges impose upon themselves and concern the nature of the subject matter and its justiciability. The courts have held that there are some powers exercised by government which are not suitable for review. In the GCHQ case (see Chapter 5) Lord Roskill gave examples of 'excluded matters', including treaties, defence, honours, the appointment of ministers and the dissolution of Parliament.

Since then the list of exclusions has been reduced – evidence of judicial activism – with the review by the courts of the Home Secretary's decision not to grant Derek Bentley (hanged in 1953) a posthumous free pardon (*R.* v. *Secretary of State for the Home Department, ex parte Bentley* (*Independent*, 8 July 1993)).

The most important and controversial 'excluded matter' is national security, on which much discussion in the GCHQ case centred. The House of Lords held that where the interests of national security are concerned, 'the court will accept the opinion of the Crown or its responsible officer as to what is required to meet it' (Lord Scarman). In his judgment Lord Scarman emphasised that the courts required evidence that national security was a consideration, a stipulation that has been repeated by the courts subsequently. However, the amount or standard of the evidence required may be slight and there is some concern that the judiciary too readily accepts the word of the executive.

Parliamentary sovereignty

National security and the other 'excluded categories' listed by Lord Roskill are all prerogative powers, but the issue of justiciability also arises with the exercise of 'policy-making' powers granted to ministers by statute. The tendency since the 1980s has been for Parliament to grant ministers wide discretionary powers which enable them to make and implement policy as they see fit, subject to parliamentary approval. Such powers have been a particular feature of legislation initiated by the government to control local government finance. A number of actions, challenging the use of the powers, have been brought by local authorities. However, in a series of judgments the courts have made clear their determination not to be drawn into political disputes, carefully defining the limits of review of powers with a high policy content.

The judicial position was demonstrated by the House of Lords in *R.* v. *Secretary of State for the Environment, ex parte Hammersmith and Fulham London Borough Council* [1990] 3 All ER 589, in which the borough council challenged the Secretary of State's decision to charge-cap on the grounds that it was unreasonable. Lord Bridge in his judgment noted, first, that the power conferred on the Secretary of State by the relevant statute involved the formulation and implementation of national economic policy and, secondly, that the exercise of this power was checked by the requirement that it must be approved by Parliament. He continued:

> The formulation and implementation of national economic policy are matters depending essentially upon political judgment. The decisions which shape them are for politicians to take and it is in the political forum of the House of Commons that they are properly to be debated and approved or disapproved on their merits. If the decisions have been taken in good faith within the four corners of the Act, the merits of the policy underlying the decisions are not susceptible to review by the courts and the courts would be exceeding their proper function if they presumed to condemn the policy as unreasonable.

An important consideration in Lord Bridge's reasoning was the fact that the Minister had to secure parliamentary agreement before his policy could be implemented. Thus if the courts reviewed the Minister's decision, other than to determine that it was in accordance with the intention of the statute and had been made in good faith, they might be seen as encroaching on Parliament's exclusive jurisdiction. Such encroachment is carefully avoided by the judges, who make a clear distinction between matters that concern 'efficiency and policy, of which Parliament is the only judge' and matters that concern 'lawfulness . . . and of that the court is the only judge.' (Lord Diplock, *IRC* v. *National Federation of Self-Employed and Small Businesses* [1982] AC 617).

This distinction recognises the constitutional importance of ministerial accountability to Parliament. However, the reliance that the judges place upon it as a check upon executive action is frequently misplaced, and suggests an understanding of constitutional theory but not of political reality. Indeed, the domination of the House of Commons by the executive not only reduces the value of ministerial accountability, it also enables the executive to pass legislation in a form which limits review by the courts. Thus, the Secretary of State for Education was warned by the Attorney-General that the hasty drafting of his Education Reform Bill (1987–8) was 'looking for judicial review'; the Minister pressed on and claimed success in fending off judicial review for the Bill's main provisions (Baker, 1993, pp. 229–30). Wide discretionary powers limit review by the courts, while review by the executive-dominated Parliament is of limited impact.

A rare public recognition of the reality of executive dominance was made by Lord Justice Purchas in a case concerning the administration of the Social Fund. Under the Social Security Act 1986, the Secretary of State was given exceptionally wide powers to direct how payments should be made from the Fund. Moreover, there was no requirement that he obtain parliamentary approval for whatever policy he decided to operate. All the judges in the Court of Appeal expressed concern and surprise at the existence of such unfettered powers. Lord Justice Purchas suggested that their inclusion within the legislation 'might be an unwelcome feature of a dominating executive in a basically two-party democracy' (*R.* v. *Secretary of State for Social Services, ex parte Stitt* [1991] Admin. LR 169).

Legislative drafting

The limitation of judicial review by legislative drafting can also be made explicit in terms inferring a complete exclusion of the courts. However, the judges are reluctant to accept that Parliament intended to exclude them completely and thus have interpreted exclusion clauses as a limitation rather than a complete exclusion. This may be more difficult with recent legislation where the clauses are more tightly drafted, thereby seeming to deny the opportunity for such interpretation.

It is evident that ministers do not see judicial review as a valuable constitutional function. This is particularly the case where security is concerned. The Interception of Communications Act 1985, which provides a statutory basis for telephone tapping, allows complaint by an aggrieved individual to a tribunal and is unequivocal about the role of the courts. The Act, section 7 (8), provides that the 'decisions of the Tribunal (including any decisions as to their jurisdiction) shall not be subject to appeal or liable to be questioned in any court'. Such a clause is controversial because if the tribunal's decisions cannot be questioned as to their legality, then the tribunal may be said to be above the law. A similar clause excluding the courts is also contained in the Security Services Act 1989, which provides statutory authorisation for the Security Service to enter or interfere with property provided a warrant has been issued by the Secretary of State.

Attempts to remove the possibility of review of executive decisions and actions by the courts demonstrate the tensions in the relationship between the executive and courts. The fact that there is nothing to forestall the exclusion of the courts indicates the courts' lack of a formal constitutional role. Thus the comparative weakness of the courts, together with the weakness of a party-controlled legislature, support a dominant executive and go some way to justify the polemical cry of 'elective dictatorship'.

7

CABINET GOVERNMENT
Prime Minister and Ministers

The rules of Cabinet government

The executive in Britain is remarkably free of constitutional restrictions. Once appointed in effect by the majority party, the executive inherits the ancient authority of the Crown and the legitimate power of Parliament. The political executive, in effect Prime Minister and Cabinet, acquires the power to govern, limited mainly by custom and practice and the broad tolerance of the majority parliamentary party. In other countries, constitutions are concerned with the grant and limitation of executive power, in relation to legislature, judiciary and the people. In this crucial area of executive power, the silences of the British constitution and the broad grant of prerogative and privilege are most significant.

It might even be inferred that executive power is, in this respect at least, whatever the executive says it is. In the strict sense of constitutional rules this appears to be the case, but the executive is hedged about with customs and understandings. It is here that custom and practice and the 'rules of politics' are most abundant.

Executive dominance is a development of the last century. Bagehot's description of the Cabinet (1963, pp. 65, 68) as a 'buckle' or 'hyphen' joining the executive to the legislature is still true, and marks the distinction between the British 'fused' system and the

American separation of powers. But the power relationship has changed since the mid-nineteenth century. Bagehot discerned a continuing relationship between Commons and Cabinet, controlled by the Commons. Since then the relationship has reversed, and Cabinet dominates Parliament.

The basic constitutional rules of executive power in Britain have been indicated above:

1. The office of Prime Minister depends on the approval of a majority in the House of Commons.
2. Certain prerogatives and privileges of the Crown are in effect granted to the government, that is, the political executive.

It is further accepted that there should be a Prime Minster, ministers and a Cabinet, though there is no prescription about, for example, the powers of the Prime Minister or the size of the Cabinet. However, custom and practice are confirmed in the document *Questions of Procedure for Ministers* which is prepared in the Cabinet Office and given to all ministers on appointment. It was published for the first time in 1992 (as a gesture towards open government), though the contents of earlier versions were known. Like many secret documents, its secrets turn out to be predictable and unexciting.

Questions of Procedure is an executive document. It sets out 'rules of politics' rather than 'constitutional rules', carries the authority of the Prime Minister and is subject to his discretion. Yet custom, practice and understandings are here quite hard: these are established procedures and rules, not guidelines to be changed by Prime Ministerial whim.

The Cabinet

Questions of Procedure may now be taken as the defining constitutional document on Prime Minister and Cabinet. Its brevity is no disadvantage; the US Constituton devotes little more than a page to the powers of the President. Of course, neither document is comprehensive or detailed; nor do they enter into the political contexts which determine the exercise of power. We are here dealing with the prescription of rules, not political analysis.

In *Questions of Procedure* the Cabinet is put in its place as the core of a committee structure, and the committees are referred to as 'ministerial' not 'Cabinet' committees. The Cabinet and the ministerial committees are dealt with as a unit. There is no definition of Cabinet business as distinct from committee business.

Cabinet and ministerial committee business consists, in the main, of the following:

1. questions which significantly engage the collective responsibility of the government, because they raise major issues of policy or because they are of critical importance to the public;
2. questions on which there is an unresolved argument between departments.

The significance of the committees is emphasised: 'appeals to the Cabinet must clearly be infrequent', and 'the Prime Minister will entertain appeals to the Cabinet only after consultation with the Chairman of the Committee concerned'. The Prime Minister's position as director of the Cabinet system, with power over the arrangement of business as well as allocation of responsibilities, is implied in his role as master of appeals.

It is quite clear that consideration by the Cabinet means consideration within the system of Cabinet and ministerial committees. Ministerial committees are treated as an integral part of the Cabinet structure: far from diminishing the collectivity, committees

> support the principle of collective responsibility by ensuring that, even though an important question may never reach the Cabinet itself, the decision will be fully considered and the final judgment will be sufficiently authoritative to ensure that the Government as a whole can be properly expected to accept responsibility for it. (para. 4)

Thus committees are defended, not as a derogation from, but as an effective support for, collectivity.

A consequence of this interpretation of collectivity is that the only Cabinet ministers not routinely excluded from the consideration of some major items of business are the Prime Minister and a few senior ministers whom he selects; the only Cabinet minister not excluded from any item of policy-making is the Prime Minister.

The special standing of the Cabinet itself, as distinct from the committee structure, is acknowledged in the single sentence of paragraph 9:

> These rules do not limit the right of Ministers to submit to the Cabinet memoranda setting out their views on general issues of policy.

Thus the role of the Cabinet as a court of appeal and final arbiter is confirmed, but this is not the normal mode of business.

In this perspective Margaret Thatcher's notorious domination of her Cabinet seems to have been an extreme version of the normal Prime Minister–Cabinet relationship, rather than a wildly extra-constitutional deviation. The exact nature of the relationship is partly coloured and obscured by Margaret Thatcher's personal 'style'. The force of her political drives and the ideological incompatibility of her early Cabinets drove her outside the main Cabinet channels toward policy-making in small groups and 'bi-laterals', and with personal advisers. This again is a normal element in modern British Cabinet government, though the extent and exclusivity may be in question.

Other Prime Ministers (Lloyd George, Chamberlain, Churchill, Wilson) had resorted to such political strategies, but none with Margaret Thatcher's conviction, self-righteousness and disdain for colleagues. Even so, Margaret Thatcher was from time to time constrained by her colleagues, though the few who sought independence found themselves resigning; and after a triumphal decade she herself met a sticky end, just like two previous 'over-mighty' Prime Ministers (Lloyd George and Chamberlain).

Solidarity and confidentiality

Collective responsibility is noted in *Questions of Procedure* as a rule of government management rather than a constitutional convention (that term is not used), and the solidarity and confidentiality elements rather than the responsibility are stressed: 'Decisions reached by the Cabinet or Ministerial Committees are binding on all members of the government' (para. 17), and ministers should maintain 'a united front when decisions have been reached' (para. 18). Moreover,

> Ministers cannot speak publicly for themselves alone. In all cases they speak as Ministers; and the principle of collective responsibility applies. They should ensure that their statements are consistent with

> collective Government policy and should not anticipate decisions not yet made public. Ministers should exercise special care in referring to subjects which are the responsibility of other Ministers. (para. 87) (Paragraph 88 refers specifically to matters affecting foreign, economic, defence and Northern Ireland policy.)

Further, the course and location of decision-taking should not be disclosed so that free discussion may precede the required 'united front'. This point is treated at greater length in previous versions of *Questions of Procedure*, which emphasise the need to avoid embarrassment arising if some decisions appeared less authoritative than others. In 1978 James Callaghan issued a personal minute on 'Disclosure of Cabinet Committees' (printed in Hennessy, 1986, pp. 89–90) designed to impose the silence of the grave on government decision-making.

In addition, ministers are warned about publishing 'material based upon their recollection of the conduct of Government business in which they took part' (para. 19). Ministers are referred here and later to the Radcliffe Report of 1976, which followed the publication of the Crossman Diaries. Labour Ministers seem to have kept diaries intended for publication (Crossman, Castle, Benn). Former Conservative Cabinet ministers, including Margaret Thatcher, have published memoirs which retrospectively breached the prescribed secrecy and solidarity of the Cabinet. Publication is subject to the scrutiny and possible veto of the Cabinet Secretary, moderated, it is assumed, by negotiation. Since Prime Ministers, with the distinguished exception of Sir Edward Heath, have now led the way, it seems that the rules protect complete confidentiality only for serving ministers.

Confidentiality is particularly important in relation to legal advice. *Questions of Procedure* states that advice given by the law officers, or even the fact that advice has been sought, must not be disclosed by ministers without the consent of the law officer concerned. This convention is at the 'hard' end of the conventional scale; its strength was demonstrated in the Westland affair (1986) when the unauthorised leaking of advice given by the Solicitor-General to Michael Heseltine resulted in an internal inquiry by the Cabinet Secretary, Sir Robert Armstrong, and the subsequent resignation of Leon Brittan.

The convention of collective responsibility

Thus in *Questions of Procedure* collective responsibility is presented realistically, as a sharp managerial instruction about confidentiality and solidarity, not as a revered convention of the constitution. However, there is still a case for speaking of a convention of collective responsibility in the sense of a rule the breach of which may carry political penalties.

(1) The government is collectively responsible to Parliament, which holds it to account for all its actions and may dismiss it by a vote of no confidence. Such a vote would lead to the resignation of the whole government (hence the responsibility is collective), though a new Prime Minister could reappoint all the ministers if he or she wished. This part of the convention is a hard rule, the constitutional consequence of parliamentary sovereignty, though party solidarity normally protects governments from losing votes of confidence. (In the recent examples of the fall of a government by parliamentary vote, Callaghan in 1979 did not have a normal secure majority, and Chamberlain in 1940 did not lose his.)

(2) Cabinet proceedings, including the location and processes of decision-making and the views of members of the Cabinet, are confidential. This position was partially endorsed by the judgment in the Crossman Diaries case (see Chapter 2). However, the convention has been weakened by the actual publication of the Crossman Diaries and of other diaries and memoirs, many of them after a shorter interval than Crossman observed, and by the practice of leaking, the deliberate disclosure of Cabinet proceedings and disagreements by Cabinet ministers, including the Prime Minister (Wilson and Thatcher both employed leaks as a tactic in political management).

The confidentiality of Cabinet proceedings now depends on the personal authority of the Prime Minister, and for memoirs, the authority of the Cabinet Secretary. A serving minister might be reluctant to incur the displeasure of his boss, the Prime Minister; a former minister might ultimately risk an injunction, delay and expensive legal proceedings. In practice, in relation to ministerial authors, the 'thirty-year rule' of official silence seems to be dead (and a former senior minister, and author, has said so).

(3) A rule of Cabinet solidarity is firmly laid down by *Questions of Procedure*: in public the 'united front' is mandatory. This convention meets the government's need for political protection, and is invaluable for a Prime Minister trying to hold together a divided Cabinet (and all Cabinets have their divisions). The convention is less attractive to dissident ministers, who may publicise their disagreements by leaks and speeches in the country. Such disagreements are natural and not at all dishonourable. Under the convention of collective responsibility the Prime Minister may tolerate moderately damaging divisions, but may choose to dismiss or move the offending minister.

For the minister the options lie between silence and resignation. The arguments against resignation are always strong and usually prevail: resignation normally amounts to an admission of defeat, and removes the resigner from the possibility of influence. Nevertheless resignations do occur, and in some cases (notably Eden and Wilson) the resigner's career is not fatally damaged. Under Margaret Thatcher there were three notable resignations under the convention (that is, want of solidarity) – Heseltine (1986), Lawson (1989) and Howe (1990). In each case the resigning minister was protesting about specific policy disagreements and a particular mode of government (non-collective, Prime Ministerial dominance).

These three ministers subsequently played a significant part in the downfall of Margaret Thatcher: Howe's resignation speech, with Lawson at his side, precipitated the contest in which Heseltine stood against the Prime Minister. Thus the resignations demonstrated both the power of the Prime Minister and its limits. The convention of collective responsibility is still for the most part a weapon in the hands of the Prime Minister; yet, as Michael Heseltine argued, its use is based on a tacit political contract, that solidarity in support of the Cabinet is dependent on collectivity in the conduct of its business.

(4) The convention of collective responsibility as it refers to Cabinet solidarity, has been specifically suspended on two occasions, in 1931–2 over free trade, and in 1975 over accession to the European Community. In the latter case ministers were allowed to campaign in the referendum on opposite sides, and Opposition politicians followed the same course. This unusual suspension of the convention demonstrated that it did exist; it also demonstrated the implausibility, to say the least, of accepting major disagreement on a policy of high significance among members of a Cabinet. But, implausible or not, Cabinet ministers subsequently settled down to continued service in a government with which they had serious disagreements. (Coalition governments, as in 1931, might need to settle in advance matters on which they should agree, and reserve matters of difference; but, as in 1931–2, an agreement to differ might prove awkward in practice.)

(5) Collective responsibility also provides political and legal protection for a minister whose actions or decisions are under scrutiny. Politically, a minister may be afforded collective cover by the support of the Prime Minister and Cabinet colleagues. Legally, he or she is protected from the consequences of any legal actions that might arise when acting in a ministerial capacity. Thus, when Edwina Currie was served with writs for negligent misstatement, after she had suggested that much of the egg production was infected with salmonella, the Treasury Solicitor let it be known that she would not be personally responsible for any ensuing legal actions; she was covered by the convention of collective responsibility.

The convention of collective responsibility exists and is prayed in aid by Prime Ministers at least. Other countries manage well enough without such a portentous rule, and maintain reasonable standards of confidentiality and solidarity. In Britain the convention appears to use the undoubted constitutional fact of responsibility to Parliament to enhance the government's claim to secrecy and solidarity, disguising political advantage as constitutional propriety.

The treatment of the convention in *Questions of Procedure* as a rule of managerial discipline avoids the constitutionalist hypocrisy which surrounds this convention, and has the virtue of directness. This still leaves room for liberal constitutionalists (and even modern managerialists) to wonder whether the complete shutting off of the course of decision-making from Parliament and public makes for good government.

The disposition of authority and Prime Ministerial power

To a minister reading *Questions of Procedure* it will be only too clear that he or she is joining a tightly structured organisation, of which the Prime Minister is the chief executive, the Cabinet Secretary is the head of administration and the Chancellor is the head of finance. The authority of the Prime Minister arises politically from party leadership, constitutionally from filling the office of the Queen's Chief Minister, and, as head of a government, from a formidable power of appointment and dismissal, and direction of the Cabinet process.

Questions of Procedure extends this authority to matters of organisation and allocation of functions and appointments made by ministers.

> The Prime Minister is responsible for the overall organisation of the Executive and the allocation of functions between Ministers in charge of Departments. His approval should therefore be sought where changes are proposed that affect this allocation and the responsibilities for the discharge of Ministerial functions. This applies where the functions in question are derived from statute or from the exercise of the Royal prerogative, or are general administrative responsibilities. (para. 32)

The Prime Minister's approval is required for the following:

1. The location of functions and transfer between ministers.
2. The conferment of 'courtesy titles' indicative of duties (for example, 'the Minister for Prisons'). (In these matters the Prime Minister may seek the advice of the Head of the Home Civil Service.)
3. Arrangements for superintending the work of an absent minister.
4. The appointment of Parliamentary Private Secretaries, special advisers to ministers, Commissions and Committees of Inquiry, the chairmen of public boards and departmental committees, and other members 'in cases where the appointment is likely to have political significance'. (In these matters the minister should consult the Public Appointments Unit of the Office of the Minister for the Civil Service, hence to the Head of the Home Civil Service.)
5. Any connection of a minister with Lloyd's, the international insurance market, based in London. (Investors are technically sole traders carrying unlimited liability over three years or more and it is not possible for ministers on appointment to withdraw investments – some syndicates have made heavy losses in recent years.)

6. The acceptance of gifts or hospitality (guidance to be sought if uncertain).

Any middle manager would recognise in these rules the limits of his or her own authority, the hierarchical nature of the system, and the location and identity of high authority. The disposition of political power here approaches the structures of corporate management, though with much less autonomy to divisional managers.

The mechanisms or procedures in the hands of the Cabinet Secretariat include implementation and supervision of the formal procedures of Cabinet:

1. Clearing of memoranda as appropriate with Treasury, Law Officers and in relation to EC matters.
2. Circulation of papers in good time – two clear working days plus a weekend. (In 1993 the Cabinet Secretary complained that Ministers had failed to raise in Cabinet matters previously notified, and had even on occasion raised matters unexpectedly.)
3. Drafting of Cabinet Conclusions and Ministerial Committee Minutes.
4. Notification about immediate action to a department not represented at a meeting.

The Cabinet Secretary, as Head of the Home Civil Service, also has a responsibility for the design as well as the working of the machinery of government. Thus, in cases of dispute about the location of functions, 'the Prime Minister may want to take the advice of the Head of the Home Civil Service' (para. 36).

All this amounts to high-level production management (rather more than machine-tending), leading to what has been called 'influence through process'. Again the middle manager will recognise the kind of barrier-power that such highly placed, highly skilled and highly prestigious mechanics can exercise. That influence is exerted by the Cabinet Office to secure the orderly management of Cabinet business. Since the Prime Minister is the head of the Cabinet, the Cabinet Office works 'to', rather than 'on behalf of', the Prime Minister, and the Cabinet Secretary acts as Permanent Secretary to the Prime Minister. This strengthens the Prime Minister's position: what chief executive would not be strengthened by the support of such a Rolls-Royce machine to prepare and process the Board's policy work? But the objective is efficient Cabinet government, not Prime Ministerial power.

The Prime Minister's Office

The personal hegemony of the Prime Minister is more directly served by the growth of the Prime Minister's Office. From its beginings under Lloyd George in 1916 the whole complex has grown to a kind of Prime Ministerial micro-department. The Office includes the following (1994):

1. *Private Office.* Six senior officials acting as gate-keepers, shadows and 'minders'.
2. *Policy Unit.* About a dozen officials, academics, businessmen advising on the development of policy.
3. *Press Office.* Involved in policy advice as well as press relations, since presentation suffuses the substance of policy. (Margaret Thatcher's Press Secretary, Bernard Ingham, was known to be a close adviser and confidant.) The Cabinet does not have a Press Office.
4. *Special Advisers.* For example, on economic policy or foreign policy – despite the availability of ministers in these fields.
5. *Political Office.* Deals with the Party, the Prime Minister's constituency and other supporters.
6. *Friends.* The 'kitchen cabinet' – the essential unofficial and friendly support in the lonely eminence of high office.

The Prime Minister's Office is not substantial by the measure of a great Department of State. But the Prime Minister does not bear the departmental responsibilities of his colleagues, and this entourage, together with the Cabinet Office, is well-adapted for his leadership and management roles. The extension of the Prime Ministership from a post for an individual to a specialised micro-department of state is a significant constitutional development.

The power of the Prime Minister

The basis of Prime Ministerial power is leadership of the majority party in the House of Commons. On that normally secure base the rules set out in *Questions of Procedure* together with the Downing Street institutional complex establish a framework for the relations of Prime Minister and ministerial colleagues, and for the conduct of Cabinet business. Within that framework the Prime Minister has considerable freedom to manage as he wishes, in accordance with personal style and inclinations, the nature of the business and political circumstance.

The normal rules of politics provide for a Prime Minister who is at least the chairman of a collective Cabinet. The conditions and circumstances of politics make for a more powerful Prime Minister, an active manager of the Cabinet, the chief executive of the government, and a presidential figure for the people. 'Strong' Prime Ministers include Lloyd George, Neville Chamberlain and Margaret Thatcher. Over two periods in office Harold Wilson played both president and chairman. Stanley Baldwin preferred to leave matters to his ministers and John Major set out to chair a collectivity.

Whatever the Prime Minister's intentions, he inherits a formidable structure of power, including leadership of the party, substantial powers of appointment and dismissal, the overall direction of the Cabinet, the capability for central management of the Downing Street complex, the attention of the media (and the capacity to manipulate them), and opportunities for playing the world statesman (again media exposure but also a direct impact on policy). Thus no modern Prime Minister can escape a substantial central leadership role.

However, there are countervailing thrusts towards collectivity. Most of the factors in Prime Ministerial power have a 'downside' or negative force. Leadership by consent is more effective in the long term than blunt authority. Cabinet colleagues and the party may resist domination, and require persuasion. Dismissed ministers may feel aggrieved and foment opposition. Able and active departmental ministers have a secure and substantial base for policy-making in their departments. Media exposure brings vulnerability and potential damage. At times of political success a Prime Minister can easily dominate, as Margaret Thatcher did in the middle years of her governments; but the good times do not last, and political disappointments drive the Prime Minister back to the support of colleagues, moderating personal power. At the same time there is a demand for leadership.

Thus the constitutional rules, the rules of politics and the conditions and circumstances of politics set up a triangle of inter-related forces – Prime Minister, Cabinet, departments – and, beyond them, the party. The actual distribution of power then depends on personalities and circumstances, including the problems and issues, rather than the normal rules. The nature of complex organisations indicates that a government requires direction but is by its nature difficult to lead, and most demanding of leadership when leadership is most difficult and risky. (You do not need a leader for a walk through the park; you do need a leader to cross a high mountain in bad weather.)

The constitution does not prescribe clear limits on the power of the Prime Minister – even the detailed written constitutions of the United States or the French Fifth Republic do not accurately prescribe or describe the powers of the chief executive. It is not possible to demonstrate that Margaret Thatcher's conduct of the Cabinet was 'unconstitutional'; but it may well have broken the rules and custom of politics, as indicated by a series of resignations by senior ministers and the eventual 'defenestration' of Mrs Thatcher herself. Within the limits of political prudence, thus dramatically signalled, the constitution provides for an executive base of Prime Minister, Cabinet and departments; managerial pressures and political opportunities give the direction of this structure to the Prime Minister, and custom legitimates Prime Ministerial power.

Ministerial responsibility

It is usual and convenient to treat Prime Minister and Cabinet separately from departments and ministers. The implication is that the role of ministers in Cabinet and ministerial committees is very different from that of ministers in their departments. But that is only partly true. The work may be different but the minister retains his or her departmental responsibilities, interests and perspectives; and indeed the work of Cabinet and committees is mainly concerned with policies and projects which will be implemented in departments. The Cabinet deals with priorities; the minister engages in a competition on behalf of the department. Hence it is appropriate to locate the departmental minister in the Cabinet structure, and place the convention of ministerial responsibility alongside the principle of collective responsibility.

Ministerial responsibility is the organising principle of British government. It is generally regarded as a convention, that is, a non-legal rule of procedure or conduct, but its significance for the structure of government is such that it may reasonably stand as a principle of the constitution. The principle of ministerial responsibility has significant constitutional consequences; it is about the distribution of power as much as accountability (just as the word 'responsibility' is often used to denote authority rather than accountability).

1. Ministers are formally accountable to Parliament, but they have a special position in Parliament as members of the majority party which supports the ministerial executive.
2. The principle legitimates ministerial power and delegitimates other forms of power: local, devolved, 'hived-off', supra-national.
3. The courts do not challenge, or are at least reluctant to challenge, the exercise of powers subject to ministerial responsibility. Thus the principle is bound up with parliamentary sovereignty, of which it is both a consequence and a support.
4. Civil servants act on behalf of the minister and are not accountable either to the courts or to Parliament; within limits they are anonymous, non-public, figures.

These points are fundamental and set the structure of government in Britain. Much may be said of the weakness in practice of the accountability which arises under the principle (because a loyal party majority normally allows the executive to dominate the Parliament to which it is responsible); but this does not affect the structural or constitutional significance of ministerial responsibility. A contrast may be made with other countries, for example France, the United States, with significant separation of powers and non-parliamentary executives, and without the peculiar British principle of ministerial responsibility.

Questions of Procedure lays down the Minister's duty in a portentous paragraph:

> Each Minister is responsible to Parliament for the conduct of his or her Department, and for the actions carried out by the Department in pursuit of Government policies or in the discharge of responsibilities

> laid upon him or her as a Minister. Ministers are accountable to Parliament, in the sense that they have a duty to explain in Parliament the exercise of their powers and duties and to give an account to Parliament of what is done by them in their capacity as Ministers or by their Departments. This includes the duty to give Parliament, including its Select Committees, and the public as full information as possible about the policies, decisions and actions of the Government, and not to deceive or mislead Parliament and the public. (para. 27)

In practice accountability is seriously weakened by the power of the government as a whole, sustained by its majority, and the Prime Minister in particular. In practice ministers are accountable to the Prime Minister, who appoints and has the power to dismiss them. Ministerial responsibility to Parliament is a continuing chore rather than a threat but it is not wholly lacking in substance. Ministers must in practice spend some time before the House, explaining and defending their policies and actions – answering Questions, defending legislation, policy and administration on the floor of the Chamber and before select committees, and legislation in standing committees. They cannot escape accounting in these ways, though under the protection of a party majority, accounting does not need to run far beyond simple information towards explanation and justification.

Accountability to Parliament is the major form of constitutional accountability, as distinct from political accountability to party, people and the media. Further, from time to time a formal inquiry into an alleged ministerial failure threatens to subject ministers to a serious and detailed accounting; but the record is not impressive. For example, the Bingham inquiry into oil sanctions against Rhodesia (1978) was not pursued in Parliament; the review of the Falklands (1983) revealed policy mistakes but concluded blandly that nothing made much difference to the outcome. The Scott Inquiry (reporting 1995) was unusual in the exposure of ministers, prime ministers and senior civil servants to persistent and penetrating inquiries in public, and in the timing of its work so that many of those concerned were still in office when the report was published.

The convention of individual ministerial responsibility is overlapped by the convention of collective responsibility. The latter is to do with solidarity rather than accountability, and offers effective protection to the minister for major policies and actions. Such protection may cover ministerial error too. However, the convention of individual ministerial responsibility is assumed to impose a specific accountability for ministerial error, and in the extreme may lead to the resignation of the minister. Hence the operation of the convention offers a rare opportunity to observe a more or less specific and accepted rule of the British constitution at work. It will come as no surprise to discover that the convention is honoured mostly in the breach – but nevertheless honoured in the sense that those who break the rule may acknowledge that a rule exists.

The historical origin of the convention of individual ministerial responsibility as it applies to error and resignation lies in the procedure of impeachment, a criminal indictment brought by a legislature or assembly, which in medieval times could have fatal consequences for the offender. Many modern constitutions include provision for impeachment – as in the United States, where President Nixon forestalled impeachment by resignation. In Britain the practice of holding a minister individually responsible and exacting his or her resignation avoided impeachment or forcing the resignation of the whole government. Apart from the constitutioal position, it seems to be an accepted part of social, commercial and professional morality that some errors require resignation by the person committing the error or by the person holding a general responsibility for those committing it. This appears to extend beyond the exculpation of disgrace to the honourable atonement for grievous error (involving the resignation of those in high authority, whether or not they had a direct part in the commission of error).

The convention of ministerial responsibility as applied to ministerial error operates as follows:

1. There is an acceptance that evident fault requires accounting to Parliament along a scale of information, explanation, emendation or resignation (the erring minister having some freedom to manoeuvre along the scale).
2. There is no expectation of resignation for vicarious fault, that is, a fault committed by an official, in which the minister had no part (either by laying down a policy or issuing a direct instruction).
3. Ministerial fault may be personal, relating to private conduct but affecting public standing or performance (for example, Mellor in 1992); personal/ministerial, relating to the personal conduct of ministerial office (for example, Currie in 1989); or ministerial/departmental, relating to the departmental policies and administratiion for which the minister is responsible

(Dugdale in 1954 and Carrington in 1982). Misleading the House of Commons (in the sense of direct lies on matters of fact) is also regarded as a resignation offence; it was the major factor in the resignation of John Profumo (1963) and may have contributed to the resignation of Leon Brittan (1986). (But Nicholas Scott escaped with an apology in 1994, despite condemnation by his telegenic campaigning daughter, perhaps because he was both widely respected and a necessary shield for the Prime Minister.)

4. Resignation occurs only in certain unusual conditions, which are to do with political relationships rather than constitutional rules:
   (a) evident grave fault, revealed while the responsible minister is still in post;
   (b) a minister with some sense of honour;
   (c) the parliamentary party (in the case of the Conservative Party, the Executive of the 1922 Committee) demands that 'a head must roll';
   (d) the media, and, in particular the tabloid press, are also out for blood;
   (e) the Prime Minister is unwilling (perhaps because he is unable) to support the threatened minister.
5. Mostly, despite evident and sometimes grave fault, ministers do not resign, honourable accountability being subordinated to the solidarity of government and governing party.
6. However, ministers are 'reshuffled' and dismissed by the Prime Minister from time to time, and such moves may be a substitute for immediate resignation.

Thus, the convention of individual ministerial responsibility is honoured in the breach, as far as resignation is concerned. However, this does not invalidate the principle for that is about the disposition of power as much as it is about accountability. It remains the basis of the relations of Parliament, ministers and civil service. It protects the legal sovereignty of Parliament, ties ministers formally to Parliament, supports the non-political status and anonymity of the civil service, and discourages the development of non-parliamentary authority and alternative forms of accountability. Altogether the principle of ministerial responsibility is the basis of British government, for better or worse.

8

THE STRUCTURE OF STATE ADMINISTRATION

Departments and the Civil Service

Departments

The departmental and ministerial basis of British government

British government is departmental and ministerial government; that is to say, much of the force and many of the functions of government are concentrated in departments headed by ministers, deriving their authority from the Crown and from Parliament. Such a characterisation is complementary to, and to some extent overrides, alternative characterisations of British government as Cabinet, Prime Ministerial or bureaucratic government.

Statutory authority may be limited and specific but is often broad and discretionary, giving ministers powers to make regulations, issue guidelines or codes of practice. Some ministers, notably the Home, Foreign and Defence Secretaries, wield substantial prerogative powers in addition to their statutory powers. The minister's statutory authority and prerogative powers are normally reinforced by the government's control of funding and legislation and the less formal powers to persuade and to negotiate.

The structure of departments

The history of British central government is one of institutional, indeed constitutional, improvisation. The Boards and Commissions of the nineteenth century became departments of central government, staffed by civil servants and headed by ministers, and responsible through the minister to Parliament. The main functions of government are incorporated into departments, without any consistent principle (for there is none), and with occasional attempts to emphasise particular areas of concern, for example, Energy, Economic Affairs, Overseas Development, Prices and Consumer Protection, or to provide an appropriate post for a friend or enemy of the Prime Minister.

There has been a tendency towards very large departments, as a way of securing co-ordination and representation, diminishing competition and rewarding or diverting ambitious colleagues. Some of these have failed from sheer size (the giant Department of Health and Social Security established in 1968 was cut in two in 1988), or have failed to subdue intra-departmental rivalry (Defence). However, the development of large departments (and the non-development of small departments) has changed the balance of the Cabinet. There are no longer 'non-Cabinet' departments. The Cabinet now represents all departments and is weighted in numbers towards the departmental rather than the non-departmental or super-departmental ministers. At the same time the number of 'intermediate' ministers (Ministers of State) in the departments has grown. Most Secretaries of State now lead a team of ministers. This development has consequences for departments and for the government as a whole, which now comprises about 110 posts compared with about 60 in 1900, and for the independence of Parliament.

Departments are organised in a dual hierarchy: the Secretary of State is the political head, the Permanent Secretary (Permanent Under-Secretary of State) the official head. At the top the lines are delicately drawn: the Permanent Secretary is close to the Secretary of State but junior ministers (so *Questions of Procedure* specifies) are not subject to the directions of the Permanent Secretary. Junior ministers have no legal status. Authority is vested in the Secretary of State, who may delegate functions to a minister but retains parliamentary responsibility for their exercise.

The distribution of power and the actual working of the departments is affected by three factors which are to do with the nature and practice of institutions rather than constitutional rules:

1. There is a network of inter-departmental relations mediated through official committees and informal contacts, not least by telephone, which has been a powerful solvent of formal institutional procedures.
2. The network is co-ordinated to some extent by the Treasury and the Cabinet Office, which must clear any proposal requiring funding and Cabinet approval. It may be misleading to call the Treasury and the Cabinet Office 'super-departments', but all departments are not equal and those two have both clout and what might be called 'tentacularity'.
3. Each department, like all old-established institutions, grows a departmental ethos, providing a context, a culture, a set of assumptions, which influence its work. Both politicians and civil servants have attested to the existence and strength of departmental ethos or philosophy, based on knowledge and experience, and incorporating an approach, a point of view, values. This raises a problem for a civil service trying to be the neutral servant of its political masters, for it appears to be a constitutional requirement that the civil service should not, like other élite professions, cultivate and pursue corporate loyalties, professional ethics and aspirations to independence.

All of these elements in the departmental structure of governments are affected by the recent reorganisation and fragmentation of departments, marked by the establishment of executive agencies, and the exposure of the service to the rather different drives and ethics of private commerce.

Departments, agencies and non-departments

A department of government is easy enough to identify: it is headed by a minister, accountable to Parliament, funded directly by the Treasury and staffed by civil servants. However, government does a great deal of its work by and through bodies which are not (or not quite) government departments. For example, the Post

Office ceased to be a government department in 1969, but it is still a public corporation, though subject to proposals (1994) for partial privatisation. Does it matter?

The pragmatic answer is no, as long as the letters arrive on time and stamps are not too expensive. But in fact the postal service is a major public service, based on a monopoly and involving the redistribution of resources (since the cost of inland postage is not related to distance and accessibility). Hence the form of a postal service is both a political and a constitutional matter. So it is important to know how the Post Office, and many other public bodies which are not departments and not private corporations, fit into the constitutional scheme.

This is the arena of the executive agency, the non-departmental public body and the public corporation. Executive agencies were established following the Next Steps Report of the Prime Minister's Efficiency Unit (1988). The Report recommended the 'hiving-off' of much government work concerned with service delivery rather than policy advice. The work should be organised in units appropriate for 'accountable management'. The proposals reflected similar recommendations by the Fulton Report of 1968, but this time action and implementation followed, and by 1994 almost 350,000 civil servants (over 60 per cent of the total) were working in over ninety agencies (including, for example, the Meteorological Office, Ordnance Survey, the Civil Service College, the Passport Agency, HM Customs and Excise, HM Prison Service, the Public Record Office, the Social Security Benefits Agency, HM Stationery Office, the Funding Agency for Schools and the much maligned Child Support Agency).

Agencies are units of management within departments. They are still answerable to the minister, but other details of their organisation have been left deliberately vague. Chief Executives (not a traditional civil service term) are recruited for a fixed term by 'open' competition (going outside the civil service in some cases) and paid more than equivalent civil servants. They work within a 'policy and resources framework' set by the department, but within that the Chief Executive has freedom to manage against performance targets. Some agencies now operate with greater financial independence as 'Trading Funds', and over twenty, including Customs and Excise and Inland Revenue, set their own pay structures. Although ministerial responsibility remains, Parliamentary Questions are referred to the agency, and Chief Executives have answered in public and through the media for their work (unlike Permanent Secretaries).

The reorganisation of civil service work into agencies has proceeded apace; it is expected that about 80 per cent of civil servants will be working in agencies by the mid-1990s, leaving a core of perhaps 50,000 officials to service ministers, allocate public funds and supervise and set standards for the whole system. However, the determination behind the reform drive is extraordinary, compared with previous limp efforts at civil service reform, and the survival of such a substantial core is uncertain. Agencies to advise on policy, hitherto the highest and most closely guarded function of the service, are under consideration; 'market testing' (experimental commercialisation) has been applied to professional services such as law and accountancy; and the Deregulation Act 1994 specifically allows delegation of functions by a minister to persons other than civil servants.

The agencies formally represent a restructuring within the civil service, rather than an uneasy half-way house to complete privatisation; although recent enthusiasm for 'market testing' of government services indicates that privatisation may displace the agency as the favoured form of 'hiving-off'. Privatisation implies the 'selling-off' and conversion to a private corporation, not owned by the government, though it may be subject to regulation (steel, gas and water are examples of this privatisation). In between agency and privatisation, the government may 'buy-in' services (for example, management consultancy, the servicing of defence equipment), or 'contract-out' the delivery of public services (for example, the transport of prisoners, the processing of tax returns). There may be political, indeed constitutional, objections to the further separation, devolving or privatisation of some government functions.

However, the government has demonstrated that this strategy is an effective and practicable instrument of reform, change certainly, and perhaps improvement. A decade ago private prisons or school inspectors were 'unthinkable' but the government has extended the bounds of 'thinkability' and only the great institutions of the state itself are, it may be assumed, beyond privatisation. Certainly the dominance of the old department of state in public administration has been diminished.

The public corporation in its modern form was invented in the 1920s and 1930s in the shape of the BBC, the Central Electricity Generating Board (CEGB) and the London Passenger Transport Board (LPTB), and was the standard structure for the post-war nationalised industries. In the latter cases the minister retained control through appointments and finance, leaving 'day-to-day management' to the Board. Parliament established a Select Committee on Nationalised Industries. The structure was unsatisfactory, particularly in the balance between government control and commercial autonomy, but had the merit at least of recognising the problem. The development of informal relations between minister and industry allowed the corporations to become 'something like tenants in the great ramshackle mansion of central government administration' (Johnson, 1978, p. 128).

The proliferating non-departmental public bodies have not acquired the security of tenure enjoyed for so many years by the old public corporations. Non-departmental public bodies have only squatters' rights in the 'great ramshackle mansion', or live in gardener's cottages or outhouses. Sometimes the term quango (quasi-autonomous non-government organisations) is used with the quago (omitting the negative) alongside. But quango has become a term of abuse, and both terms still leave obscure the whole space between government and non-government.

In the 1970s public complaints about quangos emphasised numbers, costs, patronage (by a Labour government), powers and utility (or lack of utility). The endeavour by Margaret Thatcher's government to 'cull the quangos' was not conspicuously successful, and many new non-departmental public bodies were established (under Conservative patronage). In 1992 there were about 1,400 such bodies, down by about one-third since 1979. But the numbers are growing, and if the non-elected bodies established to run the reorganised health, education and training services (and perhaps the new police authorities) are included, the once officially despised quangos are responsible for disbursing over £40 billion of public funds each year. Their work is thus quite substantial, even by the standards of central government (see also Chapter 13).

'Non-departmental public body' (NDPB) is a neutral term, but not very informative; it tells what is not but not what is. NDPBs have grown up in piecemeal fashion and there is no consistent principle or pattern of organisation. The Cabinet Office has

Table 8.1 The structure of NDPBs

Name	Council, Agency, Commission, Board, etc.
Established by	statute, order, ministerial fiat
Relation to central department	part of or distinct from
Staff	civil service or independent or hybrid (e.g. separate pay structure)
Governing body	large and representative or small and unrepresentative (reflecting government patronage)
Funding	government grant or independent
Audit	Comptroller and Auditor-General and National Audit Office or no public audit
Complaints	Parliamentary Commissioner for Administration, Citizen's Charter or no public channel
Functions	executive, advisory, regulatory, quasi-judicial, commercial, mixed

defined the NDPB negatively as a body (not an informal group, nor a government department) with a role in the process of national government. A minister would appoint some members, answer for its performance and hold the power to wind it up. This formula tied the NDPB into the system of ministerial responsibility without saying much about structure and form. In practice, NDPBs vary in structure under several heads: form and size, nature of governing body, mode of establishment, financing, staffing, accountability (see Table 8.1).

The Conservative government's programme of privatisation has led to the establishment of a new brand of powerful regulatory bodies (Ofwat, Oftel, etc.); and the enthusiasm of the government to bring private enterprise, capital and profit motivation into areas of public concern has led to the creation of new hybrid bodies such as HATs (Housing Action Trusts) and Housing Associations, as well as 'Government-Owned Contractor-Operated' companies (GOCOs).

At the same time, private interests establish bodies with public functions, for example to do with advertising standards, film censorship, press complaints and the organisation of horse racing; and in some areas, notably financial services, the government permits forms of self-regulation. All of these activities have a public dimension, but the proper line between public and private is obscure. In such organisations the distance from or closeness to government varies; and the intentions of government in that respect are neither clear nor consistent.

The growth of NDPBs raises a serious problem of accountability. In most of these areas there is a general case for a 'hands-off' regime, distanced from government. But the balancing of public and corporate or private interest, and of government control and autonomy, is a delicate matter. On the one side lies the danger of heavy-handed government intervention in, say, commercial or cultural matters which ought to be left to private enterprise or public autonomy; on the other, there is a danger of the private government of public interest, and usually public funds. In between, there is scope for government influence by informal means, especially patronage, subject to little public accountability.

Formally bodies established by a minister are subject to ministerial responsibility, but accountability through ministers to Parliament is weak. The courts have not developed a consistent approach to non-departmental public bodies. The constitutionalist might look to greater clarity and consistency in such matters as purpose and function, appointment, funding and openness in operation. However, the old formula of ministerial responsibility gets in the way of developing effective modes of public accountability, while the new formula of privatisation replaces public accountability with 'accountable management'.

The civil service

The development of a professional civil service

The civil service was established by history rather than by the constitution. Its modern history begins with the Northcote–Trevelyan Report of 1854. But the modern civil service was not created by this Report – few such 'big-bang' theories of creation are exactly true. Since the modern civil service had to fit into a particular constitutional and political pattern, it was necessary that that pattern developed in parallel with the administrative structure.

The driving force of civil service development was a concern for efficient administration in response to the extended scope of government and the growth of public expenditure. At the same time the idea of professional administration emerged. It was professional in several ways – permanent and thus distinct from elected politicians; appointed on merit, by competition, and not by the patronage of politicians; with formally established remuneration and superannuation; holding explicit qualifications and mastery of the skills of administration, the latter newly evident as typewriters drove the mechanical copying work of the clerk down the scale of prestige and remuneration (and across the gender gap to lowly-paid women). For the clerk-administrator of the higher civil service, the qualification came to be the literary education of the ancient universities.

While these developments were in process, the civil service acquired its own administrative structures, notably by the establishment of the Civil Service Commission in 1855 and the unification of the service under the Treasury in 1919–20. The undifferentiated secretaries and clerks of the eighteenth century had finally become part of what is recognisably the modern civil service.

The Permanent Secretary to the Treasury was originally designated Head of the Civil Service (1919). That post was separated within the Treasury (1962), moved to a new Civil Service Department (1962–81) and to the Cabinet Office (1981). The Cabinet Secretary now assumes the Headship of the Civil Service, and management responsibilities are shared between an Office of the Minister for the Civil Service and the Treasury. But the most powerful official in Britain is now without doubt the Cabinet Secretary.

In the development of the modern civil service the two major reports, Northcote–Trevelyan (1854) and Fulton (1968), are classic expositions, in the context of reform, of the nature of the higher civil service in Britain. Recently the Next Steps Report (1988) laid down principles for radical change. These are significant constitutional documents.

1. *The Northcote–Trevelyan Report (1854)*. This recommended separation of the 'intellectual' from the 'mechanical' sides of administration, recruitment in effect of Oxbridge arts graduates by open competition and promotion by merit, within a unified service.
2. *The Fulton Report (1968)*. The service was too much based on the 'amateur' generalist at the expense of specialists and

skilled managers. The Report recommended improvements in the management of the service, and in classification, recruitment and training. Departments should practise 'accountable management', establish planning units and senior policy advisers, and 'hive-off' some responsibilities to autonomous boards.

3. *The Next Steps Report (1988)*. As noted above, the Report recommended the 'hiving-off' of responsibilities to 'executive agencies'. Thus it developed some of Fulton's ideas, but with the difference that the Prime Minister put her weight behind the proposals, and they were implemented.

Further, the agency principle opened the way to the continuing deconcentration and fragmentation of the traditionally monolithic service, less hierarchical, better adapted to its various tasks, less concerned for the divide between public and private and with the high state function of policy advice separated from the managerial, service-delivery work.

The structure of the civil service

The civil service employs about 0.5 million people in its non-industrial section (most industrial civil servants, for example ordnance workers, have been 'hived-off' or privatised). this is only a small part of the whole public service, which, including local government and the National Health Service, employs over 3 million people. The non-industrial civil service has a structure of grades and groups including specialist professionals (for example, economists, scientists), a large 'Administration Group' (routine administrative and clerical work) and an 'Open Structure'(administrators and policy advisers) of about 18,000.

Legally the civil service is governed under executive (prerogative) power by Orders in Council, and Treasury regulations or minutes. Civil servants are employed 'at pleasure', and their contracts cannot inhibit the exercise of discretion to end their employment (*R.* v. *Civil Service Appeal Board ex parte Bruce* [1988] 3 All ER 686). The GCHQ case demonstrated the power of the government in matters of civil service employment (see Chapter 5).

Civil servants are in theory employed by 'the Crown', not by the government of the day. Recruitment to the service is supervised by the Civil Service Commission, a body set apart from the Departments, operating under Orders in Council and appointed by 'Her Majesty', the Commissioners being mostly drawn from outside the service. Hence ministers do not advertise for, then interview and appoint the senior officials who work most closely with them (though they may recruit personal advisers). But here is evidence that ministers can influence promotion and reallocation within the service.

The Prime Minister approves all senior appointments (at Permanent Secretary and Deputy Secretary level). Margaret Thatcher notoriously played some part in promotion to senior posts and by 1990 the highest ranks of the service reflected her personal (not partisan) preferences. Sir Robert Armstrong, in evidence to the Treasury and Civil Service Select Committee (1985), was asked whether the Prime Minister was a dominant influence on such appointments, and responded several times that there was 'discussion'. 'There are occasions when we discuss and one name rather than another emerges' (TCSC, 27 November 1985, 7th Report, Vol. II, para. 76).

In the matter of appointments within the service, ministers are dependent on the support of the Prime Minister. Ministers have found it difficult to remove a Permanent Secretary with whom relations are uneasy (Crossman, Benn, Castle), but new appointments may be more open to influence. (In 1992, William Waldegrave found a new Permanent Secretary for his newly designated Office of Public Service and Science. See Plowden, 1994, pp. 92–3.) In this crucial matter of promotion or movement to senior appointments the civil service retains substantial power as a self-perpetuating corporation of permanent and professional advisers. The 'short list' of candidates is heavily influenced by the service, and in practice only a well-informed and determined Prime Minister can overrule the Head of the Home Civil Service or the Permanent Secretaries in the Departments. It hardly needs to be added that Parliament plays no part in the appointing process.

Ministers learn that Permanent Secretaries do not act as Chiefs of the Ministerial Office (*chefs de cabinet* or ministerial aides and minders), but, in Lord (William) Armstrong's words, as 'strong individual[s] in executive charge of the whole outfit' (Expenditure Committee, 1976–7, II, 656). The undoubted power of the Permanent Secretaries fits a little awkwardly into the doctrine of ministerial responsibility.

Ministerial responsibility and civil service accountability

The fundamental nature of the British civil service derives from the convention of ministerial responsibility. Under the convention ministers are accountable to Parliament, and, just as significant, civil servants are not accountable to Parliament or in public at all. Civil servants act as delegates of ministers; their actions are made in the minister's name, not, as is the case in other countries, in their own name but on behalf of the state. The courts support this position. Although they are inclined to see the delegation of discretion as an improper abdication of authority, they accept at the same time the impracticality of the minister's being involved in, or even aware of, all decisions made in his or her name. Hence what is known as the Carltona principle (from *Carltona* v. *Commissioner of Works* [1943] 2 All ER 560) recognises the civil servant as an extension of the minister and able to exercise power on his or her behalf. This incorporation of the civil servant into the ministerial personality preserves ministerial responsibility and civil service anonymity, and thus diminishes or destroys the accountability of those who actually do the work and take the decisions.

The consequence of the traditional doctrine of ministerial responsibility is that 'non-political' officials work at far higher levels in government in Britain than in comparable countries. Three problems arise.

First, despite the doctrine, the theoretical division of labour between ministers and officials is impracticable; as you might expect, officials do participate in policy-making and sometimes take decisions independently. Of course, serious and sensitive matters should be referred to the minister with a recommendation, but in the press of business that may not always happen.

In the Scott Inquiry into the supply of arms to Iraq (1993–4), ministers, including two Prime Ministers, admitted they could not possibly see every paper passing through the office, and relied on officials to filter their paperwork. This is normal procedure for senior executives in large corporations. But in government ministers remain personally 'responsible' for decisions of which they knew little or nothing, excluding alternative lines of accountability.

Secondly, in practice the system of accountability is not as strictly ministerial as the doctrine seems to require, and accountability gains from this fraying of the system. In practice senior civil servants now appear before select committees, giving evidence in public and indeed on television. They have also figured in inquiries, notably the Scott Inquiry. The anonymity of the civil service is no longer absolute; officials do appear in public in a role which looks very near to accountability. But this is not designed to be so. The official speaks within the limits of ministerial responsibility, either in his master's voice or evasively – 'it is not for me to say'. For the Scott Inquiry, civil servants were exceptionally granted permission to answer with a freedom in relation to both ministerial responsibility and official secrets. But this was unusual: normally, the pattern of accountability does not match the actual division of labour between ministers and officials.

Thirdly, there is a potential strain on the tradition of non-partisan loyalty of the civil servant, since those working at the highest levels necessarily engage in the devising, promotion, execution and defence of policies and strategies which are rooted in adversarial partisan politics. How, for example, does a civil servant deal with an instruction from the Chancellor, a few weeks before a general election, to make a substantial reduction in the estimate for the Public Sector Borrowing Requirement? Or an instruction from his minister to minimise in any public document or statement the military potential of certain engineering material to be exported to Iraq? How does he reconcile with his code of professional ethics his professional duty to draft an answer to a Parliamentary Question which conveys less than the whole truth, and is misleading?

None of these problems has yet been seriously addressed, but the third, the dilemma of civil servants who cannot conscientiously advance a particular government policy, was highlighted by cases in the 1980s involving breaches of confidentiality. In the *Ponting* case (1985) (see Chapters 6 and 14), a senior civil servant, concerned that the government set out to deceive Parliament (by ambiguity and evasion rather than direct lie), leaked a document to a Member of Parliament and so breached the Official Secrets Act. To the government's dismay, Ponting was acquitted by a jury which ignored the judge's exposition of the law, which equated the public interest with the government's interest.

The civil service, alarmed by the implications of the *Ponting* case, moved quickly to reassert the traditional doctrine. The Head of the Home Civil Service, with the agreement of other Permanent

Secretaries – and no doubt of the Prime Minister – issued a note which has become known as the Armstrong Memorandum.

> . . .
>
> 2. Civil servants are servants of the Crown. For all practical purposes the Crown in this context means and is represented by the Government of the day
>
> . . . The civil service as such has no constitutional personality or responsibility separate from the duly elected Government of the day.
>
> . . .
>
> 4. The British civil service is a non-political and disciplined career service. Civil servants are required to serve the duly elected Government of the day, of whatever political complexion.
>
> . . .
>
> 6. Civil servants are under an obligation to keep the confidences to which they have become privy in the course of their official duties; not only the maintenance of trust between Ministers and civil servants, but also the efficiency of government depend on their doing so. (The Armstrong Memorandum: note by the Head of the Home Civil Service, Sir Robert Armstrong, February 1985, reprinted in TCSC, 1985–6, Vol. II, paras. 7–9)

A note from the civil service Management and Personnel Office (Nov. 1985) was intended to amplify the Armstrong Memorandum. It emphasised that the civil service, while accepting the employee's normal duty of loyalty, efficient service and confidentiality, bore the additional responsibility to serve successive governments, of differing political complexion, with equal zeal. The note reaffirms that 'the duty of the civil servant is first and foremost to the Minister in charge of the Department in which he is serving'. Any doubts about the propriety of a policy should be referred upwards (difficult for Ponting, whose official and political masters were all involved in the strategy he found unacceptable).

The Armstrong Memorandum reasserted the pre-eminence of ministers against unelected officials, and dismissed any aspiration or claim by the service to a corporate status of its own, to a service or departmental ethos, and excluded absolutely (by silence on the subject) any aspiration to a special position in policy-making. Nor, of course, did Armstrong have any truck with the notion of the official as a servant of the state.

Thus the memorandum failed to recognise any force in new arguments about the civil service, specifically that the process of policy-making is more complex than Armstrong allows, so that the model of the non-political civil servant is unrealistic. The civil servant is necessarily drawn into policy-making, compelled to make value judgements, and promote and defend them in public. He or she faces conflicts between the service of a minister and the service of the government as a whole, not to mention any concept of the public interest. There is no reciprocal obligation of the minister to seek and consider advice (though it is mentioned in *Questions of Procedure*). Plainly the degree of passivity (or of acting ability) prescribed by the Armstrong model is unlikely to be found in effective officials. If the thrust of this liberal and constitutional critique is conceded, then the constitutional doctrine on which the British civil service is based is clearly inadequate.

The new criticisms of the civil service reflect not simply a change in intellectual or political fashion, but also substantial change in the context and the nature of the work of the higher civil service. This has many strands. Government is much more open (if reluctantly so) to the demands of the public and the scrutiny of the media. The anonymity of the civil servant, formerly guaranteed by the doctrine of ministerial responsibility and the standing of the service, preserved by aloofness and secrecy, has been diminished by the intrusions of the media, the new select committees, some well-publicised 'affairs' (Vehicle and General, Westland, Ponting, the *Matrix Churchill* case and the subsequent Scott Inquiry), and the publication of ministerial memoirs. The traditional professional skills of the high official have been challenged by calls for 'management' rather than administration; while the appointment of outsiders and the 'hiving-off' of functions have damaged the self-confidence of the traditional career service.

The conditions of policy-making propel the high official into incompatible roles, as an independent negotiator with interest groups, a long way from the minister, but also close to the minister and dependent on him or her, working on the development, presentation and promotion of ministerial policy for Parliament and the media. The official may also face more often a responsibility to the law, both at home and in Europe. Yet the basic power of the civil servant, based on permanence, time and expertise, remains. In these conditions, it may be argued, a truly non-political civil servant could not be effective.

At the same time, the service has been used by ministers as a political instrument to achieve partisan ends – precisely how it should be used according to the doctrine of ministerial responsibility, and an answer to Barbara Castle's complaint about 'a state within a state'. It is not true that the service has been 'politicised' in the party political sense, but ministers, and Margaret Thatcher as Prime Minister, have sought commitment and action rather than neutrality and detachment. Mrs Thatcher's famous question, 'is he one of us?', had both personal and political implications.

The civil service is no longer a closed profession, dedicated to a special form of public service, and supported by its own ethos and codes of behaviour. The new, emerging service is more open to movement in and out, competitive recruitment, payment by results, and the performance and profit motivation of the private sector. The preferred new type of thrusting, 'pro-active' official, wondering about a management buy-out and an appropriate commercial salary, is far removed from the traditional administrator serving forty years for a pension and a medal, and never uttering a word that could be regarded as conveying a critical judgement on policy. Thus the higher civil service has been 'politicised' both by the conditions of its work and, in another direction, by the demands of ministers.

This brief consideration of the liberal or constitutional critique of the civil service, and an appreciation of radical but largely unrecognised changes in the service over the last two to three decades, raise significant constitutional issues.

1. Ministerial responsibility and civil service anonymity serve to diminish rather than emphasise accountability. But a publicly accountable civil servant would destroy Armstrong's anonymous and non-political civil service.
2. The non-political ideal may have been destroyed already by the politicisation referred to above and by the long tenure of one party in office. Coalition government might put further strain on the non-political ideal (a politics of bargaining and compromise might leave officials unsure how to be non-political).
3. The question of a higher or alternative duty is not easily disposed of. The service is plainly under the rule of law. The scope of law in government is expanding, with the development of judicial review and European law. Matters of illegality arise, as in the supply of arms to Iraq, or the evasion of oil sanctions in Rhodesia. Matters of conscience may arise (governments do sometimes act disgracefully) and cannot be swept

aside, given the inadequacy of the defence of superior orders and British attitudes to war crimes. The position of the so-called 'whistle-blower' (drawing attention to malpractice) needs to be safe-guarded, and more satisfactorily than just by an appeal to superiors. The possibility of appeal to Parliament as a higher body is entirely justified in constitutional morality, but not in the actual arrangements of executive dominance.

4. In a more politicised climate the notion that the neutral civil servant can serve any political master with equal commitment is belied by common experience. The unquestioning service of ministers is likely to lead to professional tensions and ethical conflicts. In other professions there is likely to be more scope for continuing argument and also opportunity for moving to an alternative employer. 'Incompatibility' is a normal problem in the higher echelons of most directing organisations (including the Cabinet) and it is unlikely to be entirely absent from the highest ranks of the civil service.
5. The high standards of probity associated with the traditional public servic ethos may be eroded by the pursuit of profit and performance as defined by accountants. Enterprise, not to say avarice, are not entirely compatible with the service of the public in matters such as health, education, justice; and the increasing involvement of the new civil servant with the ethos and practices of the market, and a commercial world in which he may later find attractive employment, is likely to transform the old public service ethos. This was not exactly what the Fulton Committee had in mind when they condemned the 'gentleman-amateur' ethos of the civil service.

None of these points is easily accommodated by the existing doctrine of ministerial responsibility. Indeed these problems of accountability and ethics are symptoms of far-reaching change. The traditional public service (civil servants working anonymously in departments of state) was centralised, professional, hierarchical, with a sharp separation between public and private. The emerging government service of the 1990s is tending towards a looser structure, a mix of professionals and outsiders; the boundaries of public and private are blurred, and the ethos of public service (arrogant as it often was) is contaminated by the financial drives of the private sector (arrogant as they often are).

9

PARLIAMENT
Constitution and Structure

The primacy of Parliament

The doctrine of the sovereignty of Parliament ascribes to the institution of Parliament both legal and political sovereignty, subject to the limitations arising from membership of the European Union (see Chapter 2). The legal sovereignty of Parliament is a pervasive and insistent fact of British politics: Parliament (the two Houses of Commons and Lords, together with the monarch) is the constitutional maker of law. Parliamentary sovereignty remains the ultimate source of power, but in practice is normally passed to the government as a power of initiative and execution. As part of that power, arising from party solidarity, the government manages Parliament for its governmental purposes. Those purposes are also the purposes of the majority in the House of Commons (the second chamber, the House of Lords, now exercises virtually no political power and very little constitutional power). So in a sense the power of government is an emanation of the power of Parliament, which for this essential purpose is in effect the House of Commons.

That is the perspective of constitutional theory; but in the perspective of day-to-day governing, the government is powerful and Parliament is weak. In practice a substantial part of the work of a legislature, notably in the preparation of legislation, is done by the executive, thus diminishing the legislative function of Parliament to mechanical amendment, registration and approval.

Nevertheless, Parliament derives both constitutional weight and political influence from its position of formal supremacy. First, government is constitutionally responsible to Parliament. Government derives its authority to govern from Parliament and remains responsible to Parliament. Even though such responsibility operates through and is diminished by party loyalty and cohesion, government still has to account to Parliament as a whole, and much of government business and politics is shaped by that accountability – the convention of ministerial responsibility, Parliamentary Questions and the work of the departmental select committees.

Secondly, Parliament is the exclusive arena for formal politics; there is no persistent and effective competition from the courts or from other political jurisdictions, provincial or local. Of course, the media provide an influential alternative forum for political debate, but much of that debate is shaped by parliamentary politics, and politicians are the chief performers.

Structure

A Parliament lasts for up to five years and is dissolved normally at the request of the Prime Minister after on average about four years. The Prime Minister's choice in this matter takes into account the state of the economy and the polls; this is of some advantage to the party in office, which rarely resists the temptation to manipulate the economy to suit the 'electoral cycle'. The House of Lords is not troubled by elections (see below).

Parliament is housed in the Palace of Westminster, a fine, mock-medieval building by the Thames, radiating history and symbolising and reinforcing the attachment of the English (at least) to their form of parliamentary government. The nature of the Parliament buildings is of some constitutional significance. This is evident in the medieval trappings and general inadequacy of the Palace, and particularly in the shape of the chamber. Both the rectangular shape and the procedure of the House of Commons make for a structure of government-and-Opposition, government versus

Opposition. Control by a cohesive party majority converts this pattern into dominant government in an adversarial and mainly rhetorical relationship with an impotent opposition.

Hence the structure of the House is as follows:

1. There is formally a roughly equal encounter of government and Opposition (not well adapted to multi-party politics), presided over by a Speaker and managed by the Leader of the House, and the Whips, who constitute 'the usual channels'.
2. In practice there is a hugely powerful government 'front bench' in a leadership relation to an influential government backbench, and in a dominant adversarial relation to the official Opposition front bench and all other backbenchers. There is only a weak sense of solidarity of the House as a whole, or of all backbenchers against the common interests of the two front benches.
3. The time of the House is largely in the hands of the Government. The government's business takes up about three-quarters of the days available, mostly on its own initiative. By contrast the Opposition and the generality of backbenchers each control a little over one-tenth of the Parliamentary days. Analysed by hours, backbenchers do rather better, because of the time allocated to Questions and Motions, taking up to one-third of all Parliamentary time. But the government still retains the larger share of time, and controls the serious business of the House. (Based on Session 1985–6 in Griffith and Ryle, 1989, pp. 11–12.)
4. The government's dominance of the business of the House, and mostly of its outcomes, is enforced by the government Whips. Their power, unknown to the constitution or to any manual of parliamentary procedure, is based on party loyalty and solidarity, the desire of backbench Members for comfortable office accommodation, satisfying committee places, agreeable trips abroad, and above all for promotion. The Whips have these good things in their gift, and wield harsher sanctions (such as making trouble in the constituency) for recalcitrant Members.
5. There is an unseen but influential relationship of Parliament to the people, mediated by MPs and press and broadcasting.

Privilege

Both Houses of Parliament lay claim to certain privileges. These are deemed necessary to enable Parliament to carry out its functions, but are also a reflection of the origins of Parliament as a High Court. The most important privileges are the right of each House to control its own internal affairs and the right of free speech. These were given statutory form by Article 9 of the Bill of Rights 1689 which states: '[T]he freedom of speech, and debates and proceedings in Parliament ought not to be impeached or questioned in any court or place outside of Parliament.'

Thus the courts cannot review the exercise of a privilege nor will they inquire into the exercise by Parliament of its power to punish for a breach of privilege. However, they claim the jurisdiction to determine both the existence and extent of a privilege. This claim is contested by Parliament and during the last century has led to major conflict between the two institutions. In recent times such conflict has been avoided through mutual respect and restraint of each side in pressing their jurisdictional claims. However, as recently as July 1993, the Speaker of the House, Miss Betty Boothroyd, felt it necessary to remind the judges (who were about to hear a case contesting Britain's ratification of the Maastricht Treaty) of Article 9 of the Bill of Rights.

Parliament's claim to exclusive control of matters arising within either House

Parliament claims the right to control its own affairs. This right is recognised by the courts, who will not interfere within the jurisdiction of either House, even when a statute has been wrongly interpreted. This was demonstrated in *Bradlaugh* v. *Gossett* (1884) 12 QBD 271, when the House of Commons refused to allow Bradlaugh, an atheist, to take the parliamentary oath. Bradlaugh claimed that this was contrary to the Parliamentary Oaths Act 1866, but the court held it had no jurisdiction to interfere.

On that ground the courts will not look behind an Act of Parliament to see if it has gone through the necessary procedures during its passage through both Houses. This was made clear in *British Railways Board* v. *Pickin* [1974] (see Chapter 2). In the House of Lords, Lord Simon declared that: 'a parliamentary examination of parliamentary procedures and of the actions and understandings of officers of Parliament would seem to be clearly more satisfactory than one conducted in a court of law.'

The recognition by the courts of Parliament's claim to exclusive control of its internal affairs was again demonstrated over the 'Zircon' affair.

The *'Zircon'* case

'Zircon' was the codename for a defence project, the subject of the first in a series of programmes, entitled *The Secret Society*, which had been made for the BBC in 1986 by a journalist, Duncan Campbell. The Zircon programme revealed how the government had concealed from Parliament the existence of the project and the related heavy expenditure. However, before the programme could be screened, the government persuaded the BBC not to show it and took out an injunction to prevent Campbell and others from revealing any information contained within the programme. The Attorney-General then sought an injunction against a group of MPs who were planning to screen the Zircon programme in a room in the House of Commons. The judge refused to grant this injunction, stating that to do so would be to infringe the right of the House to regulate its own proceedings.

At this point the Speaker of the House took on the role of 'regulator' and issued a direction that the programme should not be shown in the House until the matter had been debated. The ensuing debate referred the ruling by the Speaker to the Committee of Privileges, whilst maintaining the ban on showing the programme until the House decided otherwise or the injunction against Campbell was removed. The subsequent report from the Committee found that the Speaker had acted correctly, although a minority of committee members insisted on recording that they considered his actions had been unconstitutional. Thus the matter had been determined by the House, and the evidently heavy influence of the government does not alter that conclusion. (The film was later shown in the House of Commons and elsewhere and was transmitted by the BBC two years later.)

Freedom of speech

Freedom of speech is the most important privilege of Parliament. It allows Members of Parliament to debate any matter they wish, provides them with immunity from prosecution and protects them from actions in defamation for any comments which are made in the course of 'proceedings in Parliament'. In modern times immunity from prosecution has seldom needed to be claimed as a privilege. In 1938 Mr Duncan Sandys was threatened with prosecution under the Official Secrets Act after he refused to reveal his source of information for a Parliamentary Question on a matter of national security. The House of Commons asserted its privilege and made clear that a prosecution would be a contempt of Parliament. No action was taken against Mr Sandys. It was also because of the protection afforded by parliamentary privilege that four Members of the House of Commons were able to name 'Colonel B', an officer of the security services who was giving evidence in an Official Secrets trial in 1977, without fear that proceedings for contempt of court would be brought against them. Such proceedings had already been started against journalists who revealed the real name of the colonel.

More frequent is the claim of privilege as a protection against defamation actions. It is in the assertion of this claim that the courts are most frequently involved, for there is still uncertainty over what qualifies as a 'proceeding of Parliament' and hence the extent of the privilege. In general anything said by a Member during a debate or at a committee hearing, or anything written to a minister which concerns the subject of a debate, either already held or to be held, is covered by 'absolute privilege' from actions in defamation. This means that no action can be brought regardless of whether or not comments made are true or fair, or whether they are made with good intent or maliciously. Moreover, nothing that is said in this context can subsequently be used as evidence of maliciousness for a claim of defamation in another context. A Secretary of State for Education was successfully pursued for defamation for remarks made about a Director of Education at a (supposedly private) fringe meeting of the 1993 Conservative Party Conference. In the House the remarks would have been 'privileged'; although if used about another Member they might well have been regarded as abusive, and the term 'nutter' would have joined the Speaker's list of unparliamentary terms now notional. It has included cad, rat, swine and impertinent puppy.

Members of Parliament would also seem to be protected in other aspects of their work, for instance in correspondence with their constituents, by 'qualified privilege', which means that before an action in defamation can be successful, it must be shown that they acted with malice. Journalists are also protected by qualified privilege in their reporting of Parliament.

The extent of the privilege of free speech caused serious friction between Parliament and the courts during the last century, and in one case resulted in a bizarre sequence of events.

Stockdale v. *Hansard*

A copy of a book on the reproductive system written by Mr Stockdale found its way into a prison. In a report the Inspectors of Prisons referred to the book in a way which Mr Stockdale considered to be libellous and he brought an action against Hansard, the publishers of the report (*Stockdale* v. *Hansard* (1839) 9 Ad. & E.). The House of Commons claimed that the report was covered by privilege because Parliament had ordered it to be published; but this claim was rejected by the court and damages were awarded against Hansard. On the advice of Parliament, Hansard refused to pay, whereupon sheriffs were ordered by the court to seize appropriate property from Hansard. However, when the sheriffs tried to execute the order, they were arrested by the Serjeant-at-Arms and held for contempt of Parliament. The sheriffs then brought a habeas corpus action on the basis that the warrant issued by the Speaker for their arrest was too general. At this point the court ran out of courage and held the warrant to be legal.

The matter of parliamentary reports was resolved with the passing of the Parliamentary Papers Act 1840, which provides that any report published by order of either House of Parliament is protected by parliamentary privilege. Thus, Parliament asserted its authority in the matter of privilege, but also recognised a role for the courts in the interpretation of the statute.

The extent of the privilege of free speech continues to be questioned. In *Rost* v. *Edwards* [1990] 2 WLR 1280 the courts were required to determine whether the Register of Members' Interests constituted a 'proceeding in Parliament' and was therefore covered by parliamentary privilege. It was held that this was not the case, and thus information about the compilation of the Register could be used in evidence in court. The issue of privilege was raised again, in a context of broader significance, in *Pepper* v. *Hart* [1993] 1 All ER 423.

Pepper v. *Hart*

The House of Lords considered whether judges could use *Hansard* to determine the intention behind legislation, or whether this would be an abuse of privilege. Their Lordships had previously forbidden the use of such material. They now ruled that where the meaning of a statute was unclear or ambiguous, or a literal interpretation would result in absurdity, the courts could look at the statement of the minister in the House to ascertain the intention behind it. The Attorney-General argued that the use of *Hansard* would inhibit the minister because his words would be given 'legislative effect', and this would constitute a 'questioning' of the freedom of speech and debate, contrary to Article 9 of the Bill of Rights.

The Attorney-General was probably correct in his 'legislative effect' argument. Laws might well acquire from reference to parliamentary debate a kind of prologue or aid to interpretation. However, basing this pragmatic argument on Article 9 proved unacceptable to the court. The judgment by Lord Browne-Wilkinson in response to the argument of the Attorney-General provides a useful summary of the purpose of the privilege of freedom of speech and debate and the extent to which it can be claimed in the 1990s.

> Article 9 is a provision of the highest constitutional importance and should not be narrowly construed. It ensures the ability of democratically elected Members of Parliament to discuss what they will (freedom of debate) and to say what they will (freedom of speech). But, even given a generous approach to this construction, I find it impossible to attach the breadth of meaning to the word 'question' which the Attorney-General urges. It must be remembered that art. 9 prohibits questioning not only 'in any court' but also in any 'place out of Parliament'. If the Attorney-General's submission is correct, any comment in the media or elsewhere on what is said in Parliament would constitute 'questioning' since all Members of Parliament must speak and act taking into account what political commentators and others will say. Plainly art. 9 cannot have effect so as to stifle the freedom of all to comment on what is said in Parliament, even though such comment may influence members in what they say.
>
> In my judgment, the plain meaning of art. 9, viewed against the historical background in which it was enacted, was to ensure that Members of Parliament were not subjected to any penalty, civil or criminal, for what they said and were able, contrary to the previous assertions of the Stuart monarchy, to discuss what they, as opposed to the monarch, chose to have discussed.

Relaxation of the rule will not involve the courts in criticising what is said in Parliament. The purpose of looking at *Hansard* will not be to construe the words used by the minister but to give effect to the words used, so long as they are clear. Far from questioning the independence of Parliament and its debates, the courts would be giving effect to what is said and done there.

There remains some unease about parliamentary privilege, particularly the claim to freedom of speech, because it deprives individuals of their legal right to seek a remedy for defamation.

However, some protection for MPs is essential if they are to bring to public attention matters which they consider need investigation but about which they have insufficient evidence. Thus it was under the protection of privilege that Kim Philby was first named as a Soviet spy, John Profumo was accused of dubious social connections with a Soviet diplomat, and Peter Rachman was first exposed as a 'property racketeer'. Similarly Sir David Steel was able to publicise allegations against persons involved in Malaysian arms deals (March 1994); and Peter Hain alleged that leading Conservatives had been moved out of some Lloyds syndicates in advance of heavy losses. Yet the privilege is open to abuse; Members have sometimes named innocent individuals, who then have no way of seeking redress.

Contempt of Parliament

Both Houses of Parliament have the right to punish their own members and others for contempt. Contempt may be for an abuse or breach of privilege, but it can also apply more generally to offences against the dignity or authority of Parliament. This includes ignoring the authority of the Speaker and disorderly behaviour. An MP may be guilty of contempt if he makes false accusations, thereby breaching his privilege of free speech; if he uses unparliamentary language; if he speaks disrespectfully of the Queen; if he refuses to attend a select committee hearing after being ordered to do so by the House; or if he discloses prematurely the private deliberations of a select committee. Usually the Member is admonished or reprimanded and required to apologise to the House. In exceptional circumstances a Member may be suspended or even expelled from the Chamber.

'Strangers' may be guilty of contempt in the same way. Thus any attempt to bribe MPs or to restrict their freedom of action may be seen as a contempt. This includes threats to withdraw sponsorship from MPs; for instance, for failing to follow union policy. (Such threats were made in 1975 by the Yorkshire Area of the National Union of Mineworkers.) The press, too, may be held guilty of contempt for publishing material leaked from Parliament. In addition, any refusal of a private individual to appear before a committee of Parliament or to answer its questions is contemptuous.

Students of Essex University who interrupted a meeting of a select committee held at the University in 1969 were held to be in contempt. The journalist who posed as a businessman and offered £1,000 to Members in return for asking a Parliamentary Question (while secretly recording the conversation) may have been guilty of contempt, but not a criminal offence (1994).

Frequently no action is taken, although there have been instances of private individuals being called before the bar of the House to apologise. Various newspapers have been admonished for printing leaked information and in 1986 the Committee of Privileges recommended that the lobby reporter from *The Times* should be excluded from the precincts of Parliament for six months after he had disclosed the conclusions of a report on the disposal of nuclear waste. In fact the House took no action.

Both Houses possess stronger powers of punishment. The House of Commons may imprison a Member (in the Clock Tower) or a stranger (in a prison) for the rest of the parliamentary session. The House of Lords can order a fixed term of imprisonment. The House of Lords, but probably not the House of Commons, also has the power to fine. These powers still exist but have fallen into disuse. Perhaps that is as well, since Parliament would be acting as judge in its own cause, with far greater powers than the courts.

The House of Lords

Composition, powers, constitutional functions

The House of Lords is a relic of the division of the medieval Parliament into Lords Spiritual and Temporal and Commons. Its composition has been modified by the addition since 1958 of about four hundred Life Peers and by the annihilation of its powers by the Acts of 1911 and 1949. Thus reformed it serves as the second chamber of Parliament, and may be regarded either as a triumph of the British talent for modernisation while preserving ancient forms, or as an extraordinary manifestation of Britain's conservatism, not to say obtuseness, in constitutional matters.

The House is composed of about one thousand, two hundred peers, of which number around four hundred are Life Peers appointed by the Prime Minister under the Act of 1958, and there are twenty-six Bishops of the Church of England (the 'established' church) and twenty Law Lords (who carry out the work of the Court of Appeal). Most members of the House of Lords hardly ever attend, which, given their unrepresentativeness, is just as well; about four hundred might be regarded as working peers, and the average daily attendance is about three hundred. Party affiliations in 1992 were: Conservative, 465; Labour, 114; Lib. Dem., 58; crossbench, 263; others, 295.

The crossbenchers do not 'take a party whip' but divide roughly 2:1 in favour of the Conservatives. The 'working' peers are a little more evenly divided than this, but it is evident that the Conservative Party is able to summon up a permanent and substantial majority. A House of a modern Parliament based on selection by heredity and patronage, and weighted so unfairly towards one party, is not able to, and does not, play a substantial part in the government of a country claiming to be a democracy.

The legislative powers of the House of Lords were severely reduced, first by the Act of 1911, pushed through after the Lords had unwisely rejected Lloyd George's budget of 1909; and again in 1949, when the Labour government correctly perceived that the Lords would use their delaying power as a veto in the last two years of office. Under the two Parliament Acts, the Lords have the power only to delay most Bills by about one year (the 1911 Act allowed two years), being the lapse of one year and one session between the Commons second and third reading. This restriction does not apply to a Bill to prolong the life of a Parliament beyond five years; nor to private Bills and subordinate legislation including provisional order confirmation Bills. In the case of money Bills, that is, Bills certified by the Speaker as dealing exclusively with spending, taxing and borrowing, the Lords have no power at all; however, the definition is interpreted strictly and most Finance Bills do not pass this test.

Only four Acts have been passed under this procedure – the Welsh Church Act 1914 (disestablishment of the Church); the Government of Ireland Act 1914 (never operated because of the war and Irish rebellion); the Parliament Act of 1949 (further reducing the powers of the Lords); and the unusual, retro-active War Crimes Act 1991. However, the possibility of delay and an embarrassing constitutional clash have given the Lords a modest weapon in conflicts with the Commons. This has been used prudently out of concern for democracy and their own survival. Lord Salisbury invented rules (thus is the constitution composed) in 1947 to guide the Conservative majority in dealing with the Labour government: the Lords would not oppose any measure proposed in the party's election programme.

This was to exaggerate the firmness and exclusivity of the programme, and to give the Lords a substantial constitutional function, likely in practice to operate only against Labour governments. The Salisbury doctrine has not acquired the status of a constitutional understanding, but it continues to be argued – for example, in 1967 over Rhodesian independence and in 1993 over the Maastricht Treaty – that the Lords have a constitutional duty on

> a matter of great constitutional and national importance, on which there is known to be a deep division of opinion in the country or perhaps on which the people's opinion was not known . . . to afford the people of this country and Members of the House of Commons a period for reflection and time for views to be expressed. (Lord Carrington in House of Lords, 16 February 1967, HL Deb., Vol. 280, col. 420)

The House of Lords may not seem a natural defender of the right of the people to be heard, but in face of a whipped Commons majority the argument has some appeal. Certainly the House of Lords has been able to engage from time to time in modest conflict with the House of Commons, and thus with the government of the day. Most of the time the Lords acts as additional legislative machinery allowing the government to insert further amendments to its Bills. Adverse votes are not frequent, but the Labour government of 1974–9, which had no secure majority, suffered nearly three hundred and fifty defeats by the Lords, and even the Thatcher governments sustained an average of about twelve each year. In the 1992–3 session the Major government was defeated on twenty occasions (in thirteen cases the defeats were reversed in the Commons or, in the words of the government Whip, 'not acted on').

It is normal for such defeats to be reversed in the Commons without further action by the Lords. Occasionally there are more serious conflicts, and concessions are made by the government – for example, the Aircraft and Shipbuilding Industries Bill 1975–7 was delayed by the Lords and then passed in revised form (the

Labour government had no firm majority either to justify its programme or to force through a vote in the Commons). The Conservative government was compelled by the Lords to abandon its proposal to cancel the 1984 elections to the GLC and the metropolitan county councils, and to delay its abolition of the councils.

In a conflict with the House of Commons (in effect, the government) over the Bill to privatise British Rail (1993), the government made very modest concessions in face of some Lords' amendments to the Bill. The Lords at first rejected the amended Bill, but then gave way, arguing that they had indicated their misgivings, and, as a non-elected House, should not further frustrate the will of the Commons. A few months later (February 1994), the Lords scored a notable victory; spirited opposition by the Lords, including senior Conservatives, persuaded the government to withdraw its proposal to give the Home Secretary power to appoint the chairmen of police authorities. The Lords continued to be sharply critical of Home Office legislation on crime, law and justice. This seemed to reflect the views of elder statesmen on both sides of the House (including former Home Secretaries) about over-hasty legislation, and the influence of Law Lords and the legal profession in the deliberations of the Upper House.

The powers of the House of Lords are clearly limited both by its formal position and by democratic sentiment. However, the House has a serious constitutional role within the parliamentary functions of legislation, debate and scrutiny by questions and committee. Its chief function is as a complementary law-making machine for the government, providing for amendment in detail arising mainly from second thoughts by the government. The work of the Lords' European Communities Committee ranges more widely than the Commons equivalent and is generally regarded as more effective.

Debates in the Lords are sometimes illuminated by the special experience and expertise of its members, though that experience is unrepresentative of the nation at large, and grossly overrepresents certain interests, including the Church, the law, the armed forces, university education, city boardrooms, party politics, and in general London-based elderly males, especially Old Etonians.

The 'serious constitutional role' of the House of Lords is inevitably diminished by its curious composition and its other evident weaknesses. Its survival encourages the medieval sentiment surrounding constitutional issues, enlarges the huge powers of patronage of the Prime Minister (on average sixty peerages each year), strengthens the domination of London in the political culture, takes up valuable space in the Palace of Westminster, and prevents the development of an alternative, modern and representative second chamber.

For these reasons reform of the House of Lords is always on the agenda of constitutionalists, but it is not a popular cause, nor one favoured by the Conservative Party, nor by enthusiasts for the present dominance of the House of Commons (who do not want that dominance challenged by a second chamber with any claim to representativeness). Reform poses difficult problems for the constitutionalists. On composition, radical solutions for the Lords (abolish and start again) force a fundamental reformation of the whole constitution; but compromise, as attempted in 1968, looks feeble and irrational. This then raises questions about powers (should a more representative House not have more substantial powers?) which are dormant at present.

Further, any attempt at reform may be resisted by the House of Lords, which might argue, first, that it must itself consent to such reform, and, secondly, that Parliament may not have the constitutional power radically to change its own formation. It may be contended that the sovereignty of Parliament is the sovereignty of the 'Crown-in-Parliament', and that the House of Commons has only delegated power and cannot arrogate to itself the power to change the form of Parliament as thus understood. Hence the Reform Acts of 1911 and 1949 are of dubious validity.

In practice such argument is unlikely to carry much weight in face of a strong popular sentiment in favour of reform, which could legitimate new constitutional understandings. However, such sentiment does not exist. Preference for the status quo seems to be a fundamental part of British constitutional understandings. The case of the House of Lords shows that constitutional reformers must first devise acceptable procedures for constitutional reform.

10

PARLIAMENT
Functions and Processes

Functions

Walter Bagehot (1963, pp. 150–4), writing in the 1860s, set out the functions of the House of Commons – the ordering was deliberate:

1. Choosing, and maintaining or dismissing, the government, and guiding it ('They guide him and he leads them').
2. Expressing the mind of the people.
3. Teaching the nation.
4. Informing the government of grievances and complaints.
5. Legislation.

Bagehot's list of functions is still acceptable, though the political relation of Parliament to government is now very different. The analyst of a modern legislature might discern two major functions of Parliament within the political structure:

1. Empowerment. Choosing and supporting the government, and providing the personnel of government, including training and selection. The device of drawing a government from the legislature is characteristic of British parliamentary government.

2. Legitimating government, ensuring a minimum acceptability and consent. This function pervades all else, and seems to fit into and reinforce British political culture, in which Parliamentary institutions are salient.

The major processes to be observed in Parliament are as follows:

1. Legislation – in practice the machinery for processing the government's legislation (including finance), the process including amending, 'registering', legitimation.
2. Debate, ventilation, challenge, opposition – compelling the government to give an account of itself on the floor of the chamber.
3. Oversight, scrutiny, holding government to account in the more detailed way possible in select committees including the Public Accounts Committee (Comptroller and Auditor-General) and Parliamentary Questions.
4. Representation of the people and the remedy of grievances, including some parliamentary procedures, correspondence with ministers and the special procedures of the Parliamentary Commissioner (Ombudsman).

These analyses can be combined to give three overriding functions for the modern House of Commons:

1. empowerment;
2. accountability;
3. representation.

Members of Parliament

The constitutional position of Members of Parliament is determined by the structure and functions of Parliament. Members are bound constitutionally to their constituencies in the sense that their status depends ultimately on the votes of a majority in their constituencies; in consequence most Members spend a good deal of time attending to matters of concern to the constituency or to individual constituents. However, Members' behaviour is much more influenced by their membership of a party (local, national and above all parliamentary). The priorities are: party, constituency, Parliament, modified along the way by personal drives, ambition, individual conscience, the lure of additional employment.

Members of Parliament have added two functions of their own to those listed above: trouble-making and interest representation. Trouble-making means here persistent dissent, the harrying of government on particular issues. It is a personal development of the constitutional functions of opposition and the securing of accountability. Interest representation is a special form of the representative function carried out by political parties and all Members of Parliament. Members have always and naturally represented their own kind and their own acquaintance and contacts – knights of the shire, burgesses, farming and land-ownership, the railway interest, high finance, the trade unions, lawyers, teachers, journalists, men and women. Recently the representation of interests has become more formalised, professionalised and commercialised. Members themselves act as paid 'consultants' (lobbyists in effect) for special interests, or hire themselves as professional 'consultants' to any who will pay their fees. At the same time, outside lobbying firms have invaded Parliament.

About one-third of Members, mostly Conservatives, act as paid 'parliamentary consultants'. Up to one-half of Labour members are 'sponsored' by trade unions, receiving assistance in their political work (for example, contributions towards election expenses, constituency office expenses) in return for unspecified sympathy and service. Apart from continuing general advice and information, an interest group may be able in effect to purchase a Written Question or an Early Day Motion for a few hundred pounds, and an interview with a senior official or even a minister might be arranged for a more substantial fee. Minor amendments to legislation may be obtained; modification of major legislation may be more difficult, though not impossible, and will certainly be more costly.

None of this lobbying activity is illegal, and it may be justified as a proper enlargement of the Member's representative role, and an opening up of the structure of government to legitimate interests. On the other hand, the representation of interests is largely secret and heavily biased towards groups with substantial funding. In public the Member's position is defined by his or her obligations to party, constituents and conscience. In private and in practice obligations to 'clients' may weigh heavily. Burke's celebrated advice to his constituents – 'Parliament is not a congress of ambassadors from different and hostile interests' – is thus set in a new context. To reformulate Burke: 'You choose a Member indeed; but when you have chosen him, he is not a member for a constituency or for Parliament, but for any group which cares to offer an appropriate fee . . .'.

Clearly the development of the 'consultancy' relationship poses threats to the representative function and the time, perhaps also the integrity, of Members of Parliament. The only formal regulation is by a select committee which keeps and publishes an annual Register of Members' Interests, defined by the Committee as 'any pecuniary interest or other material benefit . . . which might be thought to affect his conduct as a Member of Parliament or influence his actions, speeches or vote in Parliament'. (Report of the Select Committee on Members' Interests (Declaration) (1974–5) HC 102, para. 102). Members are required to register any employment or sponsorship for which they receive some compensation. Members are free to report such interests as they choose. Some returns are incomplete and one Member simply refused on principle to make a report ('what principle would that be?' you may ask). The House takes no action on the report, except where an undeclared interest of some significance for a Member's activities is revealed (as in speaking in debate, or membership or chairmanship of a select committee), or where the interest represented attempts formally to restrict the Member's actions, as in the case of one or two trade unions.

The Committee reviewing in 1992 the working of the Register since its inception in 1975 recommended some tightening of the system, in particular the reporting of the actual nature of a business, the naming of clients of consultancies (where the Member is personally involved), disclosure of gifts and other benefits such as travel, the declaration of relevant interests by the promoters of Early Day Motions, the reporting of membership of Lloyd's and of substantial shareholdings (so that wealthy Members cannot report that they have no interests). The disposition of the House is to rely on trust rather than transparency and formal regulation – in marked contrast to the strict regulation applied by Parliament to local councillors. However, some tightening of the rules, or at least a greater sensitivity to the ethical issues which underlie them, may arise from the case (1994) of the two MPs out of twenty approached who responded positively to the journalist–*provocateur*'s offer of a fee for putting a Question. (The case was referred to the Privileges Committee.)

The constitutional consequences of this development of special interest representation are serious. The representational function of Parliament had already been somewhat distorted by the development of disciplined parties; the growth of special interest representation moves Parliament further from the representation of the people, which is its historic constitutional function. The commercialisation of the relationship recalls the corruption of the rotten boroughs of the pre-Reform period; all that is new is a shift in the location of corruption.

The main processes and procedures

The rules of parliamentary practice are authoritative and are written down and codified in Erskine May's *Parliamentary Practice*, the great bible or rule-book of Parliament. Here at last, it may seem, is a written part of the British constitution, precise rules to which obedience is required, not soft custom and convention. However, in practice parliamentary procedure is not of high constitutional significance; it deals with forms rather than substance and fundamentals. The constitutional fundamental is the doctrine of parliamentary sovereignty, which allocates and limits power (allocating to Parliament and limiting everything else) and controls the relations between institutions. That fundamental disposition of power is modified by custom and practice and further regulated by rules of procedure. Such rules are more to do with day-to-day operation than with the shaping of power by way of limitations and procedures for accountability.

Government control of procedure and time

The government has substantial control of the time and business of the House through the Leader of the House (a senior government minister), the Whips and 'the usual channels', that is, arrangements made with the Opposition, backed by the governing party's majority but constrained by custom and the morality of 'do-as-you-would-be-done-by' (not very sharply felt in a period of one-party dominance). The government does not have a monopoly of time, and must share with the Opposition and backbenchers (see Chapter 9), but there is enough time and control to get through most of the legislation the government needs, even if not as much as it might sometimes want. The 'success rate' of government Bills in sessions of normal length is about 95 per cent; indeed, the notion of a score in a contest between executive and legislature, as in the United States, is inappropriate in Britain.

Legislation

There is adequate provision of time for the consideration of legislation prepared and drafted by the government – debate on general principles at second reading, detailed consideration and amendment in standing committee, further consideration in a report stage and a final debate on third reading; followed by a similar procedure in the House of Lords with consideration of further amendments in the Commons. In all of this Parliament acts as a legislative machine controlled by the government, which can impose a strict timetable for debate by means of closure or 'guillotine'. Moreover, the preparatory work – inquiry, consultation, drafting – is done almost wholly within the executive (contrast this with the United States).

As far as legislation is concerned, the committee system works in support of the government. Select committees do not normally consider future legislation. Standing committees (legislative committes which are not standing, but appointed *ad hoc* for each Bill) work as amending and improving machinery on behalf of the government. The minister is well briefed and well supported by a team of ministers and officials; government Members sit (perhaps reading their correspondence or keeping in touch with lobbyists in the corridor) ready to vote as instructed by the Whips in favour of government proposals and against Opposition amendments.

Parliament is not entirely without influence in legislation. Discontent within the governing party, anticipated by the government or expressed privately (and so difficult to discover), and occasional dissent on the floor of the House lead to modification of proposals, but hardly ever to major change or abandonment (the Shops Bill of 1986 is an isolated and special case). Altogether, it is clear that the main law-making function of Parliament is to legitimate the finished product put forward by the executive.

There are special provisions for Private Members' Bills and about ten to fifteen are passed in each session. The main procedure is a ballot for a place in the limited time made available. Members may choose a favoured subject or take up a cause pressed by an interest group. They are unlikely to succeed without the support of a substantial number of Members and the sympathetic help of the government, particularly in drafting. Notable Private Members' Bills include the Abolition of the Death Penalty (1965) and abortion law reform (1967) and, less noticed at the time, a Bill to ensure the admission of the press to meetings of local authorities, introduced in 1960 by a new young Member, a Mrs Margaret Thatcher.

Subordinate or delegated legislation

Subordinate legislation is mostly delegated legislation, delegated by Parliament to the government, and made in the form of 'Statutory Instruments'. Such rules and regulations literally outweigh Acts of Parliament – three times in size and twenty times in number. They are concerned with the implementation of policy and the detail of its administration, for example the adjustment of fees and charges, the revision of standards in manufacturing, changes in restrictions arising from health hazards in agriculture or in working conditions or in pension regulations. Such examples reflect the fact that modern governments intervene in detail over vast areas of economic and social life; and it is difficult, inefficient and for the most part unnecessary for primary legislation to do more than lay down the general principles.

That rather complacent view of delegation is plainly acceptable where there is very little or no policy content, as in the adjustment for inflation of charges provided for in the legislation; but in other cases the policy content may be higher, as, for example, in the decision to levy a new charge, under a general power to make charges, or to modify substantially a restriction for health or safety purposes, or to change the conditions of entry of immigrants and visitors, or to develop in detail the rather skeletal provisions of the Child Support Act. Behind such particular considerations lies a general argument about the scope of executive power. There is virtue in a pluralist diffusion of power, some counter-balance to executive omnipotence.

Much alarm was raised over sixty years ago by an influential book written by the Lord Chief Justice, Lord Hewart, under the rhetorical title *The New Despotism* (1929). In fact, the fuss raised by Hewart's polemic was exaggerated. It reflected a *laissez-faire*, anti-collectivist outlook, also some justified concern about the excesses of executive power under the war-time Defence of the Realm Acts of 1914 and 1915, and the anti-parliamentary tendency of some leading socialists. Further, the critics of the alleged new despotism included the development of administrative tribunals in their denunciation, thus confusing the rule of law with the rule of lawyers. A government committee set up to consider the specific problem of ministers' powers (Donoughmore Committee, 1932) concluded that there was no fundamental cause for concern about delegated legislation.

> We do not agree with those critics who think that the practice is wholly bad. We see in it definite advantages provided that the statutory powers are exercised and the statutory functions performed in the right way. But risks of abuse are incidental to it, and we believe that safeguards are required, if the country is to continue to enjoy the advantages of the practice without suffering from its inherent dangers. (*Report of the Committee on Ministers' Powers*, 1932, para. 5)

The Donoughmore Committee recommended the strict limitation of the power of ministers to modify the provisions of an Act (so-called Henry VIII clauses, after the despotic Tudor king); precision in the nature and extent of the delegation of rule-making power; openness, due notice and consultation in the making of delegated legislation; and parliamentary scrutiny by a standing committee.

These recommendations have been accepted in principle, although the Deregulation Act of 1994 specifically confers powers on ministers to change or repeal non-civil rights laws by means of secondary (delegated) legislation (Henry VIII lives again!). Parliament continues to consider delegation of powers at the stage of primary legislation; when particular Instruments are laid before the House for approval by affirmative or negative procedures; and in a Joint Committee on Statutory Instruments. The Joint Committee is served by an official, the Counsel to the Speaker, but is short of time for careful consideration. Debate on the floor of the

House is rare, unless the regulation has aroused a great deal of critical comment.

Altogether, Parliament's control of ministers' delegated powers is not substantial. Parliament is generally weak in face of the executive, and especially so where delegation may be appropriate and the precise limitation of executive power is by definition inappropriate. Lord Hewart's anxieties, in an altered context, may still be justified. Parliament's role is limited: it has conceded its power over major policy to the executive. Having neither time nor expertise to deal with detail, it must fall back to its characteristic role, rather like a motorway patrol or a customs control, of deterrence by random check.

European Community legislation

The consequences for the constitution of Britain's membership of the European Community were discussed in Chapter 3. For major policy Parliament's procedures are associated with the legislation consequent upon the making of treaties (as in the case of Maastricht) and the continuing processes of ministerial responsibility. Ratification of treaties is a prerogative power, but the incorporation of provisions into law requires legislation, and there is in any case scope for debates on the general policy implied by the treaties. Ministerial responsibility and the normal processes of Parliament also require that the Prime Minister or other ministers make statements to the House on major Community business, for example after meetings of the European Council.

Community legislation, apart from treaties, is usually known as secondary legislation, that is, legislation deriving from the primary legislation embodied in the treaties. This is a matter of concern to the UK Parliament, since it has only an indirect hand in the making of the primary legislation, and the 'secondary legislation' may have a direct effect in Britain. Here the actual transfer of legislative power to the Community is revealed. To deal with such legislation the two Houses have adopted procedures similar to those used for domestic delegated legislation – and no more effective, it may be said.

The House of Commons has a Select Committee on European Legislation, the Lords a Select Committee on the European Communities. Both committees are assisted by a legal adviser and other staff, the Commons Select Committee having a clerk and three specialists. The committees deal with draft EC legislation and other documents published by the Commission for submission to the Council of the EC (the 'legislation' which is made by the Commission alone is not within the responsibility of ministers in the United Kingdom and does not therefore come before Parliament). The Committee is provided by the government with an explanatory memorandum and may also take evidence from ministers and officials including EC officials.

The Committee then reports to the House, not on the merits of the legislation, but on whether it raises questions of legal or political importance and what matters of principle or policy may be affected thereby. If the Committee so recommends, the government may endeavour to find time for debate. The Committee deals with between six and nine hundred documents each year and recommends about eighty to one hundred for further consideration (Norton, 1993, p. 118). This is now usually done in one of two special standing committees. The Lords Committee works in a similar way, but on a larger scale, with more members, more staff and sub-committees, more time and greater expertise and commitment to the European Community.

Of course, the UK Parliament has no power to amend or reject the legislation of the European Community. In any case the government is likely to apply its majority, and sometimes may have had to give its agreement before parliamentary consideration. There are no formal relations between the UK Parliament and the European Parliament. Thus the committee procedure for dealing with European legislation reflects the usual problems of time, energy and expertise for a lay parliament confronting a formidable executive bureaucracy, added to the difficulties of coping with the remoteness, unfamiliarity and inaccessibility of the European Community.

Financial procedure

Financial procedure is even more tightly controlled by government than legislative procedure. The procedural initiative in financial matters (expenditure and revenue) rests with 'the Crown', that is, the government. The current Standing Orders of the House are based on a resolution of 1706: 'This House will receive no petition for any sum relating to public service, or proceed upon any motion for a grant or charge upon the public revenue . . . unless recommended from the Crown.' Hence Opposition motions relating to finance may propose reducing the minister's salary, a procedural device for debating the subject.

In this way procedure confirms the basic pre-constitutional fact that a government spending £350 billion each year is unwilling to share financial power with Parliament, and Parliament for its part is incapable of close control or effective scrutiny of a massive and complex programme of spending and taxation. Parliament has to some extent accepted this position: the days formerly known as 'Supply Days' are now called 'Opposition Days' and are devoted to general debates; the former Estimates and Expenditure Committees have been replaced by the structure of departmental select committees. Parliament still expects to be informed (in fact financial information has improved of recent years), and endeavours to scrutinise past expenditure through the Public Accounts Committee (see below). What it cannot do in this central area of government policy-making is to take over itself the business of governing.

The expressive, teaching and informing functions

These are Bagehot's functions which include specifically the representation of opinion in the country, political information and education, and the presentation of grievances, and generally contributing to the public debate of matters of public concern. A range of procedures is available to Parliament to carry out these functions:

1. major debates, for example on Opposition Days (dominated by the front benches and ending with a government victory);
2. questions for oral or written answer (media shows for adversarial jousts, or occasions for harrying ministers and securing information; mainly for backbenchers);
3. adjournment debates (late night debates initiated by backbenchers, raising matters such as constituency grievances, poorly attended);
4. early day motions (an increasingly popular method – now over a thousand per session – of publicising a cause or a grievance, never debated; more, but not much more, than

parliamentary graffitti except when used to signal persisting and substantial discontent to party leadership, as over the Maastricht Treaty 1993).

The committees of the House

A major part of the constitutional position of the House of Commons now lies in its committees. This is not to say that 'Parliament in committee is Parliament at work' – as can be said of the US Congress. The essential constitutional functions of Parliament take place primarily in the chamber, where the government must sustain its position day-by-day. But the committees have come to fulfil certain functions crucial to the maintenance of the constitutional role of scrutiny and oversight of the government.

Select committees

In 1979 the system of select committees was reformed to provide specialist committees 'to examine the expenditure, administration and policy of the principal government departments . . . and associated public bodies' (Standing Order No. 130, 25 June 1979). Such committees are now set up in each session of Parliament – sixteen altogether, including the Committee on Northern Ireland established in 1994. The only department excluded from such scrutiny was the Lord Chancellor's Department, but that now comes within the scope of the Home Office Committee (and a junior minister answers in the House of Commons for the Department).

The reform of the select committees was intended to improve Parliament's ability to scrutinise the executive and hold ministers accountable; also to provide opportunities for serious work, and even an alternative career path for professionally oriented and ambitious backbench Members of Parliament. A more sceptical view is that service on the committees would give backbenchers harmless activity while awaiting instructions from the Whips.

Composition

The committees are cross-party, the eleven places on each committee being allocated by the Selection Committee to reflect the party position within the House. Thus since the reform, the Conservative Party has had a majority on every committee and chairs ten of the sixteen committees. Selection is in practice heavily influenced by the Whips on each side, even in this area, which is wholly for backbenchers, and for some of the time free of the predictable adversarial partisanship of the Chamber.

The select committees are each assisted by a small staff, an official clerk and one or two part-time advisers. Much responsibility falls upon them and the chairman for the effective work of the committee. But however dedicated, well-informed and skilful, the select committees are Davids in face of the mighty Goliath of Whitehall.

Powers and limitations

Select committees have the power to send for persons, papers and records. This means that in theory they can call anyone to appear before them to answer questions and give evidence and require the production of any papers and records relevant to their inquiry. In practice these powers can only be used without restriction against private individuals; otherwise they are hedged around with qualifications and restrictions. Some of these arise through parliamentary limitations (as a consequence of parliamentary privilege and procedures) and others are imposed by government.

Parliamentary limitations

The power of select committees is delegated power, and the formal authority to insist on the attendance of a member of either House or the production of documents remains with the House. Thus select committees can only invite Members, whether backbenchers or ministers, to appear and must go to the House for an order to enforce attendance. In relation to Members of Parliament, this limitation has presented few problems. It is exceptional for Members to refuse an invitation. In 1989 Edwina Currie, the former junior Minister for Health, was invited to appear before the Agriculture Committee, which was inquiring into salmonella in eggs. This was a subject of some concern since Mrs Currie, as a minister, had made a widely publicised and somewhat misleading statement. At first Mrs Currie declined to attend. After being informed by the committee chairman that if she continued to refuse to attend 'formal steps' would be taken in the House to secure her attendance, she complied with the committee's request (HC108–I, 1989).

Prime Ministers and former Prime Ministers do not normally appear before select committees. Mrs Thatcher, in refusing (1994) an invitation from the committee inquiring into the Malaysian Pergau Dam project (in which, it seemed, she had been closely involved), claimed she was following a convention – an interesting example of the rapid development of a convention which protects the executive.

Ministers and former ministers may appear before the committees but refuse to answer questions. This may be a serious problem. Edwina Currie, having yielded to pressure to appear before the Agriculture Committee, proved reluctant to respond to the Committee's questions (with, it must be said, the help of a sympathetic chairman). Even more controversial was Leon Brittan's refusal in 1986 to answer many of the questions put by the Defence Committee, which was inquiring into the Westland affair (HC519, 1985–6). Again the action a select committee can take on its own is limited. It can seek time in the House for a debate, but parliamentary time is scarce in a crowded timetable controlled by the government.

Usually committees confine themselves to expressing dissatisfaction in their reports. Thus the Defence Committee made clear its expectations of ministers and ex-ministers: 'Accountability involves ACCOUNTING in detail for actions as a Minister' (HC519, 1985–6, para. 235). The Agriculture Committee took a similar line in its report on salmonella in eggs: 'We believe Members of Parliament have a clear duty to assist select committee inquiries; . . . this is particularly true of those who may be asked to account for their actions as former ministers' (HC108–1, para. 102). Subsequently the Procedure Committee, reporting in 1990 on the Working of the Select Committees, took up the point and concluded that there was 'no acceptable reason' for ministers to refuse to answer questions (HC19, 1989–90, para. 163). However, it did not recommend either improving the committees' access to the House in such cases or giving them increased powers.

The limitations of delegated power are also evident when it comes to acquiring documents from government departments. Select committees cannot themselves order the production of papers, which requires the authority of the House. Hence, wherever possible, the select committees have sought other means of securing information. One of the most notable incidents occurred prior to the reform of the select committee system and involved the Select Committee on Nationalised Industries (which no longer exists). In 1978 the Secretary of State for Industry refused a request for papers concerning the future prospects of British Steel (HC238, 1977–8). The chairman of the Committee sought a debate in the House but failed to secure parliamentary time. The Committee therefore sought the documents from the Chairman of British Steel, Sir Charles Villiers, who, as a private person rather than an MP, had no protection from Parliament. He complied with the Committee's order, being aware that failure to have done so would have constituted contempt of Parliament.

There are other examples of select committees seeking information from alternative sources. When the Ministry of Defence refused the Defence Committee documentation concerning defence spending, the Committee acquired the relevant documents from the Press Association to which they had been leaked (HC773, 1979–80). The Department of Trade and Industry denied the Trade and Industry Committee access to documents concerning the International Tin Council, and the Committee obtained them from America where they were available under the Freedom of Information Act (HC305–I, 1985–6). However, such alternative sources for information are only occasionally available. Most of the time if a minister refuses to release documents, the select committee is left without the information it requires.

Government limitations

The lack of any formal authority to use against government departments and ministers means that select committees are largely dependent upon the co-operation of government in their investigations. However, there are significant limitations upon this co-operation, most importantly regarding the appearance of civil servants before committees. The limitations concern both the evidence that can be given by officials and the appearance of individually named officials before committees.

The rules for officials appearing before committees are contained within a Civil Service Department Memorandum of Guidance, frequently referred to as the 'Osmotherly Rules' after its author. Officials are told 'to be as helpful as possible to Committees'. There are, however, strict limitations on the information officials can give to them. Most significantly they are instructed not to disclose advice given to ministers, inter-departmental exchanges, and alternative policy options. Moreover, ministers frequently impose these restrictions on themselves as well, on the grounds of confidentiality, and in accordance with the conventions of collective and individual ministerial responsibility. Select committees may therefore find their investigations thwarted by 'a rigid interpretation of the so-called convention by which Ministers and officials are prohibited from informing the House about the ways in which government decisions are made' (HC553, 1979–80, para. 16).

Such rigidity may result in select committees being denied not just the advice that was given to ministers but also background information. This is because of a reluctance by departments to distinguish between the two, as demonstrated during the Defence Committee's inquiry into the future of the Gurkhas (*First Report from the Defence Committee*, HC68, 1988–9). Officials refused to answer questions about a departmental study on the basis that such answers concerned 'advice'. However, Michael Mates, the chairman of the Committee, insisted that he was seeking 'information' which could be separated from 'advice', and suspended the inquiry until the minister could be questioned. The dispute in this case was resolved when the minister provided the required material. However, there is often not such a satisfactory outcome.

The Procedure Committee, reporting in 1990, expressed its concern about the restrictions imposed by the Osmotherly Rules:

> We doubt whether the fabric of constitutional government would suffer fatal injury if witnesses were more forthcoming about the level at which decisions are taken and the extent of involvement of different Departments. . . .
>
> It is difficult to see why . . . Committees cannot be told in purely practical terms, what options are under consideration and their cost implications. We regard as unsustainable the Government's argument that experienced and trained officials cannot distinguish between the subject on which Ministers sought advice on the one hand, and the substance of that advice on the other. (HC19, paras 157, 160)

Despite such comments, the Committee was not prepared to confront the government over restrictions of the Osmotherly Rules, preferring to take what it considered to be a 'pragmatic' approach (HC19, para. 157) – that is, not 'rocking the boat'.

One other area of debate since the reform of the select committee system has been whether or not committees can summon named civil servants. According to the Osmotherly Rules:

> Officials appearing before select committees do so on behalf of their Ministers. It is customary, therefore, for Ministers to decide which officials . . . should appear to give evidence.

However, it continues:

> If a Committee insisted on a particular official appearing before them they could issue a formal order for his attendance. In such an event the official would have to appear before the Committee.

This would seem to be a recognition that committees have the right to call named officials, although there is a clear reluctance by government to concede such attendance. This reluctance was evident during the Westland Inquiry when the Department of Trade and Industry and the Cabinet Office refused a request from the Defence Committee for five named officials to appear before it. Sir Robert Armstrong, Head of the Civil Service and Cabinet Secretary, appeared instead, and the Defence Committee, despite protests, never tested its powers by making a formal order.

A further issue that arose in Westland was whether it was acceptable for a select committee to inquire into the 'conduct' (more easily understood as 'misconduct') of civil servants. The Defence Committee sought to establish where responsibility lay for the leaking of parts of the letter written by the Solicitor-General to Michael Heseltine. The question was whether disclosure had been authorised by the Secretary of State for Trade and Industry, Leon Brittan, or whether officials from the Department had acted on their own initiative with or without the backing of officials in Downing Street (the Prime Minister's Office). Leon Brittan took full responsibility for the leak when he appeared before the Committee. However, his failure to explain what had happened and his refusal to answer certain questions led to suspicions that his officials may have gone beyond what he had authorised. It was to determine the truth that the Committee sought unsuccessfully to interview the officials concerned.

In the aftermath of Westland the government confirmed its position regarding the 'conduct' of civil servants, and laid down additional guidelines for civil servants concerning their appearance before select committees (Cmnd 78, Appendix 2, 1986). Officials are instructed to avoid answering any questions which concern, or appear to concern, their conduct or the behaviour of other officials. Such questions, the guidelines suggest, should be referred to the minister or 'designated senior official' for 'the principles of ministerial accountability are still applicable, even if officials have acted outside or contrary to the authorisation given to them by their Ministers'.

The government insisted that its reason for issuing the guidelines was to protect individual civil servants from committee inquiries which sought to allocate blame. Such guidelines might be acceptable to the committees if they could rely on ministers always providing full explanations. However, as Westland demonstrated, this may not be a realistic expectation, and the guidelines may be seen as imposing a further restriction on the ability of select committees to secure information.

The determination of the government to maintain a firm grip upon the information that select committees acquire would seem to be undiminished. Even the establishment of Next Steps executive agencies has done little to produce a change in attitude. Chief Executives are publicly accountable for the performance of the agencies, but when they appear before select committees, they are still bound by the Osmotherly Rules.

The effectiveness of the select committees

The departmental select committees have to take their place in a system structured by party discipline and dominated by the executive. It is not open to the committees to change the course of government policy. They must work on the lower slopes of government, contributing to the context rather than the development of policy. They are most effective in a bi-partisan mode, but that in itself indicates the necessary limitations of their role, for the larger part of government in Britain is uncompromisingly partisan.

Within those limitations, the select committees may be assessed as follows:

1. They have increased the amount of government information made publicly available.

2. They have improved routine departmental accountability.
3. They have enabled some backbenchers to become expert in particular areas of policy, and provided serious professional work, an alternative career path for those disappointed of or not ambitious for office, and for Opposition Members.
4. They have produced some reports of high quality based on a unique mode of gathering evidence and testing opinion, and thus demonstrating the value of a non-adversarial, bi-partisan approach to government.
5. They have raised public awareness of the detailed workings of government, particularly since the hearings have been presented in broadcasts and figure in press reports of Parliament, as reporting of parliamentary debates has declined.

However, the effectiveness of select committees is limited by several factors:

1. their inability to summon ministers or order the disclosure of documents from government departments;
2. the restrictions imposed by the government through the Osmotherly Rules and more recent guidelines;
3. the practical problems of effective operation; in particular, the difficulties, for the chairman especially, of avoiding a lapse into fruitless partisanship or ineffectual bi-partisanship, and, for all members and staff, of persistently and systematically challenging the defensive expertise of officials and ministers;
4. the ultimate power of the government majority within each committee, and the unseen pressure of the Whips, to ensure that the government normally suffers no embarrassment, so the effectiveness of bi-partisanship is limited;
5. the lack of parliamentary time for debating committee reports – during the period 1979–85 only five reports were debated out of a total of 275 (HC Deb., 22 July 1985, cols 371–2).

In view of the difficulties of their work, the committees rely upon the co-operation of government to fulfil their function effectively. Normally such co-operation is forthcoming, and indeed some committees develop helpful, even cosy, relations with the departments. However, as Westland demonstrated, helpfulness cannot be taken for granted. Political considerations, in particular the avoidance of embarrassment to the government, may result in the withholding of information and the frustration of a committee's inquiries. So far the committees have chosen to avoid confrontation with government, for the good reason that a majority of each committee is on the side of the government, and a committee is certain to lose both the particular contest and the longer-term standing of the system as a whole.

The Select Committee on Public Accounts

The Select Committee on Public Accounts (or Public Accounts Committee – PAC) has constitutional significance because it does succeed in exposing the conduct of government and securing a measure of accountability. There are two good reasons for this unusual degree of effectiveness. First, the PAC is assisted by the Comptroller and Auditor-General and the staff of around eight hundred of the National Audit Office (NAO). Secondly, it deals with, or at least is structured to deal with, administration rather than policy, the past not the future, costs not substance. With that support and within those strict limits, the PAC demonstrates the possibility of making government answerable to Parliament.

The PAC is the oldest of the select committees, first appointed in 1861 by Gladstone, a cost-cutting Chancellor of the Exchequer, who wondered aloud whether income tax could be abolished. The PAC has been reappointed annually since then. It has fifteen members, with a majority for the governing party but as chairman a member of the Opposition with experience of financial office. The Committee is granted the usual powers to send for persons, papers and records, and to report from time to time. In particular, it takes evidence from departmental Accounting Officers, not the accountants but the Permanent Secretaries with ultimate responsibility for all expenditure, and, in the case of the Agencies, from the Chief Executives.

The inquiries of the PAC have always been based on the reports of the Comptroller and Auditor-General and his staff of government auditors. The National Audit Act 1983 strengthened the position of the Comptroller and gave him a firm base in the House of Commons. He is in effect appointed by the House of Commons and is an officer of the House; he heads the new NAO (previously the Exchequer and Audit Department), and appoints his own staff who similarly are not civil servants. Budget and staffing are supervised by a Public Accounts Commission of the House of Commons which has only one ministerial member (the Leader of the House of Commons). The Comptroller directs his own work, but takes account of the views of the PAC not the Treasury.

The Comptroller and his staff work in a more or less systematic cycle of reviews. More than one half of the work lies in auditing the accounts of departments and other public bodies receiving over half their income from public funds (with the much-disputed exception of the nationalised industries; and local government, which has its own Audit Commission). Auditing here means checking that proper accounts have been kept, money has been spent as appropriate, and standards of financial probity and good practice have been maintained. However, a still substantial part of the Comptroller's work (about 40 per cent) is directed under the Act at examining 'the economy, efficiency and effectiveness' of the department concerned.

It is not intended that this 'value-for-money' audit challenges the policies implied in a department's operations; but it is inevitable that inquiry into costs, effectiveness of implementation, controls, achievement of objectives, consideration of alternatives raises questions of policy. For example, any critical examination of the costs of defence technology or privatisation must throw doubts on the policy itself. In some cases, for example the gross undervaluing of bus stations in the selling off of public transport, the fault may lie in implementation; but in the numerous and persistent cost overruns discovered by the NAO in defence spending doubts arise about the whole financial basis of policy. Thus the Comptroller and the NAO, backed by the PAC, act to some extent more as management consultants than as auditors, but unlike management consultants in business the Comptroller arrives uninvited, ranges where he chooses, reports to outsiders and comes back again to monitor improvement.

All this is at least irritating, possibly nerve-racking, to the departments under scrutiny, and within limits the process secures accountability. The reports of the Comptroller and the PAC are considered in the departments before publication and may be amended; departments do thus have a first chance to defend themselves. Thereafter the reports are published. There may be a debate on one or at most two days in the House, and the more scandalous accounts of government mismanagement and extravagance may enjoy a headline in the press.

However, governments do not in practice make fundamental changes to policy, even in the face of the persistent demonstration of inefficiency, waste and overspending; and the pace of improvement in cost controls is painfully slow. The main effect of the PAC and its associated audit operation lies, like all such audits, in the systematic pressure on officials to stay within the rules and avoid extravagance. There is an impact on the departments – but not enough to diminish the annual crop of scandalous waste uncovered by the Comptroller.

It might be concluded that in the massive operations of a government spending over £350 billion each year, waste and corruption could be a great deal worse; so some credit, and perhaps more power, is due to financial scrutiny and in particular the PAC. On the other hand, one former senior Treasury official, Sir Leo Pliatzky, has argued that the PAC and the NAO have gone further than was intended or is proper. Departments may be irritated or embarrassed by reports. '[A]t the end of the day a Department may still feel that its reservations about the NAO's comments are inadequately reflected.' (One can imagine a junior official using more colourful language.)

> [A]s seen from Whitehall, the NAO has from the first been pushing at the frontiers of its remit and encroaching on policy issues – an encroachment which, from the point of view of the executive, has to be discouraged if the National Audit Office and the Committee on Public Accounts are not to develop into a court of appeal sitting in judgment on government policies. (Pliatzky, 1989, p. 91)

If Pliatzky's perception is correct, then the PAC is pressing the potential of the select committees to the limit; and the limit is set by the government at the point at which they begin to have an impact on government policies.

Conclusion

The place of Parliament in the British constitution is systemically fundamental but functionally limited. 'At the heart of the "unwritten" constitution is the requirement of the Bill of Rights for the holding of free and frequent elections which puts the Government under sentence of death from the day of its election' (Griffith and Ryle, 1989, pp. 523–4). This is the 'Westminster model' of British government, often denounced as a façade and certainly less than the whole truth, but still the iron framework by which British government is shaped. In that framework Parliament is a necessary legislative machine, a forum for debate and an instrument of scrutiny. At the same time the functions of Parliament are limited: Parliament does not govern or initiate, and is itself largely controlled by the executive.

Yet Parliament can never be taken for granted. Like most such representative bodies, committees, boards, councils, senates, it has to be worked through, persuaded, its consent sought not assumed; control by the executive is imperfect. Ministers recognise the need for effort and the possibility of failure by conceding to Parliament at least the respect involved in time expended and anxiety endured. Moreover, Parliament is the arena in which ambitious Members stake their claim to office in competition with each other and incumbent ministers. The latter know very well that their case has to be made effectively in the House. The relief felt by ministers when Parliament is in recess, and the consequent slump in political news, both show the impact of Parliament on the conduct of government.

11

THE PEOPLE IN THE CONSTITUTION
Elections and Parties

Elections

Elections and parties both lie within a broad definition of the constitution, because of their functions in structuring government. This is evident in the case of elections, which are established and regulated by law. Elections are a crucial mechanism in the structure of British parliamentary democracy, developed historically and under the pressure of popular protest and reform movements. The mechanism is imperfect but still broadly conforms to the requirements of a modern system of 'free and fair elections', as set out, for example, in the European Convention on Human Rights. The following conditions may be regarded as appropriate and are, within limits, met in Britain:

1. universal adult suffrage (in practice restricted to citizens), with an open and inclusive process for registration;
2. constituencies (electoral districts) fairly drawn and of approximately equal size (necessary but not sufficient for fairness in the British ballot system);
3. all constituencies regularly contested;
4. elections at an established maximum interval;
5. elections decisive for the formation of a government;

6. no bar to candidature;
7. outlawing of corrupt practices;
8. secret ballot without intimidation;
9. the media not controlled by one group of candidates.

It is evident that the British system, like most others, cannot score full marks on each of these heads. Nevertheless, the system is generally accepted as free and, less surely, fair, subject to substantial reservations about the ballot method, and some concern about the finance of national campaigns and the influence of the partisan press.

The ballot method

The control of Parliament flows from elections in single-member territorial constituencies, conducted by the simple plurality method ('first-past-the-post'). The advantages and disadvantages of this method compared with methods of proportional representation will not be rehearsed in full here. The ideal consequence of the simple plurality method in conjunction with disciplined national parties is held to be strong but responsible and responsive government – the classic alternating two-party Westminster model. In practice the effects have been less consistent than this: third parties have been squeezed but minority or coalition governments have not been avoided. Dominance by the Conservative Party with little alternation is the normal pattern, but no government since 1945 has commanded a majority of the popular vote, still less a majority of those entitled to vote.

Thus the claimed advantages of 'strong and responsive' government have not been consistently achieved; yet the price paid in fairness and proportionality has been high. In particular the ballot system has left minorities unrepresented and small parties gravely disadvantaged; it has supported in unchallenged power government by the largest minority, while excluding a majority made up of several minorities. Altogether the virtues of 'first-past-the-post' have been much exaggerated, though it has roughly reflected shifts in popular opinion and has succeeded in providing legitimate (or at least reluctantly accepted) government.

Forms of proportional representation have been advocated to meet the defects of the simple plurality system, and to gain the benefits of fairness by greater proportionality and representation of minorities. Proportional representation is already used in Northern Ireland for elections to local government and the European Parliament, and Britain is now the only member of the European Community not to use a form of proportional representation for European elections in accordance with the implicit intentions of the Community.

There are various systems of proportional representation based on the several elements of the vote:

1. preferential voting, first, second, third, etc. (but having more than one vote, without preference, also provides for some refinement of choice, as in the two-member constituencies common in Britain until 1885);
2. counting by elimination (of bottom candidate) or by quota (the target for winning a seat);
3. in single- or multi-member constituencies (five or seven members is regarded as the best basis for the single transferable vote), or in a single national constituency (as in the party list used as a supplementary voting system in Germany);
4. a second ballot (as used in presidential elections in France) may also contribute to proportionality.

The ballot system could be reformed by ordinary legislation, though it would be customary to consult other parties (and indeed the people) and ensure a substantial measure of consent. It is conventional to proceed by a Speaker's Conference – there have been six plus a Royal Commission since 1900. A Speaker's Conference is in effect a commission representative of the political parties, chaired by the Speaker. It is expected to reach more or less agreed conclusions, and in consequence is often unable to reach conclusions at all.

There is evidently a strong case to be made for proportional representation, but there are counter-arguments and counter-interests. Any government or Member of Parliament elected under the existing method stands to lose by reform. Some forms of proportional representation threaten the historic and much loved territorial constituency. Worse, and constitutionally more significant, most forms of proportional representation are likely to undermine the existing pattern of political parties. The effect of proportional representation (the intended effect) is to nourish the smaller parties, and diminish the dominance of the two large parties. Coalition government is likely to become normal, and small parties are likely to hold the balance of power.

This would amount to a radical change in the workings of government and in the understandings and conventions which derive from and reinforce the dominance of the executive, based on a party majority in a sovereign Parliament. The present structure is based on the principle of 'winner-takes-all': power is not shared, nor even much challenged, except within the majority party. Hence a shift to a proportional system of voting would have a profound effect on the constitution. Parliamentary sovereignty would remain, but Parliament itself, and the structure of governance it supports, would be transformed. Whether it would be more or less democratic is difficult to say.

Constituency boundaries

In a structure based on single-member territorial constituencies, the drawing of boundaries in relation to a changing and mobile population is crucial to the outcome of elections. There is an unavoidable arbitrariness in the adjustment of boundaries, and continuing disparities in the size of constituency. Political parties press their own interests, do deals with each other and naturally complain when decisions run against them. A Member of Parliament may in effect be deprived of his or her seat by the redrawing of boundaries. The procedure is designed to be impartial and fair, but in some areas the task is so difficult as to raise a question about the desirability of a voting structure based on single-member constituencies.

The rules and procedure for the drawing of constituency boundaries are laid down in the consolidating Parliamentary Constituencies Act 1986. This provides for four Boundary Commissions for the four countries of the United Kingdom, reporting every ten to fifteen years (three to seven years between 1945 and 1958). Major re-distributions preceded the elections of 1974 and 1983.

The Commissions are chaired by the Speaker, assisted by a superior judge, two other commissioners (often lawyers, never Members of Parliament) and advised by the Registrar-General (of population) and the Director-General of Ordnance Survey, in practice by their expert staffs. The Commissioners report to the

Home Secretary, who lays the reports before Parliament, together with draft Orders in Council, giving effect with or without modification to their recommendations. Any modification by the Home Secretary would thus have to be open and defended. After approval by both Houses, the Orders are confirmed and made effective for the next election.

The procedure for local elections is slightly different. The Local Government Boundary Commissions determine the number of councillors appropriate to the authority and approve local ward boundaries, but these may be proposed by the local councils themselves (parish boundaries must be respected). Constituencies for European elections are amalgamations of parliamentary constituencies, drawn up by the Boundary Commissions. The provision of additional seats for the United Kingdom, under the Maastricht Treaty, raised an awkward problem of rapid redistribution in a system which is at present grossly disproportionate.

The Parliamentary Constituencies Act lays down certain rules for the Boundary Commissioners in drawing up constituencies:

1. The total number of seats is now 651 (one having been added to accommodate the rapidly expanding population of Milton Keynes).
2. Every constituency now returns a single member (multi-member seats were common in the nineteenth century and persist in some local government areas).
3. Scotland, Wales and Northern Ireland are entitled to a minimum of seats (71, 35 and 16, respectively), and as implemented (72, 38, 17) are overrepresented by 12, 5 and 1, respectively – the Celtic bonus.
4. The City of London shall be a single constituency ('why?' you may well ask).

The above rules are mandatory; all others are subject to some discretion, and reflect difficult negotiations and/or bad drafting; and the unavoidable fact that the Commissioners have to balance as best they can obscure and incompatible considerations:

5. So far as practicable, local government boundaries should be respected (specifically in English counties; and London boroughs should not be divided).

6. Account should be taken of 'special geographical considerations, including in particular the size, shape and accessibility of a constituency' (in practice this is a bonus for rural areas and islands).
7. 'The electorate of any constituency shall be as near the electoral quota [the divisor of the total electorate providing equal electoral districts] as is practicable, having regard to the foregoing rules.'

Considerations of practicability and release from strict application are applied to these rules. The hierarchy or priorities are confused. Thus the Commissioners must have regard to the local government boundary rule but it need not be strictly applied if it leads to an excessive disparity. The judges in the *Foot* case, 1983 (see below), conducted a detailed analysis of the rules, spending some time on the significance of the word 'But'. In practice the rules are guidelines, and this status is emphasised by the addition of the clause: 'It shall not be the duty of a Boundary Commission to aim at giving full effect in all circumstances to the above rules', and may take account of the inconvenience attending on alterations.

The process of review allows for representation and appeal, following the publication of provisional recommendations – though the appeal may be heard by an Assistant Commissioner, appointed *ad hoc*, and not well-informed about the area or the previous deliberations of the Commissioners.

Inevitably the Boundary Commissions have achieved only a fair approximation to equal electoral districts within the four countries of the United Kingdom (the disparities between the countries are 'built-in'). But the main problem is the rapid movement of population, and especially the process of suburbanisation of cities and the countryside. Proposals sometimes appear to be desperate and arbitrary attempts to meet the problems of an expanded electorate and a rapidly shifting population under contradictory rules and sharp political pressures. Oxford and Cambridge illustrate different approaches to similar problems. In Cambridge a single concentrated constituency has been fashioned from the city itself. In Oxford two constituencies have been created by dividing the city and making up numbers by the addition of Abingdon, which thought of itself as an ancient riverside, market and industrial town, not an integral suburb of Oxford.

The political parties are often displeased by the Commissions' recommendations. The Labour Party tends to lose its old city-centre strongholds because of declining population, but the Conservative shires may be upset by suburban development. In 1969 the Labour government in effect refused to implement the recommendations of the Boundary Commissions, first by legislation (defeated in the Lords) and then by securing the rejection of the Orders. Their (not entirely persuasive) defence against the charge of partisan bias was that the Commissioners had worked on local government boundaries which were about to be radically revised.

Given the very broad discretion given to the Commissions, their recommendations are not easily open to review. In 1983 the Labour Party, through its Leader and senior members, applied for judicial review, seeking to restrain the Commissioners from proceeding with their recommendations (*R.* v. *Boundary Commission, ex parte Foot* [1983] QB 600). It was argued on their behalf that the Commission had failed to achieve the fundamental objective of equal constituencies, and that they had in particular failed for that purpose to exercise their discretion to create constituencies which crossed county and London borough boundaries. The Court subjected the Rules to a lengthy and rigorous analysis (the words 'hammer' and 'nut' come to mind), and concluded that they had not been misinterpreted, and that discretion had been exercised reasonably; and therefore rejected the application.

The courts properly declined to repeat the work of the Commission, and claimed to consider only whether they had misconstrued their instructions. But the distinction is a fine one. The courts cannot improve a fundamentally unsatisfactory procedure. The truth is that many of the problems faced by the Commissions have no rational solution; the rules acknowledge this by their imprecision. The Commissions are subject to very little external accountability. The structure depends on the integrity and patience of the officials who do the work. But in default of persuasive objective criteria the system is open to contamination by considerations of party advantage; indeed it may be argued that there is virtually no other rational basis for the detailed determination of boundaries.

Hence there is a case for rewriting the rules and for including the supervision of boundary delimitation in the responsibilities of a Commission on Elections. However, the fundamental weakness rests in the attempt to devise single-member territorial constituencies in a country which is no longer divided naturally into medieval boroughs and shires. This is another argument for a radical reform of the ballot system.

The timing of elections

Elections for local government and the European Parliament are held at prescribed times; parliamentary elections are held at the choice of the Prime Minister, subject only to a maximum interval of five years and the necessity to seek a dissolution from the Queen. However, the Queen is unlikely to refuse a dissolution requested by a Prime Minister except in the circumstances set out in Chapter 4 – either the unavailability of an alternative Prime Minister or the lack of a decent interval since the last election. It is usual to regard the decision to 'go to the country' as one for the Prime Minister alone. It is true that it is not a decision for the Cabinet as a whole, and responsibility to Parliament does not arise. But Prime Ministers naturally consult senior colleagues, Whips and party chairmen, and of course public opinion polls, so the decision is not unlike many others taken in the bi-laterals and bunkers of the central executive territory.

The choice of the date of a general election gives the governing party a considerable advantage. The Opposition parties can be kept guessing while the government carefully plans an election to take advantage of polls and policies, the latest economic news (if favourable) and any summitry opportunities for the Prime Minister. The election can also be timed to fit into the government's management of the economy. The consequences of these calculations of political advantage are not always edifying – for example, the generous pre-election budget followed by the post-election crisis budget when the tax benefits are recouped, and the tendency for Prime Ministers to tease the Opposition, the media and the people about the date of the election.

Elections belong to the people, not to Prime Ministers, and there is a case for fixed-term parliaments, perhaps of four years, with provision for earlier dissolution if the government has lost its parliamentary majority (allowing scope for monarchical discretion in granting a dissolution). This would not preclude the management of the economy for electoral purposes, but that is inherent in a democratic polity. More frequent elections (for example, three-year parliaments or with one-third of Members retiring every two years, like US Senators) might make government excessively dependent on electoral favour: this is part of the 'strong government' argument in favour of the present structure.

The franchise

Britain may be described after 1688 as a constitutional monarchy with Parliament playing an indispensable part in government. However, it was not until the Parliamentary Reform Act of 1832 that Britain began to be a democracy in a modern sense. The Act abolished many of the old 'rotten boroughs' and 'pocket boroughs', bringing about a fairer distribution of seats, and extending the vote to about one-fifth of adult men. After further reform legislation (1867 and 1884–5) about three-fifths of men were eligible to vote.

But entitlement to vote without any kind of property qualification and without a bar to women was not achieved until 1928; even then the 'fancy franchises', votes for the occupiers of business premises and university graduates, survived until 1948. The age of entitlement to vote was reduced to 18 in 1969. Thus Britain has been governed under the principle of 'one person, one vote' for only fifty years – and, it may be remembered, entered the twentieth century with a hereditary peer as Prime Minister and a Cabinet including nine peers. Despite Magna Carta and a Parliament dating back to the Middle Ages, Britain is comparatively a young democracy.

Since the demise of the property qualification, entitlement to the vote is not now an area of much dispute, but it is still of some constitutional interest. For example, if residence is the basic qualification for voting, where do students reside? Should Australian or Irish people living in Britain, as distinct from just visiting, be entitled to vote? With regard to residence, it has been accepted that students may reside in two places, and are entitled to vote either in their home or in their college constituency. Student voting in a college constituency might affect the outcome if the students are concentrated and the constituency is marginal, but this is not true of most college constituencies, and in any case students as a whole are not heavily biased towards one party. The student vote is more likely to have a noticeable impact on one or two local government wards rather than a parliamentary constituency.

Owners of second homes, like students, are entitled to choose where to exercise their vote. That may be regarded as a dubious privilege attaching to property: for example, is it fair that an English businessman from the Birmingham suburbs should vote in a Welsh-speaking rural constituency in North Wales? The answer is that, fair or not, it is legal, though the courts in Scotland have been stricter in ruling against the owners of holiday homes, on grounds of purpose, length of time and 'quality' of residence. Such considerations led an English court to rule that the peace campaigners camping outside the USAF base at Greenham Common were indeed resident, fully committed to their place of residence by a quite precise purpose (*Hipperson* v. *Electoral Registration Officer of Newbury* [1985] QB 1060). Such problems are inherent in a structure based on small territorial consituencies.

Electoral title is also raised by questions of citizenship and by British citizens living abroad. The law is liberal in the matter of citizenship. All categories of British citizen, citizens of other Commonwealth countries (known collectively as 'Commonwealth citizens'), and all citizens of the Republic of Ireland are entitled to vote. There are historical reasons for the liberality towards the Commonwealth and Ireland, reinforced by the practical difficulties of discriminating, and the possible damage to race relations. British citizens living abroad are treated less generously: they lose their vote after five years. Other EU nationals are not entitled to vote in Parliamentary and local elections. However, under the Maastricht Treaty all citizens of the Member States, being citizens of the European Union, are entitled to vote in European elections (for the European Parliament).

The process of registration for the vote has always been regarded as straightforward and efficient, but it seems likely that the comprehensiveness of the Register is declining. The Register of Electors (for all elections) is compiled every year in October by the local Electoral Registration Officer, working by mail and by house calls and supported by public advertisement. The great merit of this procedure is that it requires no initiative and very little effort by the individual elector. But the Register, which comes into effect five months after compilation and lasts for one year, goes out of date quickly through death and removal. Young persons may be registered on attaining the age of 18, but the provision of a 'rolling' register for all has been resisted on the grounds of cost and practicality. Further, the 'poll tax' discouraged some reluctant or resistant tax-payers from entering their names on any official list, thus further degrading the Register. The Electoral Registration Officer is under no statutory obligation to ensure adequate representation, and it might be difficult to justify or devise a procedure for that purpose.

Candidates

In the by-election in Christchurch in July 1993 there were fourteen candidates, including those described as 'Anti-Maastricht Anti-Fed League', 'Sack Graham Taylor' (then manager of the England football team) and, less comprehensibly, 'I am for King' and 'Alfred Chicken' (these three collected 121 votes altogether).

Evidently there are few restrictions on standing as a candidate (except for those on some senior officials in central and local government). Only ten signatures are required for nomination, and in parliamentary elections no connection with the constituency has to be demonstrated. A deposit of £500 must be provided and is forfeit if the candidate receives less than 5 per cent of the votes cast. (In Christchurch eleven of the fourteen candidates predictably, and one assumes quite cheerfully, lost their deposits.) The deposit was first set at £150 in 1918, equivalent to over £4,000 in the 1990s; so a candidate may well feel that the current sum of £500 is well spent for the publicity, including a free mail shot to every elector. A more restrictive approach would present problems: a higher deposit might discourage worthy political groups; a requirement for more signatures of local electors is not difficult to meet, and cannot easily be checked.

The Electoral Registration Officer is not in a good position to reject nominations on the grounds of irrelevance or frivolity. For example, in Glasgow Hillhead, 1982, a by-election in which the SDP leader, Roy Jenkins, was standing, a second Roy Jenkins presented himself, claiming (truthfully) that he had already used the name for nine months, and the SDP he represented was actually founded before the other Roy Jenkins' SDP. He was allowed to stand and the electors of Hillhead proved able to distinguish the 'real' Roy Jenkins from the 'impostor'. It was no doubt helpful that the 'real' Roy Jenkins was a politician of high national salience; but in the European election of 1994 electors were more confused by a candidate standing in a Devon constituency for the Li*t*eral Democrats. He gained over 10,000 votes and the seat was lost by the Liberal Democrats.

In Finchley in 1983 a second Margaret Thatcher appeared, claiming to live in a flat called 'Downing Street Mansions', and standing for the Conservationist Party. His (or her) agent was called Regan (address: 'Whitehouse Mansions'). The Electoral Registration Officer rejected the nomination. The candidate sought judicial review, but lost again on the grounds that the candidature was an abuse of the right of nomination and an obvious unreality. This looks like a sensible personal opinion rather than a legalistic judgment. Indeed, the Appeal Court found the grounds unsatisfactory, but still dismissed the appeal, arguing that the motives of the candidate were malign, as was admitted. (*R* v. *Barnet and Finchley ERO, ex parte Bennett* [1983], unreported; see Rawlings, 1988, p. 119)

Election campaigns

It has been accepted for over a hundred and fifty years that the conduct of election campaigns should be regulated by the law in order to limit expenditure and prevent corrupt practices. The rampant corruption of eighteenth-century elections was reduced by the series of Parliamentary Reform Acts which extended the franchise and redistributed constituencies. This radical cleansing of the hustings was completed by the Corrupt and Illegal Practices Prevention Act of 1883. The Act is based on the campaign in the constituency since that was where the serious campaigning took place; for example, the expenditure of the Conservative Party in each contested constituency in the 1880s was between £2,000 and £3,000 on average – equivalent to well over £100,000 today. Over a century later, when most serious campaign activity goes on at the centre, the constituency principle still holds, and the massive expenditure of the parties on the national campaign is unregulated. It is a neat illustration of the use, or perhaps misuse, of a Victorian constitution in radically changed conditions.

The principle that election campaigns are local was upheld in the *Tronoh Mines* case (*R*. v. *Tronoh Mines Ltd* [1952] 1 All ER 697). It was held that an advertisement in support of the Conservative Party placed by the company in *The Times* during the 1951 election campaign was general political propaganda, only incidentally in support of any particular candidate, and so was not 'corrupt'. At the same time local campaign activity and much smaller expenditures are quite strictly controlled. Nineteenth-century practices including 'treating' ('regaling, feasting, entertaining' in return for a vote) and any payment which might be regarded as bribery are effectively outlawed; campaign expenditure is limited by a formula based on the size of the constituency (with a slightly larger allowance for rural seats) to about £7,000 for each candidate, and has to be accounted for.

These limits make for difficulties in the running of a constituency campaign despite some ingenuity in accounting, anticipation or deferment of printing bills, giving the agent unpaid leave while she helps in the campaign, and so on. Yet central expenditure by the major political parties is now more than double the total of spending in the constituencies, and falls completely outside the statutory regulation of maximum expenditure. Nor do the standards of truth and honesty established by the Advertising Standards Authority apply to political advertising.

The judgement of truth and honesty must in the end be left to the voters, but there is clearly a case for some quantitative regulation of expenditure. The case is based on the old reform principle of 1883, that money should not be able to buy votes or excessive influence, and the modern understanding that parties should compete on 'a level playing field'. The present position is defended, mainly by Conservatives, on the grounds that financial disparities are overrated (see below), especially while broadcasting time cannot be purchased; that individual freedom should be respected, and even the rich, or at least businessmen, are entitled to defend their interests; and that the practical problems of defining and controlling expenditure are insuperable.

Regulation in the sphere of opinion and free speech is indeed both repugnant and difficult; what, for example, should be done about the tabloid press, which is not at all devoted to the concept of a level playing field? Even the regulation of expenditure by the political parties raises problems of drafting and application, specifically the definition of kinds of expenditure – by whom, and when? Moreover, the creative accounting used in the constituencies could certainly be exploited at the centre. Yet the case against some form of regulation is not entirely convincing. The truth is there is a law, quite draconian where it applies, to regulate election expenditure, so the principle is conceded; but that law, being over one hundred years old, applies to local campaigns only, and is ill-suited to the conditions of modern elections and does not achieve the objectives implied by its principles.

In contrast to national advertising and the press, broadcasting is at present closely regulated. Both the BBC and the commercial companies (under the supervision of the ITC and Radio Authority) have responsibilities for fairness, balance and impartiality. For the BBC such responsibilities arise under the terms of its Charter and Licence; for the commercial companies there is a statutory obligation under the Broadcasting Act of 1990. The special arrangements for broadcasting during elections are made by a committee of senior politicians and broadcasters. The main issue is the allocation of party election broadcasts between the parties. This is proportionate to the performance of the parties in the last election, thus raising the question of measurement by seats or votes, and a threshold and fair allocation to small and regional parties. The two major parties and the Greens and the Nationalists hold different views on fairness in these matters. (In the elections for the European Parliament in 1994 more generous rules, based on number of candidates, provided single broadcasts for hitherto unknown parties, the UK Independence Party and the Natural Law Party. The latter advocated an unusual form of jumping known as 'yogic flying', and gained 100,000 votes in the United Kingdom.)

Behind the allocation of party election broadcasts lies the general coverage of election campaigns, and the response of the broadcasters to the 'media events' carefully designed by the parties for television. Compared with the highly partisan press, the reporting of elections by the broadcasters is remarkably fair and balanced, and challenges the deceptions and dishonesty of the political parties. Even so, small and new parties have a very thin time, and the governing party tends to get more than its fair share of media coverage, more at least than any other party, simply because it is the government and can make news. The presentation of the election is determined by the parties rather than the broadcasters; or else by the partisan press which is able and willing to manufacture its own news values. Thus in an arena which is formally and informally regulated a measure of fairness is achieved; but overall the media reinforce the centralisation and adversarial partisanship of British politics.

The regulation of election broadcasting offers an interesting case of regulation in the sphere of opinion. It happens because of the development of broadcasting in Britain as a regulated public service, a kind of half-nationalised industry; and it may well be weakened as satellite technology leads to the expansion of foreign-based commercial broadcasting. Thus regulated national broadcasting may turn out to be an episode in the history of global communication; and the corrupt and illegal practices outlawed in 1883 may return in a form which leaves voters little more freedom than their bribed and corrupted Victorian ancestors.

Other elections

This chapter has been mainly concerned with parliamentary elections, which determine the party composition of the government and so dominate political activity. Other elections, for local government and the European Parliament, are less significant politically, since local governments are subordinate to the Westminster Parliament, while the European Parliament still has only a limited influence, even within the European Union itself. Local and European elections are dominated by the political parties, and tend to reflect popular sentiment towards the government. The 'turn-out' of voters is low. Thus the voters register their own assessment of the political and constitutional significance of these elections.

Both local and European elections display the familiar problems of a simple plurality ballot system. The distortions of 'first-past-the-post' have led in some local councils to permanent single-party dominance based on a minority vote ('just like Westminster', you may say). The drawing of boundaries is especially difficult both for the wards of a few thousand voters in District Councils, and for the massive European constituencies of roughly half-a-million voters. The original 78 Euro-constituencies were drawn up by the Boundary Commission as amalgamations of Parliamentary constituencies. The additional six seats offered following the Maastricht Treaty were an embarrassing gift, now tacked onto the unwieldy structure. Northern Ireland, often treated as an exception (as in local government elections), constitutes a single constituency, with three members elected by the single transferable vote.

It is intended that the European Union adopt a uniform ballot system for elections to the European Parliament. Since most

Member States use methods of proportional representation, it is certain that a uniform system would be proportional, and Britain would have to modify or abandon its historic commitment to simple plurality. It is also proposed that all citizens of the Member States be entitled to vote in local elections wherever they reside – a step towards a common citizenship of the European Union.

The referendum

A referendum is a form of election, a reference to the people of a choice of policy, constitutional change or other government action. There have been local referendums in Britain, for example, over Sunday opening of licensed houses in Wales, and over the status of Northern Ireland; and referendums in Scotland and Wales in 1979 to confirm or reject the devolution legislation. The only national referendum was that held in 1975 to confirm Britain's accession to the European Economic Community, under the terms of the Labour government's 'renegotiation'.

The idea of a referendum was revived in 1993 as an appropriate device to secure the approval, or rejection (as some hoped), of the Maastricht Treaty, and again in 1994 in relation to any further integration and, in particular, the establishment of a single currency. It was argued that in the 1990s, as in the 1970s, the party system (divided within parties rather than between them) was failing to present a choice to the people; hence there was a constitutional problem, not merely a transient difficulty in party management.

The referendum is used in some other countries, for example in Switzerland, in some states and localities in the United States, and, for constitutional matters, in the Irish Republic. It is literally an outlandish device, but comparatively not a constitutional abnormality. It has one great advantage: it submits a significant question to the people. But against such democratic virtue there are a number of problems and disadvantages:

1. the status of the referendum, whether advisory or mandatory;
2. the appropriate majority to constitute approval (in the devolution referendum a minimum of 40 per cent of the electorate was set);
3. the form of the question (few issues admit of a simple 'yes' or 'no' answer);

4. the mode and financing of campaigning;
5. the separation of the issue from current politics.

Apart from these problems arising from the procedure itself, there are serious political and constitutional difficulties. The people may not be well-informed judges of the issue. In the United States people like to vote in favour of public goods, such as libraries and swimming pools, but against the taxation to pay for them. Change and reform are unpopular, and most people approve of the status quo; for example, they may favour staying in the European Union, but not joining in the first place. The referendum question gets caught up in current political disputes. Thus Dicey advocated a referendum on Irish Home Rule in 1915, not on constitutional grounds, but because he believed it would support his own position on Ireland. The people may well support causes such as capital punishment, restriction of immigration and the impoverishment of single parents, which middle-class liberals abhor (but, of course, middle-class liberals are a minority). These arguments are not totally convincing, and certainly do not destroy the powerful case for letting the people decide.

However, in Britain there are substantial constitutional arguments against the referendum. First, the constitution is based on representation and responsibility, not on direct government by the people, or even by Parliament. This applies to all issues, including constitutional or other 'fundamental' matters. It may be claimed that this structure meets the arguments about trusting and not trusting the people, by according to the people only an indirect power to decide specific questions, but an overriding, indeed sovereign, power to dismiss the government.

Secondly, the fundamental basis of the constitution, supporting the structure of representation and responsibility, is parliamentary sovereignty; but a referendum delivering a mandate to Parliament, or even an advisory referendum, carrying the special legitimacy of popular approval plainly invades parliamentary sovereignty. It might thus be argued that the referendum is unconstitutional, as well as being contrary to the British structure of democracy.

These were the arguments used in 1993 against the submission of the Maastricht Treaty to a referendum: 'That is not the way we decide such matters in Britain.' But that argument seemed less convincing to opponents of the Treaty. They, and other advocates of the use of referendums, could argue, like Dicey, that a referendum was not unconstitutional, simply unusual. Moreover, the referendum does not interfere with the legal sovereignty of Parliament, for anything determined by a referendum is not in itself law. It still needs to be enacted and thus in theory it could still be voted down or amended. In practice Members are likely to accord authority, even sovereignty, to the evident will of the people (that is why we no longer have the poll tax).

If some part of this argument be accepted, then there is a case for the referendum on some matters of significance, especially constitutional reform which would change fundamentally and irreversibly the way we are governed. In a democracy the submission of an issue to the people can never lightly be dismissed.

Political parties in the constitution

Political parties are now the driving mechanism of modern democracy, but they operate largely outside the constitution, and mainly outside the network of sub-constitutional regulation. Nevertheless, their importance is recognised in the constitutional penumbra of conventions, understandings and expectations.

Political parties enjoy the fullest recognition in those constitutions in which they are more or less incorporated into government as directing, organising and mobilising instruments of the state, as in the old Soviet Union and some single-party countries. But this is a quite different kind of party from that found in Western democracies, where the political party is characteristically engaged in competition for governing power. In such countries the parties have a position at the edge of the formal constitution. The US Constitution (1787) makes no mention at all of political parties, which had not then been invented. The Constitution of the French Fifth Republic includes one broadly drawn Article:

> Political parties and groups participate in the expression of the suffrage. They are formed and carry out their activities freely. They must respect the principles of national sovereignty and of democracy. (Art. 4)

In Britain in practice the constitutional position of political parties is set by the arrangements for elections, the conduct of parliamentary business and the organisation of government. A political party is a user of the constitution rather than being itself a part of the constitution; but the dominant position of parties as monopoly users (in a particular way) of the constitution blurs the distinction. For example, Prime Minister and Members of Parliament, both at the core of the constitution, are also and essentially emanations of party. The party uses the constitution but colonises it. If a customer analogy were employed, the parties would seem to take over the shop.

It is evident that the political parties in Britain have taken over the competition for parliamentary seats and the organisation of a majority in Parliament to support Prime Minister and Cabinet, wielding the authority of government. Other parties oppose the government, and the largest forms the official Opposition, recognised by the payment of a salary to the Leader and to the Leader in the Lords and to four Opposition Whips (the Leader of the Opposition also gets a government car). Parliamentary business is managed by the party Whips. Thus political parties are a necessary mechanism of the 'Westminster model' of the British constitution, which comprises party government within a parliamentary framework.

The structure of political parties

Given the major significance of political parties in the working of government, the structures of the parties themselves are clearly of constitutional significance. Parties are shadowy and fragmented organisations, operating in several forms and locations:

1. the parliamentary leadership;
2. the national organisation, including some elective positions;
3. the members coming together in regional and national meetings, notably the annual conference;
4. the members in their constituency associations, and their elected officers;
5. the voters, both occasional and the loyalists (supporters) – constitutionally unattached but essential to the success of the enterprise (rather like customers).

It is not easy to tie these disparate elements into a coherent organisation with some claim to function in a democratic manner in the service of a democratic constitution; in consequence, despite aspirations and endeavours, political parties are inherently fragmented.

The Conservative Party has not attempted to organise itself in a fully democratic structure. It has a Leader elected by the parliamentary party; a Central Office headed by the Leader, who appoints a Chairman; and there is a National Union of Conservative and Unionist (constituency) Associations. Thus the Conservative Party is elusive; it is not an entity, and not legally an unincorporated association, like other political parties.

The Labour Party, by contrast, is a more coherent organisation, with a democratic ethos and structure; but it is hampered in its effectiveness and its democratic aspirations by its unwieldy federal organisation, which reflects its historical development as, in part, the parliamentary arm of the trade union movement. The structure of the party is designed to accommodate some four million or so members of affiliated unions who pay a 'political levy', alongside constituency associations now recruiting little more than one-quarter of a million members. In consequence – and it is arguably an entirely democratic if electorally damaging consequence – trade unions hold substantial power within the main structures of the party, the annual conference, the National Executive Committee and the constituency parties, and wield considerable influence in the development of policy, the selection of parliamentary candidates and the election of the leader.

The reforms of 1993, pressed through by John Smith, the Labour leader, provided for the election of the leader in an electoral college divided by thirds between the Parliamentary Labour Party, the constituency associations and the affiliated trade unions, voting by individual levy payer, not in a block. Previously the trade unions held 40 per cent of the vote, usually exercised as a block vote by the union leaders. The new procedure, based on the principle of 'one member one vote', did not strictly achieve its ideal (a levy payer is not a member; some members had more than one vote), but it seems to have had a significant effect on the leadership election of 1994.

The Liberal Democrats have a strong democratic ethos and, as a recently re-formed party, no historical justification for a structure less than plainly democratic. Selection of candidates and the election of the Leader is by a poll of all members. This is the one member, one vote principle which by history and structure the

Labour Party is unable, and the Conservative party unwilling, to achieve.

The financing of political parties

Political parties offer a good example of the modification of formal constitutional structure by financial considerations – the phenomenon of 'he who pays the piper calls the tune'. Politics is an expensive business, and the subscriptions of members are not sufficient to run large and complex organisations and to mount the monstrous election campaigns now customary, and expected by the media. The Conservative and Labour parties draw a substantial part of their funds from their corporate sponsors, allies and friends. In the case of the Labour Party, the trade unions have provided up to 80 per cent of their funds. For the Conservative Party, industry and commerce have made massive contributions, amounting perhaps to between 55 and 60 per cent of the party's central income (Hansard Society, 1981).

The details of Labour Party finance are fairly clear, for the role of the trade unions is established and open. The financing of the Conservative Party is obscure. Local associations, compared with other parties, are generally larger, more affluent and more energetic in organising coffee mornings, 'Autumn Fayres', dinners and the like; so the party does generate a substantial voluntary income. However, contributions from industry and from overseas business have been massive. Some of these are not acknowledged, some are disguised as contributions to other sympathetic propaganda organisations, and the party itself, having no formal structure, has not published full accounts. It denies that any influence is conceded in return for donations, and contrasts the evident and preponderant influence of the trade unions in the Labour Party.

The present position of party financing is unsatisfactory in some respects. First, there appear to be substantial differences in the resources of the parties (already noted in the conduct of elections). The Houghton Committee found Conservative income in 1973–5 about twice that of the Labour Party and seven times that of the Liberals. Recent evidence of large donations by overseas businessmen suggests that the disparity persists. The evidence of expenditure by the parties confirms inequities, notably in expenditure on advertising and the employment of agents.

The normal inequalities between the parties are moderated by state aid for elections, especially the provision of free television time and the banning of political advertising on television. If allowance is made for this assistance, the inequity between the three major parties is about 5:4:3 (Conservative : Labour : Liberal) – hardly fair, but not grossly unfair. The bias of the tabloid press towards the Conservative Party, which is not to do with party finance, is probably more significant.

Secondly, the corporate donations to the parties (almost exclusively to the Conservative Party) are largely unregulated, in contrast to trade union political contributions. The latter are strictly regulated by legislation enacted by Conservative governments, imposing ballots and opting-out procedures. Corporate donations are usually legalised by reference to the general objects of the company, and are reported in company accounts, though shareholders are not consulted. Donations may be made indirectly to propaganda organisations and to companies specially formed to minimise publicity and tax liability.

Thirdly, while the Conservative Party enters into no contract or formal obligation, and there is no structure of formal representation, as in the Labour Party, it is evident that donations create obligations and expectations – policy sympathy, invitations to Downing Street, tax privileges for overseas businesses, and even honours. It is denied that there is a connection between the flow of honours to businessmen and their contributions to the ruling party; just as it would be denied that road-building policies are influenced by civil engineering companies which contribute to party funds. The problem here is that there is no sharp dividing line between the corrupt and the incorrupt, and there is a gap between business ethics (which include the dubious practice of lavish corporate 'entertainment') and the stricter standards of the public service.

The financing of political parties is one area of British political life which is tainted by a non-criminal corruption. There is no cause for surprise. In a highly competitive system, parties need money, while companies and trade unions need sympathetic governments and are ready to purchase goodwill. However, there may be cause for concern, since there is a sharp difference in the rules applying to the chief purchasers of goodwill. Professor Ewing concluded: 'In Britain company political donations are for all practical purposes unregulated by law, while trade union political expenditure is subject to detailed and restrictive legislation' (1987, p. 73). It may be added that small groups and individuals are not at all in the business of the purchase of goodwill by massive donations, and cannot compete with the big corporations, including the trade unions.

The prohibition of corporate political donations is both undesirable (a gross restriction of freedom) and impractical (easily evaded); but there are other approaches to reform. First, political parties could be compelled to publish full annual reports of their accounts, including the disclosure of major donations, any right to privacy being subordinate to the public interest in information about the political structure. Secondly, the expenditure of the parties could be reduced by the banning of some kinds of advertising during elections (this is not a proposal that appeals to newspaper proprietors). Thirdly, the dependence of the parties on private funding could be reduced by the extension of public financing.

State funding was proposed by the Houghton Committee in 1976 but not implemented, except for the provision of aid for the parliamentary activity of Opposition parties. Fairly substantial assistance for elections was already provided, and advertising on television and radio was already banned (a radical measure of equalisation). The case for state funding is evident enough: parties fulfil essential constitutional functions, and should not be disabled or seriously disadvantaged by differences in funding. Many other countries have found the argument persuasive and have solved the practical problems. The case against state funding is to do with practicality, the encouragement of highly valued voluntary political activity, and the acceptance by the Conservatives, and perhaps too by Labour, that their own financial sponsors are entitled in a 'free country' to use their own resources to protect and promote their interests.

Altogether, there are grounds for some concern about the political parties as near-monopoly forms of political participation. The quality of party political activity is generally poor, membership is low, participation is weak and accountability is fragmentary and distorted. Despite the centrality of political parties to the working of the Westminster model constitution, they remain inevitably marginal to the constitution itself. The Basic Law of the Federal Republic of Germany sets out as proper constitutional objectives that political parties should conform in their internal organisation to democratic principles, and 'must publicly account for the sources of their funds' (Art. 21). Even these limited but desirable objectives are not entirely achieved in constitutionless Britain.

The mandate

The doctrine of the mandate brings together elections, parties and government in a bond of responsibility. 'Doctrine' here means a more-or-less accepted idea, falling short of a convention. According to the doctrine, the mandate arises when a party submits a programme to the electors, usually in the form of a manifesto, a substantial document published by the party leadership at the beginning of an election campaign. If the electors give the party a majority, they are deemed to have signified approval of the programme (survey evidence indicates that the approval of the voters is general rather than specific, and by no means inclusive).

In its softer version, the mandate is a legitimated prospectus but not a binding contract. The majority party is entitled positively to pursue its programme, subject to any modification arising from second thoughts or new conditions, inhibited from doing what it promised not to do (usually increasing taxes) at least without explanation and apology, and discouraged from pursuing policies not presented to the electors. Some defenders of the residual delaying powers of the House of Lords have argued that the intervention of the Lords is legitimate if a government steps beyond its mandate (see Chapter 9).

The softer version of the mandate amounts to an informal agreement between party and electors, and is enforced only by political sanctions, notably the threat of voting for another party which 'keeps its promises'. The harder form of the mandate takes the term literally: the mandate is mandatory. It is a command from the electors to the party, a duty put upon the party, not an entitlement. This version of the doctrine is favoured by party activists, and all those with strong policy commitments, for they perceive correctly that the hard mandate strengthens their role in policy-making. Hence they have argued that it is unconstitutional for the House of Lords to reject legislation necessary to fulfil a pledge which appeared in the ruling party's manifesto.

The courts have taken note of the mandate as a factor in local government decisions. In the *Tameside* case (see Chapter 13) Lord

Wilberforce accepted that the new Conservative council was 'entitled – indeed in a sense bound – to carry out the policy [of reorganising secondary schools] on which it was elected'. On the other hand, in the 'Fare's Fair' case (Chapter 13) an Appeal Court judge peremptorily dismissed the mandate as a factor in the authority of an elected local government, seeing no element of legitimation apart from legality.

Putting these cases side by side, it might be thought that the judges respect Conservative manifestos more than Labour manifestos. In fact the judges indicate the permitted range of obligation arising from the mandate – a commitment to action or a mere indication of a policy leaning. A party cannot be bound by its manifesto (that would exclude all other forms of policy-making), but if it took no notice at all of its manifesto that would be demeaning to the electorate.

These are political-constitutional rather than strict legal-constitutional arguments. It would have been open to the courts in both these cases to retreat to strict legality, and hence dismiss the manifesto as of no account. However, the courts do engage in broader political-constitutional argument, and indeed must do so if their interpretation of the law is to be more than literal and mechanical. In the 'Fare's Fair' case Lord Diplock presented a more rounded view of the manifesto/mandate doctrine. He conceded substance to the doctrine on the grounds that the elected councillors believed the policy to be correct, and it had been approved by a majority of the electors; the mandate should be given considerable weight, but not a mandatory authority. This accords with the softer version of the mandate, which legitimates the general direction of a majority party, but falls short of a political command or legal authority. Perhaps not surprisingly the courts have refused to consider the mandate in relation to central government.

Conclusion

Political parties are the major channels or mechanisms for popular participation in government, feeding directly into the parliamentary structure. By comparison, interest and protest groups, while influential in some cases, lack such constitutional access and legitimacy. In a constitutional perspective, political parties shape and supplement the parliamentary functions of responsibility and responsiveness. However, assessed by the highest expectations of popular democracy, the parties do not perform very well. The constitutionalist might judge that in a pluralist democracy political parties ought not to monopolise the channels of popular representation and policy-making.

Consideration of the parties as instruments of democracy poses again the question of the ballot system in which the winner takes all. However good the parties may be in the representation and responsible development of the voters' policy preferences, the end result, following an election, is the raising to power of one party and the exclusion of all others. In this perspective the mandate appears to be a far from perfect instrument of democracy, since it appears to legitimise the policy preferences of a minority of the electorate. Ironically any form of power-sharing or coalition government remedies the exclusionary tendency of the winner-takes-all system, but weakens the link between party 'grass roots' and the leadership, since the leaders have to engage in bargaining with coalition partners.

12

THE UNITARY CONSTITUTION

The unitary, non-federal constitution

The British constitution is unitary, not federal. Characteristically a federal constitution arises from the formation by treaty (*foedus* in Latin) of a union of formerly separate governments (as in the classic case of the United States) which preserve some of their power. A federal union is thus a partial or limited union in which sovereign power is shared. By contrast the British Union came about by the absorption of Wales, Scotland and Ireland under the English monarchy. English hegemony was lightly disguised (to the English at least) by the idea of Britain as the common 'mother country' (or fatherland), and the Union was legitimised by representation in the British Parliament.

The United Kingdom was created in an age which accepted monarchical rule. Federalism was a product of rebellion against such rule. The Union was thus a pre-democratic construction and has remained so. 'Unitarism' became a habit of mind and practice, a 'tacit understanding' in Sidney Low's phrase, quoted by Vernon Bogdanor:

> Perhaps the strongest of these 'tacit understandings' is the profoundly unitary nature of the United Kingdom as expressed in the supremacy of Parliament. We find it difficult to think in terms of a separation of powers, and difficult also to think of government as a series of interdependent layers, each with its own rights and responsibilities. (1979, p. 7)

The 'tacit understanding' of unitarism was more than a potent and enduring element in political culture. It was embodied in the constitution by the fact of parliamentary sovereignty and the doctrine of ministerial responsibility.

Culture and constitution were both inimical to federalism. The Royal Commission on the Constitution (Chairman, Lord Kilbrandon), though it took as its main task the consideration of devolution, rejected federalism in a brisk page or two (Report, Vol I, 1973, pp. 152–61). Federalism would appear 'strange and artificial' to most people, and would not be acceptable. It would require a written constitution and a constitutional court; judges would tend to become political. Central economic management would be difficult. The dominance of England could not be accommodated in a federal system. 'Provincial sovereignty would lead to intergovernmental rivalry and contention.' These arguments were all persuasive, except perhaps in Scotland and Wales and the numerous federal countries around the world, including countries of the British Commonwealth. Even the Royal Commission accepted that some of the problems to which federalism claimed to offer an answer still remained.

Thus the United Kingdom of Great Britain and Northern Ireland is an unlikely union, based, like its constitution, on history rather than theory, accidental in origin, awkward in structure, yet solid and persistent despite its flaws.

The nations and regions of the United Kingdom

The United Kingdom grew initially by occupation, conquest and incorporation.

Scotland

Scotland is the least integrated, most independent, of the constituent nations of the United Kingdom. It has a long history as an independent European nation and state, and retains its own Church, law and educational system, not to mention national dress, its own version of the English language and a surviving Gaelic language, a distinctive culture and the popular patriotism of the football field. However, since the Act of Union of 1707,

Scotland has been incorporated in the Union and has no government of its own. The status of the Act or Treaty to the Scots is still disputed. It is argued that the Act limited the powers of the UK Parliament in relation to Scotland. This argument, sometimes heard in the Scottish courts, has 'neither prevailed nor been summarily dismissed', but has not found favour with English lawyers (Turpin, 1990, p. 223).

Although Scotland has no formal standing as a country, nor any sovereign power, within the United Kingdom, it does enjoy special governmental arrangements, amounting, in the perspective of an English region at least, to constitutional privilege.

These special arrangements are as follows:

1. Representation in the UK Parliament: 72 Scottish seats when only 60 are justified by proportionality; a Scottish Grand Committee to deal with Scottish Bills and a Select Committee on Scottish Affairs to cover the work of the Scottish Office (although there are problems in finding sufficient Conservative Members of Parliament from Labour-dominated Scotland).
2. A Secretary of State for Scotland with a seat in the Cabinet (in practice not likely to be a senior and influential politician, and the Cabinet itself is not the major decision-making body).
3. The Scottish Office, headed by the Secretary of State and based in Edinburgh. This is a substantial administrative unit (with about ten thousand civil servants in 1992) engaged mainly in the implementation of UK policies, but with some limited power, within the UK framework, to modify policies in their application to Scotland and to have a particular influence in matters which have a special relevance to Scotland, for example fisheries and forestry. But the writ of all the non-territorial ministries runs throughout the United Kingdom.

These arrangements plainly do not amount to a substantial degree of autonomy for Scotland. The politics of the United Kingdom are dominated by England, which contains 85 per cent of the population. The Conservative Party is the normal governing party of the United Kingdom, but has not attained a majority in Scotland since 1955 (yet a remarkable proportion of political leaders, including Prime Ministers, have had Scottish roots). High policy – economic management, taxation and public spending, foreign and defence policy – are decided, as in most federations, at the centre. In a matter such as oil, which has a special relevance to Scotland, but is also of concern to the United Kingdom as a whole, the London government followed its own, and, we assume, the United Kingdom's, interests. Scottish interests and priorities are likely to predominate only where they do not impinge on the rest of the United Kingdom and do not cost very much.

However, Scotland's 'constitutional privileges' do bring some benefit. Scotland's proportion of public spending has been substantially higher than is justified by its population – perhaps as much as 30 per cent higher for the devolved services (Kellas, 1990, p. 430). Some allowance must be made for indirect expenditure, notably on defence and administration, which is of disproportionate benefit to England. Even so, Scotland's economic gain from its special constitutional position has been significant. English regions are entitled to be envious. Hence, if Scotland were further to enhance its constitutional position, there is likely to be a demand from some English regions, notably in the deprived North and North-East, for comparable privileges.

Wales

Wales enjoys constitutional privileges similar to Scotland's – over-representation in Parliament (38 seats to a proportionately just 33), a Secretary of State and Welsh Office, a Select Committee on Welsh Affairs and an occasional Welsh Grand Committee to deal with Welsh Bills. But the limitations on genuine autonomy apply more strongly than in Scotland. Constitutionally, Wales has been integrated with England since Acts of 1536 and 1543, and physical proximity, population movement and common legal and educational systems have reinforced the bonds. Gladstone claimed that any distinction between England and Wales was 'totally unknown to our constitution'. But Wales has a powerful if diffuse culture and sense of identity, evident at international rugby matches at the National Stadium at Cardiff Arms Park and in the admirable Welsh National Opera, in the non-conformist chapels, and in the old Labour culture of the heavy industries of South Wales (now in rapid decline).

At the heart of a lively and assertive Welsh culture is the Welsh language, spoken by about one-fifth of the people of Wales. After centuries of neglect the language has been accorded a special status in the national curriculum for Wales, in public administration and in the courts, and a Welsh-language television channel (S4C) is heavily subsidised (Welsh is the most generously subsidised minority language in the world). However, Welsh cannot be spoken in Parliament, and a Member doing so will be ruled out of order, even if he or she provides an immediate translation. This is Britain's only experience in national politics of the awkward and baffling problems of linguistic politics, which afflict many other countries and are not unknown in some localities in Britain.

Wales, like Scotland, suffers from a misfit between its politics and those of the dominant partner, England, and can often claim that it has little sympathy with the politics of the UK government (though, like Scotland, it has contributed more than its fair share of leading politicians and one Prime Minister of distinction). High policy is made at Westminster and there is less evidence of policy 'clout' in the figures for public spending in Wales. On the other hand, the Welsh Office has at times deviated from Westminster priorities in its programmes, has built effective consultative relations with its subsidiary government system and has been encouraged to develop support for the Welsh language, within the limits of public finance and the tolerance of the four-fifths of people living in Wales who do not speak Welsh.

Northern Ireland

Northern Ireland presents an altogether more difficult political and constitutional problem. Within Northern Ireland two 'communities', one Protestant and (British) Unionist, the other Catholic and (Irish) Republican, confront each other in an historic mutual antagonism, fought out bloodily on the ground by near-professional private armies.

The ancient cause of dispute lies in the history of Ireland as a kind of British colony, the 'plantation' of Ulster mainly by Scottish Presbyterians in the seventeenth century, some brutal and bloody military episodes of the 1640s and 1650s and 1690 (still ritually remembered), and the famine of the 1840s. The modern form of the problem was created by Lloyd George (after the failure to create 'Home Rule' for the whole of Ireland) by the establishment (Government of Ireland Act 1920) of the province of Northern Ireland, based roughly on the largest area which could be dominated by the Protestants. Thus the Protestants were in a majority of two to one (now diminishing) in the North and a minority of one to three in the whole of Ireland.

The conflict thus drawn from Irish history is sustained by fierce communal loyalties based on a strong sense of national identity bound up with continuing and intense 'religiosity' – two-thirds of Protestants think of themselves as British, two-thirds of Catholics think of themselves as Irish. The hostility of the two 'communities' is reinforced by the experience of past discrimination by the Unionist majority against Catholics in employment and government services, bitter hostility to the security forces, including the British army, the continuing influence of Catholicism in the government of the Irish Republic, and the maintenance of the Republic's claim (still in the constitution, if weakened in practice) to govern the whole island of Ireland.

The constitutional history of Ireland has reflected these troubles. Ireland was formally united with Great Britain by Acts of the British and Irish Parliaments of 1800, and until 1918 the UK Parliament included Irish Members – who had a considerable impact on party politics and Irish policy. This parliamentary union broke down in 1916 and the Union was abrogated in 1921–2, with the 'Irish Free State' becoming a dominion within the Commonwealth and subsequently the independent Republic of Eire (1937). Six of the counties of Ulster in the North-East, dominated by the Protestant and Presbyterian culture, remained within the United Kingdom, and are indeed the fiercest supporters of the Union, which now protects them from the Republican majority in the island of Ireland. Curiously, as part of Britain's ambivalent relation with Ireland, there is no bar to the settlement of Irish people in Britain, and, once resident, they may claim the benefits of the welfare state and the privilege of the vote.

Under the Government of Ireland Act of 1920 Northern Ireland was granted a kind of provincial status within the United Kingdom. It had its own bi-cameral Parliament (Stormont), an executive headed by a Governor representing the Crown, and its own civil service. Representation at Westminster was limited to 13, later 12, but now 17. Sovereignty was retained by the Westminster Parliament. The Government of Ireland Act 1920 stated:

> Notwithstanding the establishment of the Parliament of . . . Northern Ireland . . . or anything contained in this Act, the supreme authority of the Parliament of the United Kingdom shall remain unaffected and undiminished. (s. 75)

The high policy areas were specifically reserved. All other areas of policy were transferred to the Parliament of Northern Ireland.

The convention developed that the Westminster Parliament did not intervene in Northern Ireland unless requested (and the Home Office then allocated only one middle-ranking official to Northern Ireland affairs). The non-intervention convention was happily complemented by a 'step-by-step' convention which accorded to the province the same welfare benefits offered on the mainland. This remarkable constitutional innovation was effective enough as an exercise in devolution, but it allowed scope for the Protestant and Unionist majority to deny fair treatment and civil rights to the Catholic minority. In face of civil disorder and clear evidence of abuse of power, the UK government imposed 'direct rule' on the province in 1972.

Thus ended Britain's first modern provincial government. It had demonstrated the practical possibilities of such devolved government, but had also shown that devolution does not guarantee good government, and further that finance and independence are necessarily linked in a reciprocal relationship.

England

England is by far the largest of the countries of the United Kingdom. It is slightly underrepresented in the House of Commons, to allow overrepresentation of other parts, but still has over 80 per cent of the seats. In practice the government of the United Kingdom must win a majority in England. This constitutional power of England based on its population is reinforced by the cultural dominance of the South-Eastern metropolitan area. In the multinational union England is the senior partner.

For the purposes of government England hardly figures as an entity; it is subsumed in government as the greater part of the United Kingdom. There is no England Office. In matters in which there is some devolution to the 'national regions' – education, agriculture, housing and local government – the UK ministry acts for England and oversees Scotland and Wales. It is possible to construct English regions equivalent in population and scale to the 'national regions', but regional government is poorly developed and incoherent. Administrative regions were established for some war-time purposes, and for economic planning, the utilities and the Health Service; but there were no agreed boundaries, still less any co-ordinating or political structure.

Many of the regional functions have since been abandoned or ceded to the private sector, and the five metropolitan counties established in 1974 alongside the Greater London Council (1965) were abolished in 1986. The episode is instructive for the proponents of devolution. If devolution to English regions is a necessary complement to devolution to the 'national regions', then it must be fitted into a system of local government and a political culture which is national rather than local, and regional not at all.

Devolution

Proposals for devolution to Scotland and Wales were legislated in 1978 but rejected in referendums in Scotland and Wales in 1979. The decision of the referendums on the approval of the two schemes for devolution was subject to a '40 per cent rule': approval required a positive response from not less than 40 per cent of those entitled to vote (not just those voting). Both the referendum and the rule were remarkable constitutional devices (see Chapter 11). The referendum may be justified as appropriate for a matter of fundamental constitutional concern (as on accession to the EEC in 1975 – but not for the popular approval of the Maastricht Treaty, 1993). The 40 per cent rule seems inappropriate in a 'first-past-the-post' culture, and was so restrictive as to amount almost to a veto.

In the event only 11 per cent of the people of Wales voted 'yes' to devolution. In Scotland the voters split roughly three ways, one-third 'yes', one-third 'no' and one-third not voting. By the normal rules of UK elections the 'yes' vote scored a tiny majority, but a majority nevertheless. The Scotland Act and the Wales Act were repealed a few months later by the new Conservative (and Unionist) government.

The devolution legislation of 1978 was a response to the Report of the Royal Commission on the Constitution (1973) and no doubt also to the precarious parliamentary position of the minority Labour government. The Commission was established in 1968 as a response to political discontent expressed in a sharp increase in Nationalist voting in Scotland and Wales. The establishment of the Commission did not arise from a principled concern for the structure of the United Kingdom, still less for the constitution as a whole; it was a classic demonstration of the use of a committee to defuse and postpone a problem.

A majority of the Commission favoured some reform of a devolutionary character, though the specific proposals differed. The most forceful case for a radical devolution of power from the centre to English regions as well as Scotland and Wales was made in a Minority Report (Commission on the Constitution, Report, Vol. II, 1973). The analysis of the Minority Report ranged beyond the special, partly nationalist, discontents of Scotland and Wales. The whole United Kingdom, it was argued, suffered from alienation from government, a condition of powerlessness, while the central government was weakened by 'overload'. The evidence for these arguments was by its nature open to question, though some discontent was evident at the time.

The government did not accept the case for a radical scheme of 'devolution all round'. The legislation finally enacted in 1978 provided for a form of legislative devolution to Scotland, with an Assembly supporting an executive, and a more limited form of administrative devolution to Wales. The powers of the proposed Assemblies lay largely in the spheres of local government, planning and social services. The two Secretaries of State were retained and the assemblies and devolved administrations were to be served by the UK civil service. The Assemblies had no revenue-raising powers and depended on a block vote by the UK Parliament, in practice the British government, which retained power in economic affairs. The centre, through the Secretaries of State, retained a power of 'override', though the Judicial Committee of the Privy Council could pronounce on the validity of Scottish legislation.

The schemes of devolution proposed in the Act of 1978 were plainly unsatisfactory – too much for unionists, far too little for Scottish nationalist opinion. Some parts of the schemes looked awkward and difficult to work, and the logic and coherence of the

United Kingdom and its Parliament were undermined. The 'West Lothian Question' (repeatedly posed by the Member for that constituency) challenged the role of Scottish Members at Westminster in voting on policy matters for England which for Scotland were devolved and therefore excluded from the Westminster Parliament. The problem was recognised but not resolved. Here, as elsewhere, the awkwardness, illogicality and untidiness of dividing power was apparent. This is the nature of all federal systems; indeed, some part of their democratic value lies in the spaces in the structure.

In practice, the Scotland and Wales Acts may have offered a greater measure of devolution than was intended. The assemblies would have had more political 'clout' just because they were in the business of representing strong national interests and cultures more vigorously than their constitutional position would indicate. If the Acts had been implemented, the structure would have been subject to disputes and bargaining, the characteristic push-and-pull of federalism, which may be regarded as debilitating or invigorating, according to constitutional taste. One authority, writing at the time of enactment (and before rejection), concluded that the Scotland Act was the beginning of federalism for the United Kingdom.

> [T]he Scotland Act not only effectively limits the power of Parliament, but it also introduces a judicial element into the defining of limitation. It proposes, therefore what amounts to a written constitution for the United Kingdom, establishing a quasi-federal system of government with a politically sanctified division of powers and a court to act as arbiter of the division. (Bogdanor, 1979, p. 218)

Devolution does raise constitutional issues, though these are all inevitably entwined with political issues about economic management, equalisation and public expenditure. Nationalist sentiment, emphasised by remoteness, at least in the case of Scotland (though remoteness is a cultural as well as a geographical phenomenon), intensifies the problems of structuring government; improvements in procedures, effectiveness and accountability do not satisfy the separatist.

There are three major problems concerning devolution within the United Kingdom:

1. *Asymmetry*. Devolution to Scotland, and perhaps Wales, is difficult to accommodate in a state which would otherwise

remain in a unitary form, dominated by England. The problem may be exaggerated: other federations manage to contain great disparities, and in practice the tidiness of the present system is illusory. A pragmatic asymmetry is feasible.

2. *Finance*. This is a more serious problem. If Scotland is to ask and receive more through its devolved structure, which part of England will volunteer to take less? This is the kind of basic political question which tests a constitution near to destruction. Pragmatic asymmetry may here break down.
3. *Parliamentary sovereignty*. Devolution must be accommodated to parliamentary sovereignty, or Britain must accept what would be a constitutional revolution, the divided sovereignty of a true federalism. This seems unlikely; hence a Scottish Assembly must act and be seen as a third chamber of the Westminster Parliament, dealing with legislation and administration affecting Scotland. The 'West Lothian Question' might then be settled pragmatically. However, neither nationalists nor unionists are likely to be satisfied by such arrangements, and the drafter of the constitution, and the maker of pragmatic compromises, might well lose heart.

The problem of Northern Ireland

Northern Ireland poses a special and difficult problem for the makers of constitutions. All governments relate authority to people within a particular territory. In democratic regimes the people consent to being governed through forms of representation, and these may be adjusted to take account of the diversity of territory and peoples. Hence in countries which are very large (the United States, former USSR) or contain deep cultural or social divisions (Switzerland, Canada), government is arranged in territorial units to reflect diversity and to disperse and share power. The formal division of central sovereignty and the sharing of power produce a federal structure.

Outside federalism it is usual to reflect diversity by measures of decentralisation to subordinate local governments, while retaining overriding central authority. This is the British approach to the political problems arising from diversity. It has been on the whole successful in providing an acceptable mix of centralised government with some degree of local government, more decentralised administration than substantial local autonomy. So far serious discontent with the structure of territorial government has been most evident in Scotland and Wales, and to some extent in London, but the absence of sustained, serious protest, confirmed by the referendums, seemed to show that on the mainland the government of the United Kingdom was broadly legitimate – accepted, stable and secure.

This was not the case in Northern Ireland. The history sketched above shows the making of a territorial settlement in face of rebellion and civil war. The two 'traditions', cultures or 'communities' of Northern Ireland were corralled into the province of Northern Ireland, within the United Kingdom. For the Protestants this was a legitimate settlement which gave them the protection and the union with Britain they most desired. For the Catholics the settlement was an imposition by the colonial power, a betrayal of the United Ireland to which their religious and political loyalties aspired, and a shameless contrivance of the largest territory in the North which the Protestants could dominate.

The discontented Scots and the Welsh, for the most part, accepted the territorial structure for the time being, and struggled to reform it from within. By contrast the Irish Republican Nationalists rejected the settlement of 1920 and the constitutional basis of a Northern Ireland within the United Kingdom. The constitutional problem of Northern Ireland was then that the constitution lacked the minimal consent of well over one-third (and rising) of its people, while retaining the passionate commitment of the majority. The problem is difficult enough, and is made more urgent by the long-running civil war of the Irish Republican Army against the British government and the Protestant community, and of the Protestant paramilitary forces against the IRA and the Catholic community.

The constitutional problem is similar in essence to that of many countries in which communal or cultural differences (ethnicity, religion, language, history) have been politicised and magnified by cultural or religious zeal and nationalist fervour into epic hatreds. Northern Ireland is only one of many locations for the shedding of blood in the cause of disliking your neighbours. Such historic conflicts are not easily resolved in the short term by the devising of constitutions, but a cease-fire cannot endure if it is not followed up by formal arrangements for divided peoples to live together in peace, if not in harmony and love. The making of constitutions is a necessary part of the solution to the problem of Northern Ireland.

The elements of the constitutional problem may be briefly summarised. There are four parties to a settlement:

1. The British government (at present formed by the Conservative and Unionist Party) wants to preserve British sovereignty, at least formally, and protect the position of the Protestant Unionists, but accepts some kind of institutional link with the Republic of Ireland, favours some form of devolved government, and is tired of the heavy political and financial costs of the problem – as are the British people.
2. The government of the Republic wants a recognition of 'an Irish dimension', so constitutional links between Northern and Southern Ireland, and a better deal for the Republican community in the North (no discrimination, and power-sharing), and is perhaps ready to concede in the long term a diminution in the constitutional standing of the Catholic Church in the Republic.
3. The Unionists want to retain their position in Northern Ireland, favour closer integration in the United Kingdom and resist any formal links with the South, or power-sharing.
4. Republicans want a unitary Irish Republic for the 'island of Ireland' and British withdrawal; some scope for negotiation on the position of the Unionist 'community' and power-sharing.

There is clearly no easy solution to the political problems of Ireland, and, in the short term, no solution at all. Settlement cannot be achieved by conceding to any one party to the conflict all its aspirations (that was the weakness of the 1920 settlement). 'Self-determination' by majority vote cannot work, since there are two majorities (the Unionists in the North, the Republicans in Ireland as a whole). A federal solution could not resolve the issue of sovereignty, or disagreements about boundaries and powers.

The Downing Street Declaration by the Prime Ministers of the United Kingdom and Ireland (December 1993) marked a new and serious attempt to move towards settlement of the Irish problem, in response to heightened concern in both countries at the continuing bloodshed on both sides in the civil war. The terms of the Declaration offer no solution, or even clarification, of the constitutional problem, but do indicate significant shifts in the approach of the two governments.

> [The two Prime Ministers affirmed their aim] to foster agreement and reconciliation, leading to a new political framework founded on consent and encompassing arrangements within Northern Ireland, for the whole island and between these islands. . . .
>
> The Prime Minister, on behalf of the British Government, reaffirms that they will uphold the democratic wish of a greater number of the people of Northern Ireland on the issue of whether they prefer to support the Union or a sovereign united Ireland.
>
> On this basis, he reiterates, on behalf of the British Government, that they have no selfish strategic or economic interest in Northern Ireland.
>
> [The British Government will work to achieve agreement] which will embrace the totality of relationships [and which will be] based on full respect for the rights and identities of both traditions in Ireland.
>
> They accept that such agreement may, as of right, take the form of agreed structures for the island as a whole, including a united Ireland achieved by peaceful means on the following basis.
>
> The British Government agree that it is for the people of the island of Ireland alone, by agreement between the two parts respectively, to exercise their right of self-determination on the basis of consent, freely and concurrently given, North and South, to bring about a united Ireland, if that is their wish.
>
> [The Irish Prime Minister (Taoiseach) affirmed his acceptance of the principle of self-determination, adding that the consent of a majority in Northern Ireland must] 'respect the democratic dignity and the civil rights and religious liberties of both communities'. . . . [He also promised to examine any elements in the democratic life and organisation of the Irish state and its constitution, which might be resented or seen as a threat in the North.]

It is evident that the subtle, not to say devious, drafting of the Declaration leaves the fundamental problem unresolved: self-determination in the dual majority situation does not work. At the same time, the British government seems to have moved away from Unionist commitment and towards a secular, pragmatic position, and the Irish government likewise has distanced itself from Republican fervour. The signal from the two governments is that the armed struggle has no political legitimacy, it is just gang warfare.

The specific constitutional problem can be resolved only by the lapse of time and cultural change. The European dimension may be helpful in the long term by diminishing concern for national sovereignty, and giving confidence and support to smaller political entities (Scotland? an autonomous Northern Ireland?). In the long run 'benign neglect', a mix of public subsidy and secularisation, might diminish intransigent attitudes, just as religious tensions have faded on the mainland.

Meanwhile, there is scope for endless negotiation about devolution and power-sharing within Northern Ireland, and constitutional 'links' between the governments of the United Kingdom and the Republic. Altogether there could be no better demonstration that constitutions, structures and rules need to be underpinned by a supportive culture; if not, like the United States in the mid-nineteenth century or Yugoslavia in the 1990s, they relapse into civil war; or, like the highly democratic Weimar Republic in Germany, they perish.

13

LOCAL GOVERNMENT
The Central–Local Relationship

The history of local government since the 1970s is of unusual political and constitutional disputation. Constitutional values were inherent in these disputes, but it is easy to exaggerate the centrality of the constitutional issue. In fact the central dispute concerned the ends of government, specifically the quality and cost of local social and environmental services. The great central–local debate was about the territorial and institutional shape of government through which the differing values about those ends might be asserted and achieved. It is also tempting to portray the conflict in terms of good (local autonomy) and evil (central control). Yet there is room for doubt whether local government was fully and exclusively democratic, and equally, whether the centre ever achieved anything like absolute control.

The constitutional position of local government

The constitutional position of local government reflects much of the nature of the British constitution – a stout pillar of parliamentary sovereignty and altogether less substantial flying buttresses of conventions and rule of law. The 'hard fact' is parliamentary sovereignty. Local government is the creation of the government through Parliament, which can make and unmake local authorities, bind them or empower them, sustain or restrain them through funding decisions. Boroughs which have existed for nearly a thousand years have been abolished by Act of Parliament, and the taxing powers of local government have been emasculated by legislative and administrative action. Nothing is beyond the power of Parliament. Local government can do only what the statutes permit, and the courts have developed and applied the *ultra vires* rule ('beyond your powers') with a firmness untroubled by constitutional reflection. In Britain, unlike the United States, local government is a class of local authorities, not the collective of local governments, each with the standing indicated by the term 'government'.

The 'soft constitutional context' of local government derives from history, understandings and convention, and perhaps some imprecise commitment to the 'rule of law'. Historically local government preceded Parliament itself, and has its origins in medieval boroughs (based on royal charter), shires and parishes, sheriffs and the Justices of the Peace. For five centuries at least, until 1834, this was the structure of local government. In practice it was 'self-government at the King's command' – not centralisation in modern terms, but a central control which incorporated a measure of local autonomy on good pragmatic grounds. The local Magistracy (in a broad sense) was a necessary prop to a medieval government without effective lines of communication, still less of control.

Early local government was to do with keeping the peace, though public order soon included poor relief, in early recognition of the link between poverty and crime. The later development of local government was motivated by pressing social and environmental problems, notably the need for roads and, as the towns grew, for sanitation and public health; and it was driven by interventionist and reformist Victorian governments.

The new county and district authorities established by the end of the nineteenth century necessarily reflected the constituent power of Parliament, but they were nevertheless governments of a sort, based on elections and an independent source of revenue, and with some discretion in policy – choosing between municipal socialism or passivity, with added pomp, as so many Victorian town halls bear witness. Moreover, local governments delivered essential services on behalf of the government: the centre could not manage without local government, and that practical dependence enlarged local government's constitutional position (or at least its room for manoeuvre).

The partnership between central and local government

The relations of local and central government after 1945 hovered somewhere between local autonomy and central agency in an uneasy partnership. The central government was the dominant partner, holding the ultimate statutory power, confident that it knew best, and, above all, rich. Local government enjoyed the patronage and wealth of its rich partner, the opportunities for pomp and prestige and its own kind of patronage (jobs, housing, planning permission), and listened with respect to the pronouncements of *ultra vires* of its lawyer chief clerk.

Labour governments, driven by the popular appetite for social services and the ideology of big government, were no less centralist than the Conservatives. The post-war Labour government's economic and social reforms removed major functions, including most health services and the utilities, from local government. Nevertheless, local government, though diminished in its range of functions, expanded dramatically in size. By the early 1980s it employed more than two-and-a-half million people and spent over 10 per cent of the national income. 'Spending' for the most part meant disbursing central government funds on lines laid down by the centre (especially teachers' pay); nevertheless, local government was 'big business', if less impressive than it looked.

The unequal nature of the central–local 'partnership' was evident in the series of inquiries and reports directed at local government, notably in the 1960s and 1970s – dealing with boundaries, structure, staffing, management, finance. These culminated in the major structural reforms of 1972–4, partly destroyed in the 1980s and subject to further review in the 1990s. This time the review was conducted by an itinerant Commission led by Sir John Banham, proceeding by local inquiry and extensive consultation, but generally committed to undoing the two-tier structure imposed in 1974, and carrying the overriding authority of central government to decide the outcome.

The central government's priorities lay in macro-economic management, the control of public expenditure and modest redistribution and equalisation; any commitment to local autonomy came lower in the scale of political priorities. The normal pattern was: national policy locally administered, national funding locally disbursed. Within that framework there was room for informal relationships and tacit understandings, for guidance, persuasion and discouragement, backed by the ultimate sanctions of the national government's control of legislation, substantial funding and its superior electoral legitimacy.

The reformation of the 1980s

In the 1980s, the uneasy partnership of central and local government broke down, and the constitutional standing of local government was radically weakened. Power was reasserted by the centre or passed (by the centre) to alternative non-elected local bodies, to citizens redesignated as consumers or customers, or to commercial enterprises. In a polity thus transformed, the rules of the game were tested almost to destruction, and in a score of cases the courts were called upon to resolve disputes.

The constitutional 'crisis' arose from the intense politicisation of the two sides in the conflict, divided by principle and conviction and eager for political struggle. Both had the will to fight, though the sides were not equally matched, until in the case of the poll tax the people fought the centre and thus, perhaps unwittingly, rallied to the support of local government.

On one side the cause of local government was defended most passionately by what may be called the 'urban left', radicals in and beyond the Labour Party, fighting for 'jobs and services' with little regard for prudent accounting, and a ruthless exploitation of party and union power. On the other side, the government was reasonably enough disturbed by what it saw as the profligacy of some local governments and the indulgence of their welfare policies. It seems likely that a Labour government would have been equally disturbed if less antagonistic. But the Conservative governments of the 1980s were as 'politicised' as the 'urban left', in the sense of holding radical convictions, distrusting consensus and relishing the political struggle. Constitutional change arises from such a collision of political forces.

Such considerations about the political background of the crisis need to be taken into account in any assessment of the constitutional outcome. In particular the invention of the community charge or poll tax was an attempt to restrain local spending by improving local government's accountability to its electors. Thus, the poll tax could be seen as an attempt to improve local democracy, though the tax was badly designed and turned out to be a political disaster.

The Conservative government's assault on local government

From the point of view of the Conservative government the 'assault' was a counter-attack on irresponsible power. The assault extended over four governments and fifteen years, though it included some retreats and detours. It may claim to be the second most sustained and effective attempt at constitutional reformation of modern times (the first being the reform of the civil service). It was vigorously driven from the top and, until the poll tax, by party and popular support. The condition of local government in the 1990s is for better or for worse one of the foremost achievements of the Thatcher years.

The principal changes made to local government and the central–local relationship in the 1980s are as follows:

(1) *Finance*. Initially the central grant to local government was sharply reduced from about 60 per cent of local expenditure to about 40 per cent, and then local income was limited too. Levels of expenditure were determined at the centre, there were penalties for overspending, and provision for the 'capping' of local revenue. The community charge or poll tax was designed to make local authorities directly accountable to all electors (who would all with few exceptions pay the charge) and the charge was designed to rise steeply as local expenditure increased. Later the charge was replaced by a property-based council tax. The old business rate was converted to a National Non-Domestic Rate set and collected by the national government. Altogether the local proportion of local government revenue was thus reduced to under 20 per cent. A Local Government Audit Commission was established to monitor the efficiency and 'value for money' of local government.

It is difficult to believe that these reforms of local government finance were much concerned for a proper constitutional position for local government. Neither Labour nor Conservative governments looked sypathetically at the Layfield Committee's recommendation (1976) that a proper system of local government required a substantial source of local revenue, which in practice would have to be a local income tax.

(2) *Structure and functions.* The Metropolitan County Councils and the Greater London Council were abolished. Some local government functions were taken over by new non-elected local corporations, for example Urban Development Corporations, Housing Action Trusts. Other functions were privatised, for example sale of council housing to tenants, compulsory competitive tendering for services. Schools were allowed, indeed encouraged, to 'opt-out' of control by local education authorities. The political activities of local councils were restricted by legislation following the Widdicombe Report (1986).

These changes in local government were paralleled by changes in the structure of the National Health Service, in particular the establishment of independent Hospital Trusts and the reorganisation of the old area and regional boards, and the restructuring of the Police Authorities. This is the home territory of the 'quango', the despised label for what the Cabinet Office regards with neutral accuracy as non-departmental public bodies (see Chapter 8). The number of quangos has been reduced by about one-third since 1979 (according to the government's counting), but their significance has grown, especially if the Hospital Trusts and the new Police Authorities are included. The non-elected, government-appointed quangos have invaded the territory of local government and colonised neighbouring areas; altogether they are now responsible for the disbursement of over £40 billion of public funds.

The characteristics of this major reformation of non-central government are: replacement of elected persons on management boards by ministerial appointees; substitution of managerial rhetoric (missions, strategic plans, targets, profit) for the traditional rhetoric of public service; replacement of public accountability by managerial accountancy or no accountability at all. For local government the pattern of these changes amounted to centralisation moderated by privatisation and 'quangoisation'.

Insofar as there was an underlying philosophy of constitutional reform, apart from hostility to local government in general and Labour councils in particular, it was about local government as 'enabler' and monitor, not monopoly provider and advocate of local interests. Thus, government outside the centre was developing not into inter-governmental relations, that is, structured relations between governments of unequal powers but of some minimal substance, but into local governance, a collection of discrete processes, a geographical rather than a constitutional phenonemon.

The juridification of the central–local relationship

The collapse of the traditional relationship of central and local government – the informal mutual tolerance and courtesies of partnership overlaying the constitutional supremacy of the centre – forced centre and locality into a new concern for the limits of legal powers and duties. The centre set about exploiting its sovereign legislative power to reshape and reposition local government. A torrent of legislation (over forty Acts dealing with local government in the first two Thatcher administrations) was followed by lorry-loads of circulars, directives, guidance, advice and condemnation. Local governments fought back and, more frequently than before, resorted to the courts to contest jurisdictional disputes.

This process has been called the 'juridification' of the central–local relationship (Loughlin, 1986, pp. 193–4). The term draws attention to what is in fact a rather episodic process; litigation rarely triumphed over legislation. Not surprisingly, appeal to the courts, while settling immediate disputes, did little to resolve the problems of an inherently conflictual relationship. Neverthless the 'rules of the game' were brought to the surface, and the question of the constitutional status of local government was raised.

The major cases

The following are some of the more significant cases.

1. Education – The *Tameside* case

(*Secretary of State for Education and Science* v. *Tameside Metropolitan Borough Council* [1976] 3 WLR 641)

Under section 68 of the Education Act 1944 the Minister is empowered to intervene ('give directions') if he is satisfied that a local education authority is acting 'unreasonably'. In May 1976 the Tameside Council, newly under the control of the Conservatives, decided not to go ahead with plans for the comprehensive reorganisation of secondary education approved by their Labour predecessors six months earlier and made ready for implementation in September 1976. The Secretary of State directed the authority to implement the plans, the authority fought back through the courts, lost in the Divisional Court but won in the Court of Appeal and in the House of Lords.

It was conceded by both sides that the Minister could not impose a particular form of secondary education on a local authority, and further that the new Conservative-controlled Council was entitled following the election to pursue its policy preferences (this was the doctrine of the 'mandate' which was challenged in the *Bromley* case – see below). Hence the question decided by the courts was the administrative feasibility of the reversal of policy in a matter of a few months. After a careful review of administrative detail the court decided that the authority was not acting unreasonably. The Minister had not 'directed himself properly in law', had failed to take account of all relevant considerations, excluding all irrelevant considerations. In particular, he had paid too much attention to the views of the teaching unions.

In a later case, *R.* v. *Secretary of State for Education and Science, ex parte Avon County Council* (*Independent*, 15 May 1990) the court resisted the implementation of a Conservative government's education policy. The County Council argued that their scheme of reorganisation would be damaged by the Minister's decision to allow a particular school to 'opt-out' of the public system. The court agreed, and the Minister was compelled to reconsider his decision (he did so and came to the same conclusion).

These decisions may be seen as a fine example of the courts checking an over-mighty executive; or, alternatively, as a dubious intrusion by the judges into the realm of fact, not law, so that in effect they came to review the merits, not the legality, of the Minister's decision, and thus in effect to substitute what they considered reasonable for the Minister's view.

2. Public transport – *Bromley* ('Fare's fair') and related cases

(*R.* v. *Greater London Council, ex parte Bromley London Borough Council* [1983] 1 AC 768)

The GLC proposed to cut public transport fares in London by 25 per cent, in accordance with a Labour Party election pledge. In order to pay the requisite subsidy to the London Transport Executive it was necessary to raise a supplementary rate from the London boroughs. Bromley Council contested the GLC policy. The House of Lords finally ruled that the GLC had acted *ultra vires* and hence unlawfully. The judgments were complex and by no means consistent. It was held that the GLC had failed to strike a fair balance between rate-payers and transport users; that London transport should under the Act be run on business lines, not for social objectives, and should aim to break even; and that a local authority had an overriding 'fiduciary duty' to its rate-payers, that is, to exercise thrift and to spend their money economically. (In an earlier and relevant case, *Prescott* v. *Birmingham Corporation* [1955] Ch. 210 (CA), it had been argued that the fiduciary duty precluded making a gift of free travel to one group of passengers at the expense of the rate-payers – unless, of course, legislation specifically allowed it.)

The judgment was confused in detail and depended on some dubious arguments. The 'fiduciary duty' is a judge-made concept; the 'fair balance' is a useful but slippery concept for judicial review; the interpretation of the Transport (London) Act 1969, in particular the provision that transport facilities must be 'economic', was arguably perverse, and the understanding of the economics of public transport inadequate. At the same time, the Appeal Court's dismissal of the GLC's election mandate seemed high-handed (see Chapter 11), and some of the contextual comments in both Appeal Court and House of Lords seemed to indicate injudicious heat. For example, one judge declared the GLC policy to be 'a hasty, ill-considered, unlawful and arbitrary use of power'. (On judicial arrogance, see also Griffith, 1991, p. 306.)

The consequences of the judgment in the *Bromley* case were seen to be unacceptable. In a similar case in Merseyside (though based on a different statute) the County Council's subsidised transport scheme was held to be lawful. The GLC put forward a new scheme for reduced fares which differed only in budgetary detail from the earlier scheme. This second scheme was upheld in the Divisional Court – a decision which Professor Griffith says 'bears the marks of a rescue operation' (1991, p. 135).

The *Bromley* case arose in a period of acute political tension, between the Thatcher government and Labour-controlled local authorities. As an elected body the GLC was fully entitled to be 'political'; in any case, its policies for public transport, though radical, were within the mainstream of thinking about transport policy. The courts were formally concerned with the interpretation of statutes, and that is a proper judicial function; but their interpretation was arguably wrong-headed, and their judgments betrayed some political bias, even animosity.

The *Bromley* case was fought between a London borough and the GLC, but is about the power of a metropolitan authority to make and implement a distinctive radical policy. The electors seem to have assented, the courts dissented. The government responded with new transport legislation (Acts of 1983 and 1984) which in effect nationalised London public transport and extended deregulation and privatisation. Finally the GLC and other Metropolitan County Councils were abolished (1985–6). Thus the ultimate constitutional power of parliamentary sovereignty banished both courts and local government to the margins of the polity.

3. Housing – the *Norwich* case

(*R.* v. *Secretary of State for the Environment, ex parte Norwich City Council* [1982] QB 808 (CA))

The Housing Act 1980 gave council tenants the right to buy their rented houses from the council at a substantial discount and with a guaranteed mortgage. The Act was politically controversial since it struck at what had been a major feature of housing policy, especially favoured by the Labour Party; and the allocation of housing was a valued element in local political patronage. Tenants in Norwich met very long delays in pursuing their applications to purchase, and the Minister eventually decided to intervene and sell the houses in place of the council. The Minister's right to intervene was upheld in the Divisional Court and again in the Appeal Court.

The courts were concerned to judge the Minister's powers of intervention under section 23 of the Act. The Appeal Court (Lord Justice Kerr) first made the usual disclaimer about political bias, and addressed itself to the elucidation of section 23. The section was found to be 'Draconian' in its terms and so to be construed strictly. On the other hand:

> [S]ection 23 has been framed by parliament in such a way as to maximise the power of the Secretary of State and to minimise any power of review by the court. The governing words are 'where it appears to the Secretary of State. . . .' These words make it clear that the determinative factor is the view of the Secretary of State; not the view of the local authority in question; nor any abstract standard of reasonableness to be determined by the court.

Lord Justice Kerr saw clearly that section 23 gave the Minister very great power, more than was available to the Secretary of State for Education under the 1944 Act (challenged in the *Tameside* case), but that was a matter for Parliament not for the courts. Lord Denning, on the other hand, held that the Minister's power of intervention was excessive, and should be upheld only if the council were acting unreasonably. Lord Denning seemed to be assessing the quality of the legislation, and his view did not prevail. But the uncertainty of the law, both its potential and its limits, were thus demonstrated.

4. Finance – *Hammersmith and Fulham, Brent and others*

(*R.* v. *Secretary of State for the Environment, ex parte Hammersmith and Fulham and others* [1990] 3 All ER 589; *R.* v. *Secretary of State for the Environment, ex parte Brent LBC* [1982] 2 WLR 593)

A number of local authorities appealed to the courts against poll tax capping. This might have seemed (to reformers) an opportunity for the courts to take up a liberal role as guardians of the people against an over-mighty executive. But the courts, faced with a decision which was as much political as constitutional, ducked. The separation of powers must be preserved, they declared, and a financial policy approved by the House of Commons was not to be struck down; the Minister was entitled to judge the excessive nature of local authority spending by any principles he chose. Thus irrationality was removed from the ground for review (see also Chapter 6). In the *Brent* case the courts allowed that the fairness of procedure was a matter for review, and it was held that the local authorities were entitled to have their representations heard before the Minister exercised his discretion.

The constitutional implications of 'juridification'

In the strict sense the constitutional position of local government had not changed. The courts have no basis on which to assert local autonomy; on the contrary, they can only work in the interstices of the sovereignty of Parliament, which it is their duty for the most part to uphold. Local government was and remains the creation of central government and entirely under its control. Hence, the centre's 'assault' on local government was not unconstitutional, and the courts could not hold it to be so.

The role of the courts has not been much enlarged. For the most part the courts have properly kept to the firm constitutional ground of parliamentary sovereignty, testing legality by reference to the statute, putting upon local government a 'fiduciary duty' to the rate-payers, and conceding only the right to a fair procedure. Other values, openness of procedure, rationality, proportionality have been neglected. Accusations of political bias were made and in one case at least were not groundless.

Thus, appeal to the courts and the settling of individual disputes have done little to resolve the problems of a conflictual relationship, or to reconstitute the relationship, with some regard for a balance between the centre and local government. But why should the courts take up the task of reformulating inter-governmental relations? For their part, the local authorities have continued to work through the political structure, using their national associations, the political parties and public opinion to make their case.

The law and politics of inter-governmental relations

The post-modern system of central and local government which has taken shape in the last two decades was not unconstitutional in the proper sense, nor inherently undemocratic. The central government may legitimately govern as it sees best in the national interest; and the interest of the citizen local elector lies in the quality rather than the structure and provenance of services. It may reasonably be argued that the citizen as customer has more genuine power than the citizen as voter – the Sainsbury's view of democracy. The principle of the poll tax fitted into such customer democracy. In theory you paid your money and took your choice: the poll tax was intended to reinvigorate local democracy by the imposition of electoral restraints on local councils.

In the softer sense of constitutionality it may be argued that the Conservative government's reformation of local government neglected the traditional commitment to local political institutions and the values of pluralism and participation they embodied. The partial dismantling of local government and its replacement by market and customer relations raises questions about the propriety of a market structure for some public services, the actual power of the customer in the supermarket, and the value of alternative centres of political participation and advocacy.

There is no constitutional framework for the relations of central and local government. Beyond parliamentary sovereignty (and the consequential *ultra vires*) lies empty space, central control moderated by fragmentation and poor communication. The constitutional vacuum is protected by the nature of British political culture and the persistent gap between centre and locality. On this Nevil Johnson has written:

> [T]he crucial characteristic of British local government is not so much its dependence on the centre in relation to its executive functions, but rather its political weakness and insignificance. . . . The most persuasive explanation of this peculiarity in the structure of British politics lies in the dominance over a very long period of national political elites and their relatively sharp separation from local politics understood as the maintenance of local positions of political influence. (1977, p. 128)

This weakness of the connection between centre and locality is, so to say, a proto-constitutional fact beyond the reach of the courts, the legislators or the constitutional reformers.

Reinventing government

The Layfield Committee on Local Government Finance argued in the 1970s for a reinvigoration of local government, which, if implemented, would have amounted to its reinvention. The Report (1976) raised the question:

> [W]hether all important governmental decisions affecting people's lives and livelihood should be taken in one place on the basis of national policies; or whether many of the decisions could not as well, or better, be taken in different places, by people of diverse experience, associations, background and political persuasion. (para. 63)

They concluded:

> [T]he only way to sustain a vital democracy is to enlarge the share of local taxation in total local revenue and thereby make councillors more directly accountable to local electorates for their expenditure and taxation decisions. (para. 67)

This was the last plan for the modernisation of traditional local government. The Layfield argument was taken up, but in the form of the poll tax, not, as Layfield argued, a local income tax.

In the following decades the debate about local government moved on to question the proper role of government itself at any level or in any form. At first sight this appears to abort constitutional considerations – no government, no constitution. But this is not quite the case. In practice the debate is shifted to questions of accountability of private bodies, procedures for regulation and for the redress of grievances. Thus the focus of constitutional debate shifts from structures and inter-governmental relations to the relationship of individuals to governance.

PART III

CITIZENS AND GROUPS IN THE CONSTITUTION

14

GOVERNMENT AND THE ECONOMY

Governing the economy, or, rather, the relations of government to economic activity, raises constitutional problems as well as problems of political value. There is no certainty about the proper purposes of the state as it moves from the unquestionably public sphere of law, order and security to the doubtfully private sphere of economy and social welfare. Uncertainties about purposes are compounded by the weakness of institutions, institutional relationships and procedures. Britain is especially affected by such uncertainties, not only because of the conflict of political values, but also because of the weakness of the constitutional underpinning for the marginal or arm's-length activities of the state, and the absence of any strong conception of the state.

In some cases, for example health and education, the institutions and procedures of responsible parliamentary democracy and of local government may appear to suffice; and where they do not, the provisions of the Citizen's Charter, local 'opting-out' and other forms of privatisation are intended to enhance the power of the citizen as consumer. In such matters citizens consumers may not feel they have as much power as they do in the supermarket (the latter sometimes exaggerated), but shoppers who are also voters are not powerless.

However, the government's dealings with the economy are constitutionally more problematic, due to the thinness of the constitution, once beyond the scope of the Westminster model. It is not clear what institutional and procedural patterns are appropriate in the economic sphere; in particular, how should control and accountability be arranged, and the respective 'rights' of government and citizen be protected? In Britain the expected pattern is dominance by the substantial but imperfect institutions of Westminster of a flat terrain, lacking constitution and constitutionally oriented courts and federal institutions, though increasingly disturbed by the new and significant institutions of the European Union/European Community.

This constitutional pattern may be observed in four cases: the general relationship of government and the economy; the particular case of the government and the Bank of England; the relationship of government and industry, including the special cases of the trade unions and 'corporatism'; and the regulation of industry, including nationalised and privatised industry.

Governing the economy

Governments have always intervened in the economy, perhaps since King Alfred burnt the cakes, certainly since William 'the Conqueror' set up the massive economic survey for the purposes of taxation known as the Domesday Book (1087). The tenth-century laws of King Athelstan provided for one coinage throughout the King's dominions, and control of minting. Medieval governments, like modern governments, worried about maintaining the value of the currency. They also intervened to protect and encourage industry, sometimes in bizarre ways, such as insisting that corpses be buried in woollen clothes. Later governments protected agriculture, the major industry and source of wealth, but turned during the process of industrialisation to the protection, promotion and regulation of industry – free trade, including the abolition of the Corn Laws, the promotion of railways, the reform of banking and commercial law, the provision of education and public health, even, less helpfully for earlier industrialists, the regulation of employment and working conditions.

In the first half of the twentieth century, under the impact of two world wars and persistent economic depression, governments came to accept some responsibility for the management of the economy as a whole. Partly this was an acknowledgement of the development of the study of economics: governments were slowly persuaded that a national economy could be 'managed', though not without some regard for the more difficult problem of managing the international economy. This was the economic consequence of the great economist and prophet John Maynard Keynes. Contemporary governments struggle with the problems and the possibilities in what is now a complex global economy, beyond the imaginings of William's Domesday surveyors.

The management of the economy (the endeavour, whether or not it could be done successfully) represented a massive extension in the objectives and reach of the state: this was the constitutional consequence of Mr Keynes. The making of economic policy, in this new over-arching sense, was, like foreign policy, formally managed through the usual channels of parliamentary politics, characterised by formal ministerial responsibility and actual ministerial dominance. In practice, the process was enmeshed in confidential communication with financial and international interests, and inevitably marked by secrecy, complexity and elusiveness. Quite often only the historians will be able to say what exactly a government's economic policy was at any one time, and then with little confidence; so, if the Chancellor was misleading himself, it might seem unfair to accuse him of misleading Parliament and people.

Thus, decisions with profound consequences for the well-being of the people are largely shielded from full exposure to parliamentary and public scrutiny. For example, the huge losses to the Exchequer arising from the doomed attempt to sustain the value of the pound in the Exchange Rate Mechanism in September 1992 have not been fully revealed. The GATT negotiations have a massive influence on people's lives but are necessarily conducted in secret, with little parliamentary participation. A public sector pay policy is informally announced by the Chancellor of the Exchequer, and later, with no explanation, modified . . . and so on.

Changes in interest rates, which have substantial consequences for the distribution of income, are agreed between the Treasury and the Bank of England, in response to what is assumed to be the ineluctable power of the financial markets. In a remarkable move towards more open government in this most arcane sphere, the Chancellor decided in 1994 to publish the minutes of his meetings with the Governor of the Bank to discuss interest rates; by the standards of British government secrecy this was a modest constitutional reform.

It is evident that, in the management of the economy, policy choices of massive importance are made beyond the reach of normal parliamentary politics, and indeed largely outside collective responsibility. To a very large extent this must be so. Apart from the general problems of decision-making by an assembly, there are special problems involved in financial and international relationships. Economic policy has to be fashioned in an environment hostile to national sovereignty and, within the nation-state itself, resistant to the sovereign power of governments.

For the constitutionalist there are two resolutions of the problem of apparently extra-constitutional power. First, the responsibility mechanisms of the familiar Westminster model apply to economic as to other areas of policy. After four to five years of obscure and secretive policy-making, a government submits to a crude but effective judgement about its relative success with the economy. Mismanagement of the economy, as perceived by the citizen consumer, citizen worker (or non-worker), citizen taxpayer, may be punished; and the threat of punishment ought to ensure good behaviour and improved performance. That, at least, is the theory.

Secondly, formal international organisations may bring some order and even openness into the control of the economy, and provide a framework in which nation-states might recover useable power. This is to conclude that the European Union may be an appropriate constitutional response to the loss of national power to govern the economy; and is potentially more democratic than a national structure no longer capable of effective governance of the economy. If this is not the case, or does not prove to be the case, then the ancient machinery of the Westminster model will need to be modernised.

The Bank of England

The Bank is a major national institution, so 'part of the constitution' (as the Prime Minister, Lord North, said in 1781). Though nationalised in 1946, it still behaves with considerable independence arising from its standing as the representative not of the government, still less of the people, but of 'the City' and high finance. Despite nationalisation, Governors have treated Parliament and even Chancellors of the Exchequer with disdain, and Labour Chancellors with hostility. Fending off the Select Committee on Nationalised Industries (1969–70) the Governor pronounced: 'We are not a nationalised industry; we are a nationalised institution'; the Bank's mission was 'preserving the fabric of the financial system without anybody knowing' (quoted in Moran, 1980, p. 73).

Denis Healey, Chancellor in the Labour government of 1974–9, wrote of the Bank 'seeing itself as the guardian of mysteries which no ordinary mortal should be allowed to understand' (1989, p. 374). But the problem for the Chancellor and the Governor – and for the constitution – was that the Bank was the government's intermediary with the financial markets, and these were private, independent and international. In face of the brute power of the markets, the constitutional and political structures of the state are weak, if not entirely powerless.

The Bank was established in 1694 to raise money for the government (funding the debt), but acquired other functions, in particular under the Act of 1844 a near monopoly of the issue of bank-notes. Since then, and particularly in the twentieth century, it has evolved into a modern 'central bank', with the major responsibility for the 'health' of the currency (on which the judgement of a banker may differ from that of a politician or a citizen with a mortgage but without a job), and the management of interest rates.

The functions of the Bank of England include the following:

1. the production and issue of bank-notes;
2. acting as the government's banker, in effect maintaining its current account, and borrowing money for the government by the issue of the government bonds known as gilt-edged stock;
3. the support and protection of the currency by the management of interest rates and the gold and foreign currency reserves, including intervention in the foreign exchange markets;
4. supervision of the banking system;
5. acting as the intermediary between the government and the financial world.

These are functions of enormous significance for the well-being of the country and the people. The Bank has often been criticised for its errors of judgement and its bias in favour of the interests of the City rather than workers and the unemployed (as in the inter-war years); for the evident bias of some Governors against high-spending Labour governments; and for the failure to prevent some damaging collapses in the secondary banking structure. It is plain that the position of the Bank in relation to the government is of high political and constitutional importance.

Like other nationalised industries, the Bank appears to lie somewhere between independence and government control. The nationalisation Act of 1946 did not in practice make much difference to the Bank. The stockholders were bought out, the Treasury was given a specific power (Clause 4) to give directives to the Bank 'in the public interest', and Governor and the Court were nominated by the Chancellor of the Exchequer. In practice, apart from a token trade unionist, Governor and Court reflect the established interests of the City. The Governor participates at the highest level in the making of macro-economic policy, pitting the clout of the markets against the government. The Treasury has its own expertise and its own doctrinal differences and may be inclined towards its own perception of 'reality'; but at the end of the day the markets win.

This may not look like an appropriate constitutional position for the Bank in a democracy; but there is room for disagreement about the borderlands between the public and the private sphere, and the proper scope of the constitution. In most countries the central bank is not nationalised but private. However, there cannot be an absolute division, and even where the bank is independent its relationships with government are prescribed to some extent by government; in particular, for example, the central banks in Germany, Switzerland and the United States (the Federal Reserve) have a statutory duty to preserve the currency.

The granting of full independence to the Bank of England has been advocated in Britain on the grounds that its functions, especially in relation to the currency, are properly located in the private sphere and are indeed contaminated by the influence of government. This is a remarkable admission for democratic politicians to make: politicians cannot be trusted, democracy is corrupting – so much for government by the people! On the contrary it may be that the case for independence underestimates the extent to which monetary policy can be separated from the overall control of the economy, and involves essentially political values. (Is it for bankers to determine the economic well-being of the people?)

Nigel Lawson, when Chancellor of the Exchequer, submitted a proposal for an independent central bank to the Prime Minister in 1988. This was based on a division of responsibilities.

> (a) The Bank would assume sole responsibility for the operation of monetary policy, with a statutory duty to protect and maintain the value of the currency. It would thus be responsible for setting short-term interest rates and monetary targets.
> (b) The Government would remain responsible for determining the exchange rate framework – for example, whether we were part of any international agreement. . . . The Bank would then be responsible for the conduct of exchange rate policy within that framework. . . .
>
> [Thus t]he Bank would be obliged, as is the Bundesbank, to conduct monetary policy within the framework of the Government's economic policy as a whole, but only so far as that is consistent with its primary function of safeguarding the currency. (Extracts from the Chancellor's minute to the Prime Minister, 25 November 1988, in Lawson, 1992, pp. 1060–1)

In Nigel Lawson's scheme the Court of the Bank would continue to be appointed by the government, though possibly subject to the approval of a select committee of Parliament. The Governor would appear regularly before a select committee (he may appear from time to time at present) but this should be 'set up in a way which did not subject the Bank to unwarranted Parliamentary pressure'.

The case for an 'independent' Bank of England was not accepted by the Prime Minister. It was pressed again by Chancellor Norman Lamont (1990–3) and again rejected on the grounds that parliamentary acountability would be inadequate. The Prime Minister's concern was probably as much for ministerial power. However, backbench Members of Parliament might well have more influence on an independent bank, accounting to a select committee, than they do on the nationalised Bank.

It is clear that the Bank of England exercises substantial powers over the economy, and the relations of government and Bank are therefore of high constitutional significance. The relationship is complex. The Bank operates both independently and in a range of dependent or quasi-dependent relationships – on the instructions of, in consultation with, on behalf of the government. For example, in November 1993 the precise timing of a reduction in interest rates, almost certainly decided upon by the government, was left to the Bank; it might otherwise have been announced as part of the Budget, one week later. On the other hand, the decision (1994) to publish the Minutes of the Chancellor's regular meetings with the Governor to consider the state of the economy and the level of interest rates seemed to accord the Bank a standing – a constitutional standing – commensurate with substantial influence.

Thus the case of the Bank of England shows a pragmatic adjustment to the realities of the relationship of government to centres of private power. In the shadowlands between the public and the private spheres no sharp lines are drawn, market power is acknowledged and accommodated; on the other hand, there is some recognition that a governing relationship of this kind cannot lie totally beyond the framework of the constitution.

That conclusion is strengthened by the impact of membership of the European Union and European Community. The Community aspires to a full economic union underpinned and powerfully signalled by a common currency and a European central bank. Britain started down this path by joining the European Monetary Union and, after some agonising, the Exchange Rate Mechanism (1990). Two years later it proved impossible to sustain the pound sterling in the ERM and Britain withdrew. The British attitude to full monetary union and a single currency is now reluctant if not hostile. Thus the old problems of the proper relations of the government and the Bank of England are set in a radically new constitutional context by the Europeanisation of British government.

Government and industry

Government has many kinds of relationship with industry, ranging from ownership and control to influence and regulation, to support and sympathy, or separation, stand-aside and hands-off. The constitutionalist is interested in the relationship because it involves the use, abuse or non-use of government power. For political and constitutional analysis the key questions are: 'who does what to whom?' (a political and constitutional question), 'who gains or loses thereby?' (the political question) and 'by what rules and procedures?' (the constitutional question). The chief actors are ministers on one side, producers, industrialists, businessmen, employees, trade unionists on another, and customers, consumers and tax-payers on a third. It is this third side of the triangle which imports a high political and constitutional significance, a public interest overriding the private interests of industry and private agreements made between industry and government, and employer and employee.

Control and bargaining

Government has the power of command over industry by the formal constitutional powers of law and taxation, and subsidiary powers of licence and regulation. Thus the statutory powers taken by governments in the 1970s to control wages and prices (for example, under the Counter-Inflation Act of 1973 and the Price Commission Act of 1977) amounted to a massive intervention in private industry; but so too is taxation and the granting or withholding of licences (for example, for the exploitation of North Sea oil and gas, or television franchises).

Governments also wield extensive powers of near-command derived from their great wealth and practical capacity to take action and to spend, including the buying of shares, the granting of subsidies and loans on favourable terms. Governments are the largest purchasers of goods and services in the country (the largest customer of British Telecom, for example), and thus wield enormous power to confer benefits or impose disadvantages on industry. This power of government as customer/contractor was used in the 1970s to secure compliance with non-statutory incomes policies. It is particularly evident in the defence industries, for which the government is virtually the only customer (so far only governments buy tanks and fighter aircraft). The prosperity of the business is bound up with defence policy and procurement.

In these matters government has the legal and financial resources to secure compliance in the last resort, or earlier if necessary. But relationships are not normally conducted in conditions of last resort, and governments, despite their power, still depend on the other contracting parties. Even where contracts are not involved, the government keeps its ultimate powers in reserve.

Hence the normal relationship of government and industry is not simple command and compliance but bargaining, negotiation, pressure and counter-pressure.

Most bargaining is conducted by ministers and officials in secret – for example, the 'voluntary' agreement between the tobacco companies and the government about tobacco advertising. This agreement serves the interests of the manufacturers and the advertisers and the Treasury (and perhaps the Treasurer of the Conservative Party too), but it is against the public interest because of its effect on health and the finances of the Health Service. Most decisions on monopolies and mergers are made informally by bargaining and mutual agreement. The disposition of the market for coal was arranged between the Coal Board and the CEGB in the 1970s and drastically rearranged between the privatised gas and electricity industries in the 1980s, to the ruination of the coal industry. The role of the government in these negotiations is obscure, but it is likely that the government was aware of the probable outcomes.

The immense bargaining power of government arising from its wealth and practical capacities has been called *dominium* compared with the *imperium* of law, literally dominion and empire (Daintith, 1989, p. 197). Daintith argues that Parliamentary accountability is lacking, and the use of the powers of *dominium* 'may conflict with values like democracy, procedural fairness, or freedom from arbitrariness, which we may feel that our constitution should protect' (p. 194).

An alternative or complementary perspective would give more emphasis to the balance of power between government and industry. Though in the last resort the balance may be tilted towards the government, the normal relationship does allow the effective pursuit of private interests. This appears to be true in the case of the defence industries, which, according to numerous reports from the Comptroller and Auditor-General and the Public Accounts Committee, have been able to operate in largely uncompetitive conditions, to the grave disadvantage of the tax-payer. The 'military–industrial complex' is a special case of the normal collaborative arrangements between a powerful government and far from impotent economic interests, which pursue their bargaining between public and private interests largely outside the framework of parliamentary accountabilty.

Trade unions and corporatism

Government's relations with trade unions display some of the characteristics of the government–industry relationship. Government has immense power, both in law and 'dominion', but the private associations are not lacking in clout and at times have had the capacity to bargain rather than conform. However, the relationship differs from the government's relations with manufacturers and employers. The government recognises the right to join a trade union and, within some limits, to 'withdraw labour'; it needs stable and harmonious industrial relations and contented and productive workers. But it does not need the unions as much as it needs industry, and it has a greater power by law to regulate, reshape or diminish them.

The trade unions are by definition defenders of a sectional interest, but fatally lacking in influence except by the strike and other forms of 'industrial action', often involving public disruption affecting fellow-workers and engendering popular hostility. In face of the disruptive capacity of the unions, the government stands for the defence of the national interest and the maintenance of law and order, and plausibly denounces (with Dicey's blessing) breaches of the 'rule of law'. This is plainly a very unequal contest.

The trade unions' shrewd response to this situation was to establish the Labour Party and campaign for parliamentary and governing power. This has given them the benefits (not always apparent to trade unionists) of a sympathetic government with a working majority for just ten years since the beginning of the twentieth century when the Labour Party was established. The response of governments has been an uneven mixture of encouragement in peaceful times and hostility in face of strikes and militancy. Nevertheless, fearful of the consequences of industrial disharmony, governments have made serious attempts to come to some settlement or concordat with the unions.

This process of appeasement (using the term without its pejorative Munich associations) was pushed forward by the two world wars and was continued by both Labour and Conservative governments after 1945. It came to a climax in the 1960s and 1970s. The objective was to secure wage restraint, the institutional device was the incorporation of the trade unions along with the employers in more or less formal structures of consultation and negotiation – notably the National Economic Development Council (1962) and the agreement of the Labour Party with the trade unions known as the 'Social Contract' (1972). In 1976 and 1977, in a bizarre constitutional innovation, some parts of the Budget were made subject to good behaviour by the trade unions (they behaved well enough in 1976, but not in 1977). Since the two major economic interests were in a very limited way incorporated into the government structure, these arrangements have been called, rather portentously, 'corporatism'.

Such limited 'corporatism', or quasi-corporatism, did not achieve its objectives. Trade union leaders were unable, and in some cases unwilling, to deliver wage restraint, and the Labour government, though generous to a fault with its legislative concessions to the unions, was unable to deliver rapidly rising prosperity. Corporatism collapsed with the prolonged series of strikes in 1978–9 (the 'Winter of Discontent') and the fall of the Labour government. Mrs Thatcher's government abandoned any kind of bargaining with the unions, or even talking with them; indeed, trade union leaders have hardly been seen in Downing Street since then. Instead the government relied on high unemployment, strict legal constraints and a well-prepared exemplary defeat of the miners (1984–5) to tame the unions. The strategy proved more successful than corporatism in moderating union militancy.

In a constitutional perspective, the government–trade union relationship is a special case in the relations of government and major economic interests. In a pluralist polity the trade unions have the right (as do we all) to have their interests seriously taken into account, a claim to be consulted on matters affecting their interests, and some encouragement to organise themselves for this purpose, including the exploitation of the institutional machinery of parliamentary democracy. The use of their economic power to bargain with the government is not a constitutional right but a political fact.

In all these respects the unions resemble the banks, the 'City', the manufacturing industries, British Airways and so on. The problem for the unions is that whereas the Chairman of the Stock Exchange or British Airways can dine with the Prime Minister and exert his pressure in private (another form of corporatism), the unions, having no 'dining power', must take to the streets. In the sixties and seventies they were sometimes invited to parley in Downing Street over more modest 'beer and sandwiches'. The taking of food and drink is a factor of some significance in political and constitutional relationships. Both BA and the unions pursue selfish interests as hard as they can; both may try to be ruthlessly coercive. It does appear, however, that the big industrial and financial corporations achieve their ends more often and more easily than the trade unions.

This is disturbing news for the constitutionalist. The balancing of private interests against each other and by a measure of the public interest, insofar as that may be discerned, is a major task of a democratic government, committed to political pluralism and constitutional procedures. It is not evident that these crucial relationships of government with economic interests are conducted towards these ends through open constitutional procedures.

Regulation

Regulation of industry refers to the application of rules to a specific area of the operations of industry, usually in an institutional framework providing continuity and some predictability. The regulation of safety and working conditions in mines and factories is an obvious and venerable example. Regulation developed in the nineteenth century in relation to, for example, railways, land-use, emigration, as a form of control which was less than a department (executive, operational, headed by a minister) but more than a court. The function of regulation was quasi-judicial rather than managerial, but more continuous, expert, interactive and in effect more managerial than a court.

Following the privatisation of the nationalised utilities the practice of regulation and the number of regulatory bodies have grown. Regulatory bodies 'represent a constitutional innovation for the United Kingdom' (Graham and Prosser, 1991, p. 176), in contrast with the United States where regulation, notably of competition, has a long history. By comparison with the United States, Britain's simple institutional structure and undeveloped constitutional culture is not well-suited to the absorption and support of such elusive functions dating back to the early nineteenth century.

Such regulation is contentious when it threatens the profitability of an industry, as the nineteenth-century factory-owners argued; and contemporary industrialists are no less hostile to the attempts of modern governments to change the basic economics of an industry by the regulation of pricing and competition policy. This has arisen under both the nationalised industries and the recently privatised utilities. In the first case the government was especially interested in the control of prices and purchasing. In the case of the privatised utilities, which all tended to monopoly, the government was concerned to ensure a level and quality of service and apply some surrogate for competition. Both nationalised and privatised industries, in different ways, raised constitutional problems about the public interest: it was a fallacy of the ideologies of both left and right that ownership, public or private, on its own resolved questions of public interest.

Nationalisation

The post-war nationalisation statutes generally gave the appropriate Minister power to appoint the Board and to give general directions in matters relating to the national interest. 'The responsibility of deciding what is in the overriding interests of the nation rests with the Minister because it is only by resting with him that it can rest here', so Aneurin Bevan declared in the House of Commons on 25 February 1952 (HC Deb., vol. 496, col. 818). The Board was responsible for commercial policy and day-to-day management.

This division of function inevitably broke down under the weight of the economic and political consequences of the management of these major national industries. In practice ministers intervened in matters such as pricing, wages and purchasing, placing the government's judgement of the 'public interest' against the industry's assessment of its commercial interest. In the case of the airlines, governments intervened with the regulatory body, the Civil Aviation Authority, to discourage competition with the nationalised British Airways (see Chapter 6). The Labour government wished to protect the nationalised airline, the Conservative government to fatten it for privatisation. If there was a public interest in competition, governments did not recognise it – and behaved in that respect like almost all other governments.

It may seem reasonable for the government to claim to be the guardian of the public interest, but the claim is not entirely persuasive. The economist may argue that the public interest lies in an efficient and prosperous industry, requiring a commercial rather than a political assessment. The constitutionalist may still believe the government has a right to assert an economic judgment, but will argue that government intervention must be made by agreed procedures, openly, fully explained and subjected to accountability in Parliament.

Privatisation

Privatisation of the nationalised industries may have solved the problems of commercial efficiency (at least that was the intention), but the question of public interest and accountability remains. The process of privatisation was itself a remarkable demonstration of the power of government, rather more striking than the earlier process of nationalisation, most of which applied to the old heavy industries which were already subject to extensive war-time controls.

The process of privatisation began in 1981, and within a decade over half of the public sector was transferred to the private sector; this included the denationalisation of major state corporations such as British Gas, British Telecom and British Airways, and the disposal of shares in companies such as Rolls-Royce and Jaguar. At the same time many local government activities (for example, refuse collection, house maintenance) were opened to commercialisation or competitive tendering.

This process of privatisation was the most massive reformation of the structure of the economy since the nationalisation programme of the 1945–51 government – or perhaps since the dissolution of the monasteries in the 1530s. Huge sums of money were involved. A sceptic might think that the government sold the nation's property back to its owners (but only those who could afford to buy shares), rewarded them in most cases with substantial premiums (the shares were under-priced), and on the way gave generous fees to the City institutions and advertising agencies, which had assisted the government in this selling of the family silver. The proceeds to the government from privatisation in the course of the decade amounted to about £25 billion. The operation was of course entirely constitutional and popular, but appeared a little buccaneering compared with the bureaucratic character of the establishment of the public corporations of 1945–51.

Further it was evident that privatisation did not mean total independence for the newly private industries. The government continued to be involved, in some cases as part-owner (through the device of a special 'golden' share, as in British Petroleum and British Airways), otherwise by regulation and by informal pressures, assisted by the practice of what the French call 'pantouflage' – the migration of former ministers and civil servants to the boardrooms of the industries.

The landscape of regulatory bodies is now well-populated. Like other quangos or NDPBs they are part of the extended state which lies behind the classic structure of Minister–Department–Parliament, and which carries out substantial governmental functions in something of a constitutional limbo. There were bodies with regulatory functions before the 1980s crop of post-privatisation agencies. For example, the Independent Television Authority (ITA) was established in 1953 to 'regulate' commercial broadcasting; other early examples include the Monopolies and Mergers Commission (MMC), the Commission for Racial Equality (CRE), and the Equal Opportunities Commission (EOC). In the 1980s a new generation of agencies was established to regulate the privatised utilities – Office of Fair Trading, Oftel, Ofgas, Ofer, Ofwat. In the case of the financial services industry (already private, but requiring regulation to preserve its international standing and to protect its customers) a structure of self-regulation was established with government blessing – a notable concession to a powerful and favoured private interest.

The constitutional position of the agencies is peculiar. They are in effect non-ministerial government departments. The Secretary of State, having made the legislation and issued the licence, appoints the Director-General, who acts as his advisor. But the Director-General has an independent authority to enforce the terms of the licence, to review and publish information about the activities of the industry, to investigate complaints and protect consumer interests, and to promote competition. The last, clearly an essential function in dealing with monopolies, is the most controversial, and involves the Director-General in relations with other agencies (MMC, OFT), the Minister and the Department (DTI), and possibly the Restrictive Practices Court, and with the laws relating to competition (including EC law). This does not look like a simple pattern of regulatory institutions, nor possibly an effective one. But this is not a simple problem. If neither public nor private monopoly works in the public interest and the market proves to be imperfect, then a regulated market appears worth trying.

The economic problems of regulated competition in a supposedly free economy are severe, and challenge the constitutional standing of the agencies. If the agencies must, on the one side, threaten the profitable operation of the industry or, on the other, fail to protect the public interest (government and/or the consumer), then they need to be endowed with legitimacy, accountability, and what Americans call 'due process'. While the statutory basis of the agencies is sound enough, their status is ill-defined (part-government, part-autonomous) suspended awkwardly between government and the interests they were set up to regulate. The accountability of the agencies to Minister and Parliament is weak, and their relations with clients problematic. Who, it is asked, regulates the regulators?

For example, British Gas has had an uneasy relationship with Ofgas, and the Chairman of British Telecom complained in July 1992 about the interference of the regulators:

> We believe [in] . . . the need for the regulator to stick to preserving the overall public interest, leaving management to decide how the business is to be run, free from regulatory interference. Regrettably, the trend in regulation in the UK . . . appears to be towards greater intervention in management, without a clearly expressed vision or set of long-term objectives.
>
> Regulators can be tempted to embark on a course of social engineering, or to tinker with operational matters in response to short-term political or media pressures. Paradoxically, there is a real danger that regulated privatised businesses may be subject to more state interference than they were as nationalised industries.
>
> It is also unclear how the regulators themselves are to be held accountable. The regulated industries have little right of appeal and, in practice, no effective recourse to judicial review. In our case, our only course, if we fail to agree with Oftel even on minor issues, is to allow the matter to be referred to the Monopolies and Mergers Commission. (AGM address by the Chairman of British Telecommunications, 30 July 1992)

The complaint relates both to the decisions of the regulators and the fairness of procedures – openness, participation, consultation, even-handedness.

There are no easy solutions to the problems of accountability in the regulatory agencies. There is a delicate balance between 'light touch' regulation, maximising commercial freedom, and a heavier hand, maximising the public interest. Accountability by ministers (ministerial responsibility) is notoriously weak, and in any case ministers' powers are restricted. Judicial review is available in some cases as a remedy against the regulators, particularly in relation to 'due process', but the courts are properly reluctant to intrude in areas of ministerial responsibility, and are best suited to the remedying of particular wrongs, rather than the development of good administrative and regulatory practice.

The European Community plays a part in regulation, particularly in competition policy and the control of mergers (EEC Treaty Art. 86). The Community works in this area in part informally, by negotiation and bargaining. Its regulatory processes may be criticised as much as the British ones as lacking in openness and accountability, though the Commission is a little more accessible than the British government, and procedures are open to review by the European Court of Justice (Graham and Prosser, 1991, pp. 203–4).

That may still leave Parliament as the last resort regulator of the regulators. A select committee might indeed open up the process of regulation, compel the parties to regulation to state their case in public, and thus contribute to the identification of the public interest in the arena of Parliament designated by history for that purpose.

Conclusion

This account of the relationship of government to economic activity reveals both the importance of the relationship and the thinness of its constitutional underpinning. For the constitutionalist, here is the characteristic weakness of the British constitution: the absence of a developed constitutional law and constitutional courts; an easy dependence on a weak Parliament; and the lack of any substantial structures of government outside the centre. The advantages of flexibility and pragmatism signify in practice that the government may do as it likes. By contrast the United States and France, for example, have constitutions and constitutional courts;

the United States has a federal system and the notoriously centralised French in practice enjoy regional government and a localised political culture. Both have a strong legal tradition in which law is a check on government, not simply an instrument of government power.

It must be conceded that for governments the economy is a difficult area in which to maintain the constitutionality of their actions. Public and private interests mingle and compete, and government itself cannot easily reconcile its political and constitutional duties. In Britain such resolution must lie in Parliament rather than the courts, which have limited standing and lack the expertise to function effectively in the economic sphere. Parliament is weak, but is still the only constitutional body which may provide a legislative mandate, exact accountability, ensure open and fair procedures and a reasonable quality of expertise and efficiency. This is presently not done well, or even much at all, in relation either to the government's macro-economic policymaking or to the control or regulation of industry.

The only alternative to a reinvigoration of Parliament is the invention of a substantial level of regional government, which can certainly engage in the regulation of industry as in the United States, or, more likely, the extension of the European Union/European Community into this area to provide a 'form of constitution for economic life' (Graham and Prosser, 1991, p. 253).

15

THE LIBERAL POLITY
Secrecy, Free Speech and the Media

The limits of free speech

A constitutional democracy requires the fullest freedom of speech compatible with national security and limited confidentiality for some stages of policy development. The balance is difficult to strike, and governments, reluctant to accept the risks and embarrassments of open government, are willing and able to tip the balance in favour of protection and secrecy.

Of course, Britain is still a free country by the standards of the twentieth century. Within broad limits most people are free to speak and write, to read and listen. The media are not controlled by the government, and public criticism of the government is a normal part of daily life. This is infuriating for governments, and they do what they can, within the conventions of the traditionally liberal polity, to limit damage and avoid embarrassment. At the same time, the media are naturally defenders of their own freedoms, including commercial freedom, rather than protectors of the citizen's rights. In the absence of any constitutional guarantee of freedom of speech, those rights depend on the law and its interpretation by the courts. Thus the citizen's freedom of speech is far from absolute: it is restrained by the culture of government, by the nature of the media and by the law.

First, Britain's constitutional and political culture is pervaded by secrecy, and much of the workings of central government takes place behind closed doors. The culture of secrecy is encouraged by the adversarial system which operates both in Parliament and the courts and inhibits the open exchange of information. In the dispute over the supply of arms to Iraq, revealed by the Scott Inquiry (1993–4), ministers and high officials asserted the political necessity for 'economy with the truth', the half-truth ('truth is a difficult concept', said one official). A distinction seemed to be made between misleading and lying, and William Waldegrave, the Minister responsible for progress towards 'open government', likened politics as played in Parliament to poker rather than chess.

In constitutional practice secrecy is evident in the conventions of accountability which serve as prescriptions of confidentiality, and support the rule whereby Cabinet and other official documents are kept secret for thirty years or longer. In the courts the need for confidentiality is used by the government as a justification for the non-disclosure of documents (see Chapter 5). In addition, the civil law of confidentiality has been applied to public life in an attempt to control further the release of information. This lack of public access to information concerning the governing process in Britain limits the processes of participation and accountability for both the citizen and Members of Parliament.

Secondly, the massive and monopolistic nature of the media derogates from full freedom of speech. This is paradoxical. The media are not controlled by the government, engage in vigorous commercial competition and practise free speech for themselves. The citizen thus gains a choice, but it is a limited one. The opinions of the great proprietors and editors are sometimes propagated without much regard for the opinions of readers or the requirements of truth and honesty in journalism. The broadcasting organisations (the BBC and the 'terrestrial' commercial companies supervised by the ITC) do not work to the same commercial and partisan drives, and their contribution to a pluralism of opinion and a genuine freedom of speech may be judged the greater.

Thirdly, the government engages in 'management' of the media, using briefings, leaks, informal persuasion, threats about stricter regulation, honours, and, in the case of the BBC, threats about the licence fee and the renewal of its charter. Further, the government provides for regulation of the media, mainly concerned with intrusion into privacy, the portrayal of sex and violence and the use of offensive language, through 'arm's-length' bodies such as the Broadcasting Standards Council and the Broadcasting Complaints Commission, and the industry-based Press Complaints Commission.

It is not possible here to enter into a full account of this struggle between media and government for the attention and loyalty of the citizens; but it is the context in which a formidable battery of laws affecting freedom of speech applies.

Secrecy

The Official Secrets Act

In law the culture of secrecy is reflected most obviously in the existence of an Official Secrets Act. The first Act was passed in 1911 in response to panic about alleged German spying. Such was the climate that the Bill passed through all its parliamentary stages in one day and the notorious 'catch-all' section 2 was never debated. This section made it an offence for any public servant or anyone employed under a government contract to reveal any information either about their employment, or obtained in the course of that employment, unless such disclosure had been 'authorised'. This meant that the revelation of quite trivial information, for example about prices in a government canteen or the number of daffodil bulbs planted in Kew Gardens, was a criminal offence.

Despite the absurdity of the breadth of section 2, it did allow for a defence of disclosure in the 'public interest'. This was successfully used by Clive Ponting in 1985 (see Chapter 6), and another 'leaker', Cathy Massiter, a security officer, was never prosecuted for her revelation that the telephone of a member of CND had been tapped for 'political purposes'. In fact these much-publicised cases were unrepresentative of the working of the Act; in the past there had been many successful prosecutions under section 2. But whether effective or not, the Act's reputation was low, and, from the government's point of view, it did not provide sufficient deterrence against politically embarrassing revelations.

In 1989 it was replaced by a new Act. This created six classes of protected official information, including security and intelligence, defence, international relations, crime and special investigations, and information entrusted in confidence. The Act applies to Crown servants and government contractors, and it also imposes a lifelong duty of confidentiality upon members of the security services and upon those who are 'notified' by the Home Secretary that they fall within that category.

In addition, the Act makes it an offence for journalists and editors to publish any protected information if they have grounds for believing that it has been disclosed without official permission. There is no 'public interest' defence, thus making clearly illegal disclosures like those of Ponting and Massiter, which caused political controversy and embarrassment rather than damage to national security. The effect of the Act is that 'it will be difficult to learn anything of security and intelligence operations other than what the Government chooses to make public' (Robertson, 1993, p. 169); to which the government might respond, 'so what did you expect then?'

National security

There is a persuasive case for secrecy in the interests of national security, and for allowing government to be the judge of the matter. However, it may be thought that governments exaggerate the need for secrecy and the value and effectiveness of security operations. Revelations of the penetration of the security services by foreign agents, and the apparent ubiquity of the double-agent (working for both sides), suggest that the secret services were not after all so secret. Certainly the Cold War was exploited to promote the security services and to reinforce the government's own culture of secrecy, and the ending of the Cold War has not much diminished either.

Governments use national security as a ground for the evasion of parliamentary scrutiny, for the non-disclosure of documents in legal actions, for seeking injunctions to prevent the publication of material and as a justification for executive actions which might otherwise have been held to be illegal or at least embarrassing. The traditional attitude of the courts has allowed such claims to succeed. Judges have considered national security to be a concern of the executive and not the courts, as demonstrated by the statement from Lord Parker made early this century in the *Zamora* case:

> Those who are responsible for the national security must be the sole judge of what the national security requires. It would be obviously undesirable that such matters should be made the subject of evidence in a court of law or otherwise discussed in public. (*Zamora (The)* [1916] 2 AC 77)

There has been little change in judicial attitudes since that time. The courts are reluctant to consider matters relating to security even when individual rights are at stake. In *R* v. *Secretary of State for the Home Department, ex parte Hosenball* [1977] 3 All ER 452, an American journalist, who was being deported, failed to secure the details of the charge against him. Lord Denning declared that 'in national security cases even natural justice must take a back seat'. Such reasoning has been reflected in subsequent deportation cases, where it has been held that expulsion on the grounds of national security requires no further explanation.

This reluctance of the courts to look behind claims of national security was also evident in the GCHQ case (see Chapter 5). The House of Lords ruled that the duty of fairness, which required that the unions be consulted before changes were made to conditions of employment, was overridden by national security considerations. In what seemed to be a modification of an absolute acceptance of the executive's claim that national security was an issue, the Law Lords stated that they required evidence that security was the consideration; but in practice, the evidence required was slight.

Confidentiality

Confidentiality goes hand in hand with national security. The law of confidentiality was first used in a public law context by the Attorney-General in an effort to stop the publication of the Crossman Diaries (see Chapter 7). It is based on the premise that no one should profit from the disclosure of information which has been given in confidence, and it was the basis of the action against Peter Wright, a retired member of MI5 and author of *Spycatcher* (1987).

Peter Wright and *Spycatcher*

The government made a sustained attempt (1986–8) to prevent publication of all or parts of *Spycatcher*. In the book Wright claimed that MI5 had been involved in the burglary and bugging of political parties and trade unions. He further claimed that the service had been involved in a plot to destabilize the

Wilson government and that a former head of MI5, Sir Roger Hollis, had been a Soviet agent. For those who were inclined to be sceptical about the value of the security services, such revelations fully justified publication; for others, Wright had damaged the integrity, not to mention the reputation, of the security sevices.

Wright was living in Tasmania and could not be prosecuted under the Official Secrets Act (section 2 of the 1911 Act was then the relevant legislation) as he was outside the jurisdiction of the British courts. The British government therefore brought a civil action in the Australian courts, seeking to prevent publication on the grounds of confidentiality. The government also obtained temporary injunctions in the British courts against the *Observer* and *Guardian* newspapers to stop them printing extracts from the book or reporting Wright's allegations. These injunctions were subsequently held to apply to other newspapers as well.

However, whilst the government was successful in the British courts in preventing publication on the grounds of confidentiality, it was unsuccessful in Australia, and suffered damaging publicity when the Cabinet Secretary, Sir Robert Armstrong, conceded that he had been 'economical with the truth' (the phrase brilliantly captures the official approach to information, or how to deceive without actually telling lies). In the end, after all avenues of appeal had been explored, the British government had to concede defeat. In fact only one of the eleven judges called upon to give judgment in the Australian courts found for the British government.

The loss of the action in Australia, together with the publication of *Spycatcher* in the United States, resulted in the subsequent lifting of injunctions against the British press, despite the opposition of the government. In its ruling the House of Lords recognised that members of the security services owed a lifelong duty of confidentiality. However, it refused to issue permanent injunctions largely because the availability of the book in the States meant that its contents could no longer be considered secret and thus confidential.

The duty of confidentiality was given legal form shortly afterwards in the Official Secrets Act 1989. The Act recognises no exceptions and thus imposes a stricter framework than the judges recognised. It would seem that the *Wright* and *Ponting* cases influenced the shape of the new legislation.

Free speech

There is no constitutional or protected right to free speech in Britain. This contrasts with the situation in countries with a Bill of

Rights. Thus whilst the First Amendment of the Constitution of the United States provides that Congress 'shall make no law . . . abridging the freedom of speech, or of the press', the extent to which free speech obtains in Britain is dependent upon the liberality of the legislators and developments within the common law. The courts recognise free speech as an important legal principle, and take note of the European Convention of Human Rights. However, they can only uphold free speech as a 'right' when there is no law that limits its operation (hence not really a right at all).

Such laws arise from a variety of sources, including those that restrict freedom of assembly and thereby reduce the opportunities for the public expression of opinions. Thus the soap-box in Hyde Park as a symbol of free speech in Britain may be misleading. Hyde Park Corner is governed by a non-typical by-law, the liberality of which is not reflected elsewhere. Indeed, by-laws frequently impose restrictions preventing the gathering of a crowd which might obstruct highways, pavements and shopping malls. Similarly there are restrictions on marches and demonstrations which again act to limit the occasions when opinions can be freely and publicly expressed.

In addition, some public order offences relate to the use of language. For example, section 4 of the Public Order Act 1986 concerns the use of threatening, insulting or abusive words which might provoke violence, whilst sections 17–23 contain the offence of incitement to racial hatred. There are also offences of obscenity, sedition and treason, which limit what can be said: so too does the offence of blasphemy, although only in relation to the Christian religion. The narrow application of the law of blasphemy was drawn to public attention by the Rushdie affair, when Muslim leaders, offended by Rushdie's book, *The Satanic Verses*, were unable to use the law against the author. This gave rise to calls for the law of blasphemy either to be extended to all religions or removed from the statute book.

The law of defamation is a major restriction of freedom of speech. Both spoken and written words can be defamatory, the actions being for slander or libel respectively. Libel can be a criminal offence but usually actions are brought for damages in tort (civil wrong). A statement is defamatory if it tends to expose another to hatred, ridicule or contempt or to cause him or her to be shunned by reasonable persons. It is a defence that the statement was true, or was a fair comment on a matter of public interest. Moreover, if the statement was made in a situation covered by absolute privilege, as in proceedings in Parliament or in the courts, there can be no action. If qualified privilege applies, for instance to the press reporting of proceedings in Parliament, then it is necessary to prove malice.

The law of defamation is criticised because of the high costs involved in bringing or defending an action and the unreasonably high damages sometimes awarded by juries. This means that whilst the law works to limit the exercise of free speech when it is used to defame the wealthy, it does little to deter the making of defamatory statements against less affluent members of society. Thus the wealthy are protected from fair criticism as well as libel, while the poor are exposed to the full rigours of freedom of speech.

More restrictions upon free speech arise from the requirements of national security and the Official Secrets Act (as outlined above), and from the law of confidentiality. This applies in a private as well as a public context such that an individual cannot profit from the disclosure of confidential information obtained from his or her employer, or even, in certain circumstances, from his or her spouse.

Free speech and the media

Most of the above constraints apply to newspapers and other publications. In addition governments make some use of prior restraints. These are intended to prevent or delay the publication of material, which may well not have been the subject of legal proceedings if it had been published. Hence prior restraint is equivalent to censorship.

Prior restraints include the 'D-Notice' system and injunctions imposed by the courts. The D-Notice system, established in 1912, is voluntary and has no legal authority. It is administered by the Defence Press and Broadcasting Committee, which consists of government officials from departments concerned with national security together with representatives of the press and broadcasting. This Committee issues D-Notices addressed to newspapers and broadcasters, and dealing with categories of information which 'the government considers it has a duty to protect, and which it asks editors and publishers to refrain from publishing, as being particularly sensitive for reasons of national security' (Defence Press and Broadcasting Committee, 12 January 1992). The Notices are advisory only for both the government and the media.

Injunctions act as a legal prior restraint upon publication. In the United States such a restraint is generally considered unacceptable, on the ground that the press should be free to 'publish and be damned'. Thus newspapers can publish what they choose but must be prepared to accept the consequences if they have acted unlawfully. In Britain injunctions are granted by the courts in 'exceptional cases'. These include cases where it is argued that publication will damage a person's reputation, breach commercial or government confidentiality, or be against the interests of national security. On this basis injunctions were effectively used by the late Robert Maxwell to prevent the publication of allegations against him. They also served to prevent or delay disclosures concerning the effects of the drugs thalidomide and primelod, both of which, it was alleged, had been responsible for producing deformities in babies.

The government has also been active in seeking injunctions, particularly since the law of confidentiality has been extended to public employees. Such applications engage the judges in balancing the public interest (of the citizen) in disclosure against the public interest (of the government on behalf of all) in secrecy. However, there would seem to be a judicial tendency to lean towards the need for confidentiality, particularly where interlocutory (temporary) injunctions are concerned, the justification being that such injunctions act only to delay publication and not to prevent publication altogether.

Interlocutory injunctions are obtained from a judge in chambers on the basis that legal action is pending against the publishing party. It is merely necessary for the party seeking the injunction to show it has an arguable case, and that damages would not constitute a suitable remedy. It was on this basis that the government secured injunctions in the *Spycatcher* saga, and postponed the showing of *The Zircon Affair*, which alleged that the launching of a spy satellite had been kept secret from Parliament (see Chapter 9). In that affair legal proceedings were never brought, the Attorney-General deciding subsequently that there was no case. Nevertheless, the injunction served a useful purpose, for by the time the programme was broadcast, public interest had waned.

The granting of injunctions clearly conflicts with any right to free speech, and in *Spycatcher* it was argued that their use was contrary to Article 10 of the European Convention of Human Rights. This argument did not find favour in the British courts, the House of Lords noting that Article 10 allowed for restrictions 'in relation to certain prescribed matters, which include "the interests of national security" and "preventing the disclosure of information received in confidence" ' (*Attorney-General* v. *Guardian Newspapers* (No. 2) [1988] 3 WLR 776).

Subsequently, however, the European Court of Human Rights (ECHR) proved to be more receptive to a joint petition by the newspapers concerned. The ECHR reaffirmed that for freedom of speech to be restrained, there had to be a 'pressing social need' for such restraint. It accepted that the initial interlocutory injunctions were justified on the grounds of national security and confidentiality, but held that these grounds were no longer valid once the book had been published in the United States. The United Kingdom had therefore breached Article 10 in continuing to prevent publication beyond this time. The ruling of the ECHR indicated that it attached a greater weight than the House of Lords to freedom of speech, and that its interpretation of what constituted a 'pressing social need' was correspondingly more restrictive.

The Contempt of Court Act 1981

A failure to comply with the terms of an injunction constitutes contempt of court, an offence which can be punished by imprisonment. It is also a contempt while a case is before the court to publish information which may create a 'substantial risk that the course of justice . . . will be seriously impeded or prejudiced' (Contempt of Court Act 1981, s. 2 (1)). This restriction on freedom of speech is seen as necessary to ensure a fair trial. More controversial is the requirement that journalists and editors must reveal sources of information, if ordered to do so by the court, or risk being in contempt. Prior to the passing of the Contempt of Court Act, the making of orders was entirely dependent upon judicial discretion. However, section 10 provides that disclosure of a source may be ordered only if it is 'established to the satisfaction of the court that disclosure is necessary in the interests of justice or national security or for the prevention of disorder or crime'.

The protection of sources

The effect of section 10 was discussed by the House of Lords in *Secretary of State for Defence* v. *Guardian Newspapers* [1985] 1 AC 339. The *Guardian* had published a copy of a memorandum which originated from the Ministry of Defence. It concerned the installation of cruise missiles at British bases and had been delivered to the newspaper anonymously. The Secretary of State demanded the return of the document, which had been specially marked, so that the identity of the 'leaker' could be determined. He accepted that the publication of the document itself had not constituted a risk to national security, although it had been politically embarrassing. However, he argued that the existence of a 'leaker' within the department was a threat to security.

The House of Lords ruled that section 10 created a presumption that a journalist was entitled to protect his or her sources. This meant that the onus was on the party seeking the information to provide sufficient evidence to satisfy the court that one of the grounds stated in section 10 applied. On a split decision (3–2) the court held that the sworn statement from the Ministry of Defence, asserting that it was necessary to discover the source of the leak for security reasons, constituted sufficient evidence. There were strong dissenting judgments from Lords Scarman and Fraser. However, it would have been difficult for the House of Lords to find other than that the source should have been revealed because by the time the case reached the court, the 'leaker' was known to have been a young clerk, Sarah Tisdall, and she had already pleaded guilty to a charge under section 2 of the Official Secrets Act.

The presumption that journalistic sources are protected was upheld subsequently by the House of Lords in 1988 in a case concerning 'insider dealing' (*Re an Inquiry Under the Company Securities (Insider Dealing) Act 1985* [1988] 2 WLR 33, in which Lord Griffiths stated that the effect of section 10 was 'to recognise and establish that in the interests of a free and effective press it is in the public interest that a journalist should be entitled to protect his sources unless some other overriding public interest requires him to reveal them.' The 'overriding public interest' here was the prevention of crime. As with all statutes, the precise effect depends in part on judicial understanding of the breadth of exceptions and the nature of the evidence needed to sustain them.

Government control of broadcasting

Television and radio operate under the same restrictions as the press. In addition, the Broadcasting Act 1990 (section 10) renewed the Home Secretary's power to give notice to the Independent Broadcasting Authority to refrain from broadcasting any matter or classes of matter specified in the notice. The same power resides in relation to the BBC in clause 13 (4) of the BBC's Charter and Licence Agreement. The power is used infrequently. The application of political pressure in the form of a 'request' is usually sufficient to prevent the screening or broadcasting of a particular programme, and it was this less formal action that resulted in the postponement of Duncan Campbell's programme on Zircon.

However, in October 1988 the Home Secretary took the unusual step of issuing notices to the BBC and the IBA. These required them to refrain from broadcasting 'any words spoken, whether in the course of an interview or discussion or otherwise, by a person who appears or is heard on the programme', where 'the person speaking the words represents or purports to represent' any proscribed terrorist organisation, Sinn Fein, Republican Sinn Fein or the Ulster Defence Association, or where 'the words support or solicit or invite support for such an organisation.'

The expressed intention of the notices was to deprive terrorist organisations in Northern Ireland of a political platform for their views – what Margaret Thatcher had called the 'oxygen of publicity'. The Home Secretary feared that the appearance of representatives of such groups on television increased their standing and gave legitimacy to terrorism. This opinion was not shared by most broadcasters, who considered the notices an infringement of free speech, an unjustified limitation upon editorial freedom, and a restriction on the right of people in a democratic society to have access to the full range of opinions. The ban was evaded by the broadcasters by using an actor to speak the words of the 'terrorist' (usually Gerry Adams, President of Sinn Fein).

A group of journalists challenged the legality of the notices, claiming, among other things, that they breached Article 10 of the European Convention of Human Rights. The case went to the House of Lords, where the journalists were unsuccessful in their challenge. In his judgment Lord Ackner stressed that it was not for British judges to 'police the operation of the Convention' as it had not been incorporated into British law. All the judges could do was to use the Convention as an aid to interpretation where there was an ambiguity within a statute. He recognised no such ambiguities in the legislation which gave the Home Secretary the power to give notice. Moreover, because the Convention was not law within Britain, it was not a source of rights and obligations. Thus the question of a breach of Article 10 did not arise (*R.* v. *Secretary of State for Home Department, ex parte Brind and others* [1991] 2 WLR 588 (H. of L.)).

The ruling in *Brind* was a disappointment to those who believed that the British courts were moving closer to an acceptance of the European Convention of Human Rights as a means to uphold 'rights', such as free speech. However, it is significant that in 1993 Lord Woolf, one of the new Law Lords appointed since that ruling, declared his belief that the court would decide the case differently today. The ban was lifted in September 1994.

Freedom of information

There is in Britain no recognised legal or political right to freedom of information. The presumption has always been that the government can be trusted to tell the public what it needs to know, and the Official Secrets Act is based on the premise that the executive has the right to decide what information it will make available. Throughout government the administrator's 'need-to-know' principle (give information only to those who absolutely need it) is operated restrictively (hardly anyone else needs to know; if we give people information, they will only ask for more).

Moreover, secrecy is not confined to government and its agencies, but extends into the commercial world, where minimal requirements are placed upon industry to publish information which in many other countries, most notably the United States, is required to be in the public domain. Thus in Britain the content of emissions from factory chimneys and of industrial waste is frequently kept secret, whereas in the United States the information is publicly available under the Freedom of Information Act of 1966 (many other countries, including Canada, Australia and New Zealand now have similar laws).

A Freedom of Information Act changes the norm of secrecy to the legitimate expectation that citizens have a right to information unless a justification can be made for withholding it. Such an Act allows for the protection of sensitive information (the usual categories being national security, the investigation of crime, confidentiality, diplomatic relations, the Budget and the economy) but this protection has to be justified. Governments are inclined to see freedom of information as undermining their authority and the essential processes of governing. 'Trust us', they say. The liberal constitutionalist believes in transparency, not trust; the powerful must always be exposed to persistent and rigorous scrutiny.

There is already legislation which allows access to some information. For example, the Data Protection Act 1984 provides for individuals to have access to data concerning themselves which is kept on computer, and there are a number of Acts, notably the Local Government (Access to Information) Act 1985, which require local authorities to make information available to the public. Central government has an ideological commitment to open government at the local level, but its commitment to greater openness at the centre has so far proved to be limited. However, there have been some moves towards more open government, including the appointment of a minister with a specific responsibility for this area. The result so far has been the publication of *Questions of Procedure for Ministers* (see Chapter 7), a modest unveiling of the security services, publication of the minutes of the Chancellor's regular meetings with the Governor of the Bank of England, and some relaxation in the availability of public papers (former ministers, including Margaret Thatcher, writing their memoirs, seem to have unilaterally abandoned the 'thirty-year rule').

However, proposals for a Freedom of Information Act have been dismissed. The government, and other opponents of statutory Freedom of Information, argue that a great deal of information is already available (for example, through the parliamentary select committees), that some part of the activities of government (policy-making, negotiations, national security, dealings with personal matters) must remain confidential, and that openness of government can be achieved by other means.

It has to be conceded that a Freedom of Information Act does not automatically produce open government. Much of the massive amounts of information produced is of little significance, and skill in selection and searching is necessary. Another limitation lies in the necessary exceptions, and the way these are interpreted by the courts. Further, the operation of a Freedom of Information Act is likely to be expensive (though experience in other countries shows the point may be exaggerated); and the main beneficiaries of access to information are commercial companies and criminals and not the ordinary citizen.

There remains a persuasive case for a Freedom of Information Act. Access to information improves the quality of the questioning of government by the public and its representatives, and discourages the government's normal high selectivity in revealing information. But the fundamental importance of a Freedom of Information Act lies in the changed culture and expectations that it brings, a culture of openness and transparency, in place of secrecy and opacity. In a constitution dominated by the executive, such an Act might play a part in redressing the balance.

16

GOVERNMENT AND THE AGGRIEVED CITIZEN

The constitutional arrangements for the redress of grievances have developed haphazardly in response to perceived needs, and they lack system and coherence. The law and the courts play a relatively small part, at least in comparison with other countries, and most of the ways in which the citizen can seek redress are political, administrative or quasi-judicial rather than legal. However, the role of the courts has been increasing, particularly during the 1980s with a fourfold growth in the number of applications for judicial review. Further, the courts play an important role in the prevention of grievance by their continuing concern for procedural fairness, including the encouragement of consultation in the decision-making process.

Political or administrative redress

The simplest procedure open to an individual aggrieved by administrative action (as distinct from policy, which is a matter for the ballot box) is a direct complaint to the administrative body concerned. This is encouraged by the Citizen's Charter, which now applies to many areas of government. The Charter is concerned to impose upon public bodies clearly defined duties, generally related to the meeting of minimal standards, and to provide the citizen or consumer with an avenue of complaint, if these are not met. In some cases, British Rail for example, there is an entitlement to compensation. Direct complaint to the responsible official has also been encouraged in the case of the Next Steps executive agencies, many of which operate under Charters.

However, there are still many areas of government which are not covered by the Citizen's Charter or are not considered suitable for the Next Steps programme. These are areas where a considerable degree of discretion operates, for example immigration, or in the policy areas of central government. In addition, there are some functions where responsibility is divided. Thus whilst the Benefits Agency has certain delivery obligations towards its clients, what it delivers, that is, the amount of benefit or the entitlement to it, is the responsibility of the minister.

An individual, aggrieved by administrative action, can also complain through his or her Member of Parliament. Complaints coming under the direct responsibility of a minister are usually raised, at least initially, in correspondence to the department, but a few may form the basis of written or even oral Parliamentary Questions. Success for the aggrieved citizen is dependent on the tenacity of the MP and the responsiveness of the minister and his officials. The most likely outcome is a quick, courteous but firm justification of the decision or practice complained about.

The establishment of Next Steps agencies has reduced the areas for which ministers will answer themselves. Such agencies are still the direct responsibility of ministers, but ministers suggest that Members of Parliament should contact the Chief Executives directly, rather than approaching the minister. (This has always been the case with matters concerning the day-to-day running of the nationalised industries.) Initially, this delegation of responsibility for answering complaints caused concern amongst Members, as, unlike ministerial replies, responses by Chief Executives were not included in *Hansard*, and thus not publicly circulated. However, answers by Chief Executives are now recorded in *Hansard* under a general authorisation given by the relevant minister. Some concern remains that ministers may refuse to respond on agency matters, even where an agency response has not satisfied the Member of Parliament, or where responsibility is unclear and policy matters are involved.

Ombudsmen

The Parliamentary Commissioner for Administration

The office of the Parliamentary Commissioner for Administration (PCA, or, after the Swedish exemplar, Ombudsman) was created by the Parliamentary Commissioner Act 1967 to provide protection for the individual against injustice arising from administrative malpractice. The PCA is appointed on terms similar to those governing the tenure of office of High Court judges, which are designed to preserve independence from government and political pressure. The first three Commissioners were all retired senior civil servants, and the staff are mostly civil servants on secondment. In that way the Ombudsman was rooted in the administrative structure. However, independence has grown with age and experience. The Commissioner acts within a parliamentary framework in the sense that he investigates complaints brought to him by Members of Parliament, and reports to a committee of the House of Commons, but his reports are published and he has attained an independent standing.

Jurisdiction

The terms of reference of the PCA are to investigate complaints by members of the public who claim 'to have sustained injustice in consequence of maladministration' (s. 5 (1)). 'Maladministration' was not defined, but it was intended to refer to the manner of the making and implementation of a decision or procedure, and the Act specifically exempts 'the merits of a decision taken without maladministration . . . in the exercise of a discretion vested in [a] department'. The Minister responsible for the Bill, Richard Crossman, mentioned 'bias, neglect, inattention, delay, incompetence, ineptitude, perversity, turpitude, arbitrariness' as examples of what might constitute maladministration. This was too broad to be entirely helpful.

Later the select committee proposed that maladministration should include a decision which was 'thoroughly bad in quality', or a decision which gave rise to hardship or injustice. The PCA has been cautious about incursions into the merits of decisions (merit as substantive policy), but seems to have interpreted his remit broadly to include

> corruption, bias, unfair discrimination, harshness, misleading a member of the public as to his rights, failing to notify him properly of his rights or to explain the reasons for a decision, general high-handedness, using powers for a wrong purpose, failing to consider relevant materials, taking irrelevant material into account, losing or failing to reply to correspondence, delaying unreasonably before making a tax refund or presenting a tax demand or dealing with an application for a grant or licence, and so on. (de Smith and Brazier, 1989, p. 649)

In practice such concerns inevitably move into the consideration of the merit of a decision, and thus across the blurred interface of administration and policy.

The Commissioner can investigate actions taken 'in the exercise of administrative functions' by or on behalf of the departments of central government (s. 5(1)). The range of bodies which come within the PCA's jurisdiction was considerably extended in 1987. It includes bodies such as the Equal Opportunities Commission, Sports Council, Legal Aid Board, Charity Commission, the Royal Mint, and Scottish Tourist Board. The regulatory bodies, such as Ofwat and Oftel, established with the privatisation of the monopoly industries are also included.

However, there are serious limitations on the work of the PCA. He can only investigate complaints submitted in writing to a Member of Parliament and referred by the Member. He has no jurisdiction to deal directly with complaints from members of the public, and the aggrieved individual is dependent on the interest and services of a Member of Parliament. (In practice if the PCA receives a serious complaint directly from the public, he will inquire of the Member of Parliament about proceeding with investigation.)

In his 1983 Annual Report the PCA commented upon his inability to investigate on his own initiative:

> So far as I know I am alone among the hundred or so national ombudsmen of the world in having no powers to investigate on my own initiative apparent maladministration which has come or been brought to my notice. . . . I have felt it a reflection on a parliamentary democracy which prides itself on its considerate attitude towards its citizens that this country alone should impose such a restriction. (HC322, para. 8)

This indirect relationship between the PCA and citizens was justified as a proper support to the relationship of the Member and constituents, and as a means of protecting the Parliamentary Commissioner from an avalanche of inappropriate complaints, many of which would be better dealt with directly by the department concerned or would be outside the PCA's jurisdiction.

In practice these arrangements have not proved entirely satisfactory. Referral rates vary among MPs: roughly two-fifths of Members do not refer any complaints in any one year, and the rest refer two each on average each year. Members of Parliament have not fulfilled their gate-keeping or filtering role very adequately. The PCA stated in his Annual Report for 1990:

> As in previous years, most of the cases considered by me for investigation . . . were rejected. The proportion of cases accepted for investigation was 23 per cent. (HC299, para. 81)

Over half the complaints were rejected because they did not concern administrative actions.

The PCA cannot investigate all complaints concerning administration within government departments and other public bodies. Schedule 3 of the Act lists 'matters not subject to investigation'. The most significant exclusions relate to public service personnel matters; here the government has continued to argue that it is not appropriate for the PCA to investigate complaints brought by employees against their employer, and contractual and commercial matters. This exclusion has caused concern to the PCA, since the relationship between a citizen and a department or public body, in particular NDPB, may often be of a contractual nature.

A further limitation under the Act is that the PCA cannot investigate cases where the person aggrieved has, or had, a remedy in a court of law or a right of appeal to a minister or a tribunal. However, the Act does allow that he may investigate a complaint if he is satisfied that in the circumstances it is not reasonable to expect the legal remedies to be sought or to be of use. The PCA has exercised this discretion liberally, accepting complaints despite the possibility of a successful legal challenge.

This was the case with the investigation by the PCA in 1975 of the raising of television licence fees, which also came before the courts (for details, see *Congreve* v. *Home Office* [1976], Chapter 6). The PCA did not find that there had been maladministration, although he considered that the Home Office had been inefficient and had shown a lack of foresight. The court found the action to be unlawful. The difference in outcome indicates that maladministration does not necessarily relate to the lawfulness of the action. The administration can still be 'good', or at least not bad enough for an injustice to have been done, even if based on an unlawful premise. Thus although there may be some overlap in the role of the PCA and the courts, their concerns are different.

Procedure

Until 1993 the discretion of the PCA as to whether or not to investigate was regarded as absolute, the courts having held his decision to be non-reviewable. However, in *R.* v. *Parliamentary Commissioner for Administration, ex parte Dyer* (*Independent*, 23 October 1993), the Divisional Court held that the PCA's decisions were open to review by the courts, though it was recognised that the Commissioner's discretion was wide. If the PCA decides to embark on an investigation, he must provide the principal officer of the department or public body concerned and any person against whom allegations are made with an opportunity to comment on the allegations. Investigations must be conducted in private but in other ways the PCA has more powers than a court. He can determine his own procedure for investigation. Like a court he can administer oaths. He can interview anyone he considers necessary to his inquiry and call for any documents which would be required to be produced in civil proceedings in court.

Ministers cannot claim public interest immunity or confidentiality to protect these documents as they can in a court of law (see Chapter 5). The only restriction with regard to evidence relates to Cabinet documents. Moreover, if his inquiry is obstructed, or if there is 'any act or omission . . . which, if the investigation was a proceeding in the Court, would constitute contempt of court, the Commissioner may certify the offence to the Court' (s. 9 (1)). The court will then take the appropriate action.

Once his investigation is complete, the PCA produces a report. He can be restrained by notice from a minister from including in the report any information which 'in the opinion of the minister . . . would be prejudicial to the safety of the State or otherwise contrary to the public interest' (s. 1193). A copy of the report goes to the relevant Member of Parliament, the principal officer concerned, and to any other person against whom allegations were made. Moreover, if the PCA considers that injustice has been done and this injustice has not been remedied, he can lay a special report before both Houses of Parliament.

The PCA works to a special select committee of the House of Commons, may submit reports at any time, and renders an Annual Report. It is of some significance that the Select Committee on the Parliamentary Commissioner for Administration survived the general reform of the select committees in 1979, despite the Procedure committee's preference for each departmental Committee to take over the investigation of maladministration.

The effectiveness of the PCA

Much of the caseload of the PCA is concerned with complaints about the Inland Revenue and the Department of Social Security, departments which affect the citizen's most sensitive concern, the pocket. In 1990 the PCA completed 177 investigations, which, on average, took fourteen months each. In 74 cases he 'found the complaint against the body principally concerned wholly justified'; in 83 cases he 'found it necessary (whilst not upholding the main complaint) to criticise at least some aspects of the body's handling of matters'; in the remaining 20 cases he 'found no justification for the complaint in 18 cases and made no findings in 2 cases' (Annual Report, 1990, HC299).

In those cases where there has been injustice, the PCA may suggest a remedy, usually compensation of some kind, and/or an amendment to rules or procedures to ensure the incident is not repeated. The PCA has no authority to insist upon reform, remedy or compensation, but his recommendations carry weight and the Permanent Secretary may be summoned before the Committee to explain a refusal to take remedial action. Thus the Commissioner recommends, with the power of suggestion rather than command, but, unlike a judge, he can usefully make informal approaches and engage in discussion. There is seldom resistance by government to making small payments in compensation, for example back pay, or compensation for interest lost or nuisance caused by delay. This is literally the small change of politics, but of concern to aggrieved citizens.

The weakness as much as the strength of the Parliamentary Commissioner was demonstrated in the Barlow Clowes investigation, undertaken in 1988.

The Barlow Clowes affair

This was the most extensive investigation ever undertaken by the Ombudsman. He had several hundred referrals made to him which he joined into one action. The matter concerned the loss by some eighteen thousand people of the money they had invested in Barlow Clowes and an associated company. The loss was not because the high-risk investments had failed but because the funds had been misappropriated by Peter Clowes. The company had been licensed by the DTI and it was alleged that the Department had been negligent in fulfilling its regulatory function. There was much public and parliamentary disquiet because many of those affected were elderly people, seeking to provide for retirement, and mostly new investors, attracted to the market by its successes in the 1980s and the government's encouragement of private investment. They were entitled, it was argued, to protection, not from the consequences of dubious and risky investment, but from fraud.

The PCA, Sir Anthony Barrowclough, found that there had been 'significant maladministration' on five counts. These involved licensing decisions, the failure of the Department to heed the warnings given, and the inadequacy of its investigations, which, he considered, stemmed from a 'lack of a sufficiently rigorous and enquiring approach' (*Report from the Parliamentary Commission for Administration: The Barlow Clowes Affair* (1989), HC76, para. 8.13). Sir Anthony concluded that the Department was liable for compensation.

The Secretary of State at the DTI, Nicholas Ridley, refused to accept that there had been maladministration and declared: 'In the Government's view, the department's handling of the case was within the acceptable range of standards reasonably to be expected of a regulator' (HC Deb., 19 December 1989, col. 104).

Ridley's response indicated the inherent weakness of the PCA's position. However, the PCA was not willing to be disregarded, and replied that 'the grounds for questioning my findings have left me unconvinced' (para. 8.21). In the end the government paid £150 million compensation because of the 'exceptional circumstances' and in deference to the Commissioner. However, such compensation would not have been forthcoming but for the considerable political pressure applied by Conservative backbenchers, whose constituents were among those affected.

This lack of authority of the PCA to insist upon compensation, changes in procedure, or a departmental review of all like cases is understandable in the perspective of government; but it is a serious weakness of the office of the Parliamentary Commissioner. As a last resort the Commissioner must rely upon political pressure. Other factors limiting his effectiveness include the requirement that all complaints are channelled through Members of Parliament, the size of his staff and the comparatively low public profile of his work. As a result he makes relatively few investigations and very few attract publicity. On the other hand, the very presence of the Commissioner with his authority to conduct in-depth investigations has made departments think more carefully about their administration; and, for those citizens who have a grievance, the Commissioner provides a free means of seeking redress.

The institution of the Parliamentary Commissioner for Administration has some constitutional consequences. The concern of Parliament not to be by-passed has been noted, but the work of the Commissioner has some consequences too for the doctrine of ministerial responsibility and civil service anonymity. Under that doctrine the minister answers to Parliament for alleged maladministration, and the anonymous civil servants answer in private to the minister. In an early case (the Sachsenhausen inquiry, 1968) the Foreign Secretary, George Brown, protested vehemently that the establishment of the PCA undermined the accountability of ministers to Parliament and the anonymity of civil servants. In another investigation, concerning losses arising from a collapsed travel company, Court Line (1975), the minister concerned, Tony Benn, exercised his right and duty to account to the House of Commons by rejecting the Commissioner's criticisms on the floor of the House, and winning the subsequent vote.

Both Brown and Benn were correct, but Brown at least failed to see what is now much clearer, that accountability to Parliament through the PCA for these relatively minor cases of maladministration is likely to be far more effective than ministerial accountability, and its effect on the civil service is likely to be salutary rather than demoralising (as George Brown alleged). Altogether, the institution of the Ombudsman may be seen as a valuable complement to the often inadequate processes of ministerial accountability.

Local Government Commissioners: the Local Government Ombudsmen

The Local Government Act 1974 provided for Commissioners with jurisdiction to make investigations into injustices caused by maladministration in any local or police authority or any statutory authority with the power to raise money which is specified by an Order in Council (Local Government Act 1974, s. 25 (1)). As in the case of the PCA, Local Commissioners exercise discretion as to whether or not to investigate and similar exclusions apply. Again, they are not authorised to question the merits of a decision. However, in contrast to the PCA, Local Commissioners can receive complaints in writing directly from members of the public, and their reports receive more publicity. Examples of the Local Government Ombudsman's work include findings of maladministration in unreasonable delay by education authorities in the assessment of special educational needs.

The Local Government Act requires a local authority to make reports available to the public and to notify the Commissioner of the action it has taken, or proposes to take, in the light of his report. The Commissioner is entitled to make a further report if he is not satisfied with the local authority's response. He can also insist that a council which refuses to take effective action publishes statements in the local press which explain its failure to comply with the recommendations of the Commissioner.

Local Commissioners have had their jurisdiction tested in the courts, in particular in relation to intrusions into policy, and matters for which a legal remedy was available. These cases have demonstrated some resistance by local councils to administrative review by the Commissioner, and a readiness by the courts to determine that the Local Commissioners remain inside the boundaries set by Parliament in the Local Government Act. Neither the councils nor the courts are willing to yield power to the Ombudsman.

The number of complaints made to the Local Commissioners has shown a marked increase. In 1983/4 there were just over three thousand complaints. In 1990/1 there were over nine thousand. This suggests that the Commissioners have been more effective than the PCA in publicising their role and that they are more accessible. It is likely, too, that maladministration is both more frequent and more obvious at a local level, because of the direct impact of local government functions in many areas of daily life.

A proliferation of Ombudsmen

Since the 1970s, Commissioners have been instituted for Northern Ireland and for the Health Service; and in 1990 the Courts and

Legal Services Act created the position of Legal Services Ombudsman. Ombudsmen have also been established in the private sector, notably in banking and insurance. Thus specialist offices for the investigation and redress of grievance have come to be accepted as a normal and useful part of a democratic polity. The work of the Commissioners is undramatic and marginal in significance, yet it has modestly increased fairness and justice, and thus enhanced the rights of individuals.

Quasi-judicial remedies: tribunals

There are now about two thousand tribunals, not all statutory and not all actually called 'tribunal', concerned with the adjudication of disputes between the state and the citizen in the administration of regulatory legislation and welfare provision. Thus the tribunals are an important location for the redress of grievances against the state. Matters dealt with include disputes over tax assessments, compensation for the compulsory purchase of land, the grant of welfare benefits and pensions, appeals related to disability allowances, mental health and immigration. Tribunals are also used extensively to resolve employment and landlord/tenant disputes, which may or may not involve government agencies.

The structure of tribunals developed in the twentieth century without systematic thought or planning, as the functions of government expanded and the need to deal with grievances grew. This typically *ad hoc* approach to the constitution was complemented by the eventual establishment of a committee chaired by a former senior civil servant, Lord Franks, to review the problem. (Thus is the British constitution constructed.) In 1957 the Franks Committee on Administrative Tribunals and Inquiries provided the structure of tribunals with recognition, legitimation, a working philosophy and a supervisory framework.

Franks' contribution was in effect to confirm that the tribunals were neither part of the administrative process, nor quite courts of law; rather, their function lay in what might be called administrative adjudication. Hence their work must bear the characteristics of the judicial process – openness, fairness and impartiality. Following Franks, two bodies were established, a Council on Tribunals for England and Wales and a Committee for Scotland, to supervise the tribunals, and to ensure as far as possible the attainment of Franks' objectives.

Tribunals are mainly established by statute. The Tribunals and Inquiries Act 1971 provides that the members of the tribunal shall be appointed by the Minister (s. 6 (1)). The Minister also has the power 'to make, approve, confirm or concur in procedural rules', although he has to consult with the Council on Tribunals (s. 8 (1)). Tribunals therefore fall within the Minister's responsibility although their quasi-judicial nature is demonstrated by the fact that they come under the supervision of the courts, as well as the Council on Tribunals.

However, tribunals operate outside the normal court system and provide an alternative, and usually more appropriate, means of dispute resolution for the citizen. They are seen as having certain advantages over the courts:

1. Tribunals tend to be less formal than courts and their procedure is simpler. This enables the layperson to present a case without facing the procedural complexities of a court of law. Most tribunals also adopt an inquisitorial rather than an adversarial style, aiming to bring to light all the relevant facts, thus attaining truth and justice directly, rather than as the uncertain product of a battle of rival advocates. However, an adversarial procedure is used for settling disputes between parties, notably in Employment and Land tribunals.
2. Tribunals generally provide a quicker resolution of disputes than the courts – though delays do occur, for example in Industrial Tribunals, because of 'funding difficulties'.
3. Tribunals provide a much cheaper means of seeking redress than the courts. The cost of the officials and building come out of public funds and it is seldom necessary for an individual to take legal advice or to be represented. In addition, as a general principle, applicants usually receive an allowance towards costs. Applicants to tribunals may take advantage of advice agencies which offer specialist advice in presenting a case. Some of the more formal and adversarial tribunals allow legal representation, and the Council on Tribunals is of the opinion that 'there are certain tribunals where the complexity of the law and the adversarial nature of the proceedings make skilled legal representation necessary' (Annual

Report, 1989/90, HC64). However, this raises the question of cost, and legal aid is only available for proceedings before the Land Tribunal and the Employment Appeal Tribunal.

4. Tribunals are intended to be more accessible than the courts and familiar to citizens. They also provide 'open' justice, in that hearings are usually in public, and reasons for decisions may be given.
5. Tribunals are by their nature specialist bodies, unlike the courts. Members of the tribunal usually have specialist knowledge or expertise in the subject, although there is considerable variation between tribunals, and the chairman is normally a lawyer. However, with few exceptions, tribunals come under the supervision of the ordinary courts and thus can find themselves 'bound' through the doctrine of precedent by a decision of the 'non-expert' court. This not only intrudes on the function of the specialist tribunal but also reduces the ability of the tribunal to be flexible in its approach to cases.
6. Tribunals, unlike the Ombudsmen, provide the citizen with a means of redress where the merits (as distinct from the processes) of a decision are in doubt.

Thus tribunals have substantial advantages for the citizen with a grievance, and indeed for administrators faced with difficult decisions. But the system is not without weaknesses; in particular, the sheer number of tribunals and the obscurity and confusion of their jurisdictions and the absence of publicity about their purposes diminish accessibility. The proper place of lawyers and legal procedures in their work is uncertain.

This reflects the necessarily awkward constitutional position, straddling the executive and judicial functions. On the one hand, tribunals come within the responsibility of the Minister and are part of the administrative structure; on the other, they lie within the supervisory jurisdiction of the courts and their function is adjudicatory. Such 'awkwardness' is unavoidable, unless administrative justice is to be handed to the courts, and thus put beyond the reach of most citizens. In short, there is a good deal to be said for the unsystematic system of tribunals.

Apart from the tribunals, there is sometimes a right of appeal to the Minister on the merits of a decision; but this is available only if it is expressly provided by legislation. Most frequently appeal is allowed on decisions taken by local authorities or other statutory bodies, for example on planning decisions and on some educational matters.

The courts

The courts play a comparatively small role in the redress of grievances. Political, administrative or quasi-judicial mechanisms have dominated constitutional arrangements. However, because legal decisions are recorded and have legal force, their effect is significant and long term. Moreover, in certain instances the courts provide the only means of challenge and of securing a remedy.

Judicial review

Judicial review is the mechanism by which the lawfulness of a decision can be challenged on the grounds of illegality, irrationality, procedural impropriety and proportionality; but it is the way in which the decision was made and not the substance of the decision that is open to review by the courts (see Chapter 6). Judicial review is a discretionary remedy which means that the individual has to apply for *leave* from the courts to make an application for a remedy. Whether or not this is granted depends in part on the applicant's *standing* (that is, the interest he or she has in the matter). The principles of *standing* or *locus standi* enable the courts to limit the bringing of actions to those with 'sufficient interest', thereby excluding those whose motive for bringing an action against a public body is simply political or for publicity.

The granting of leave also depends on the justiciability of the subject matter of the application (is it a suitable matter for the court to hear?), its acceptance as being a matter of 'public' rather than 'private' law, the availability of alternative appeal procedures, and any statutory limitation of the court's jurisdiction (as in the case of security matters). As a consequence of the discretionary nature of judicial review, the percentage of applicants granted leave varies from judge to judge, one survey suggesting that the variation ranges from a 75 per cent success rate to only 25 per cent.

The differences arise from the very different approaches to *standing* taken by the High Court judges.

The discretionary nature of judicial review extends to the remedies. An individual has no right to a remedy, even if he or she has proved to the satisfaction of the court that the public body acted unlawfully. Remedies include a declaration – a statement of the law as it relates to the situation, which may result in the quashing of a decision. This is also the effect of the public law remedy, *certiorari*. The quashing of a decision puts the parties back to the position prior to the making of the decision, unless the decision has been quashed for being unreasonable or irrational, or being a misuse of power – in which case it remains quashed.

Other remedies sought by applicants for judicial review include *prohibition*, which prevents an unlawful act being performed, *mandamus*, which compels the performance of a public duty, and an *injunction*, which may either restrain an unlawful action or compel the performance of a particular act. Damages only exceptionally attach to an application for judicial review.

Judicial review is being increasingly seen as an important means of securing redress against a public body. The three areas responsible for the most applications during the 1980s and 1990s have been housing, including the accommodation of homeless persons, immigration, and planning and environmental issues. However, applications for judicial review are diverse. They cover matters concerned with social security benefits, education, health, licensing, local government tax or rates, income tax and VAT. New legislation is likely to produce a surge of applications in related areas to determine and test the law, and to contest its operation by public bodies. For example, Education Acts, which increased parents' rights and provided for the 'opt-out' of schools from local authority control, gave rise to a small flood of applications for judicial review.

As well as public law actions against public bodies, the citizen can also bring actions for damages in private law. In general the principles that apply to private individuals and companies also apply to public bodies. Thus damages can be sought for breach of contract or for negligence, nuisance, trespass and other torts. However, the citizen faces the heavy costs and uncertainties of litigation, especially against Crown bodies armed with substantial legal and financial resources and significant immunities and protections. Thus it is rare that an action for breach of a statutory duty lies against the Crown, for the Crown is not bound by legislation unless by express words or necessary implication. In most circumstances the legal system protects the state better than its citizens.

European Community law and the European Convention on Human Rights

British citizens have rights accorded to them under European Community law and the European Convention on Human Rights and can bring actions in the courts if these rights are breached by the government or its agencies.

All individuals within the European Community can claim rights under Community law which must be upheld by the national courts. This is known as the doctrine or principle of direct effect (see Chapter 3). In Britain such claims have been particularly effective in the area of sex discrimination in relation to equal pay for equal work and pension rights, where British legislation has been more restrictive than Community law, or has been subject to a restrictive interpretation by the courts. An individual, wishing to claim rights under EC law, brings an action in the British courts. The court may, in some instances must, refer matters of Community law to the European Court of Justice for resolution. The national court then applies the ruling from the ECJ to the case before it. Where the government is failing to fulfil Community obligations, an individual may also approach the Commission and ask it to bring an enforcement action against Britain.

British citizens also have rights under the European Convention on Human Rights, of which Britain is a signatory. However, the Convention has not been incorporated into British law and thus rights cannot be claimed directly in the national courts. Action has to be taken to the Commission, which then decides whether the case should go to the European Court of Human Rights in Strasbourg. The ruling of the Court is generally accepted by the government, which may already have taken action to correct or compensate for any infringement of the Convention. This may involve a change in the law as in *Malone* v. *Metropolitan Police Commissioner* [1979] Ch. 344.

The *Malone* case

Malone had been prosecuted for handling stolen goods. During his trial, it emerged that the Home Secretary had authorised the tapping of his telephone. Malone sought a declaration that the Home Secretary had no legal authority for issuing a warrant and thus the tapping of his phone was unlawful. He further claimed that the action was in contravention of his right to privacy and, in addition, breached Article 8 of the European Convention on Human Rights which entitled everyone to 'respect for his private and family life, his home and correspondence'. The judge, Sir Robert Megarry, noted that the tapping of Malone's telephone was carried out at the telephone exchange; there had been no need to enter Malone's property. He therefore concluded that the issuing of the warrant by the Home Secretary had not been unlawful as it had not authorised the breaking of any law. He stated that the right to privacy did not exist in English law, and, he reluctantly concluded, any action under Article 8 of the Convention on Human Rights could not be enforced by the English courts. Mr Malone therefore failed in his action.

Malone was, however, more successful before the European Court of Human Rights, which held that the tapping of Malone's telephone violated Article 8. There had to be rules and remedies which provided adequate safeguards against the abuse of power. Such conditions were necessary before the invasion of privacy could be justified to combat crime or protect national security. The judgment from the European Court of Human Rights resulted in the passing of the Interception of Communications Act 1985, which put telephone tapping on a statutory basis. However, the Act may be in contravention of Article 13 ECHR, which requires that there is an effective remedy for every violation of a right. The Interception of Communications Act provides that an individual who believes his or her phone is subject to an unauthorised, or wrongly authorized, tap may complain to a specially constituted tribunal, but the Act forbids the raising of matters relating to telephone tapping in court and excludes the courts from reviewing the exercise of tapping powers. The European Court of Human Rights may not consider this remedy effective.

Individuals have been successful in the European Court of Human Rights on a variety of issues, including the use of corporal punishment in schools, the rights of prisoners and of immigrants, the right not to join a union (under a closed shop agreement), and the rights of homosexuals. Cases have also been brought by journalists and newspaper proprietors on the basis of Article 10, which upholds the right to freedom of expression (see Chapter 15).

The European Convention on Human Rights has limited effectiveness in providing a remedy for an aggrieved individual: first, because it may be five or six years before judgment is given; secondly, because all the national avenues for seeking a remedy have to be exhausted before the Commission will consider the case; thirdly, because the British government may derogate from its obligations under the Convention. Derogations may be made in time of war 'or other public emergency threatening the life of the nation' (Art. 15). However, they are allowed only 'to the extent strictly required by the exigencies of the situation'. Britain has made a number of derogations in respect of Northern Ireland in response to the terrorist campaign.

Conclusion: the citizen and the state

The account of grievance procedures brings us back to the consideration of the nature of the whole constitutional and political structure. In a constitutional democracy the citizen may expect (indeed, has a right to expect) to exert some influence on the government through the political structure, to have his or her interests taken into account by processes of consultation and communication, and to have access to procedures for the speedy and effective remedy of grievances. In this perspective Britain seems to lack a coherent and accessible system for the redress of grievances with clear procedures, advertised options and appropriate remedies. Even so, the rather unsystematic collection of grievance procedures reviewed here may seem a reasonable response to the problems of a complex society aspiring to be constitutionally democratic.

Recent reform by a Conservative government aiming to reduce the power of the state in some areas has altered and improved the position of the citizen aggrieved or burdened by the state. The Citizen's Charters, providing for published standards for public services, and simple complaints procedures, have the great virtue of acknowledging the problem of redress of grievance, and strengthening the rather ragged culture of public accountability. The political motivation of the Charters (arguably simple hostility to public services and the need to disguise government underfunding), and the lack of popular interest, should not in the longer term detract from their constitutional utility.

Further, grievances against the state are certain to be diminished by the 'rolling back of the frontiers of the state', through the policy of privatisation and 'contracting-out' pursued by Conservative governments since 1979. However, this simply shifts the problem to the redress of grievances against private corporations. Where these are monopolies or cartels, or otherwise act in concert to restrict service of the client or customer in a competitive environment, the citizen/customer with a grievance suffers the same old problems in a different context. Hence the regulation of privatised industries is of growing significance (see Chapter 14).

Thus diminution of the state is unlikely to diminish grievances. However effective the procedures for the redress of grievances, the pursuit of redress is likely to bring the aggrieved citizen/client/customer into conflict with fellow-citizens, major private corporations and the government. Hence the citizen needs political as well as judicial and quasi-judicial structures; in a hostile environment administrative justice is no substitute for the protection of a well-founded constitution.

17

LAW AND ORDER

The basic function of government is to maintain a minimum of peace and order, thus keeping at bay that state of nature in which the seventeenth-century philosopher Hobbes famously thought life to be 'nasty, brutish and short'. Law and order, in this sense of public order, is concerned, on one side, with the structure of the courts and the workings of the legal system, and, on the other, with the exercise of the powers given to the police, the military and the security services as agents of the state to ensure the maintenance of the public peace.

Here the criticisms and anxieties of the civil libertarians confront the assurances of those who believe that Britain is a notably free society enjoying the blessings of the rule of law (sometimes narrowly understood as to do with 'law and order'). Of course there is right on both sides. The civil libertarians may sometimes be unduly suspicious, seeing an MI5 agent behind every curtain; yet there is complacency in the 'rule of law' school. On the whole, vigilance in the cause of liberty is to be preferred.

The structure of the courts

The law courts have their origins as royal courts; hence criminal cases are still brought in the name of the King or Queen, and senior barristers are called Queen's Counsel. Such distant but still

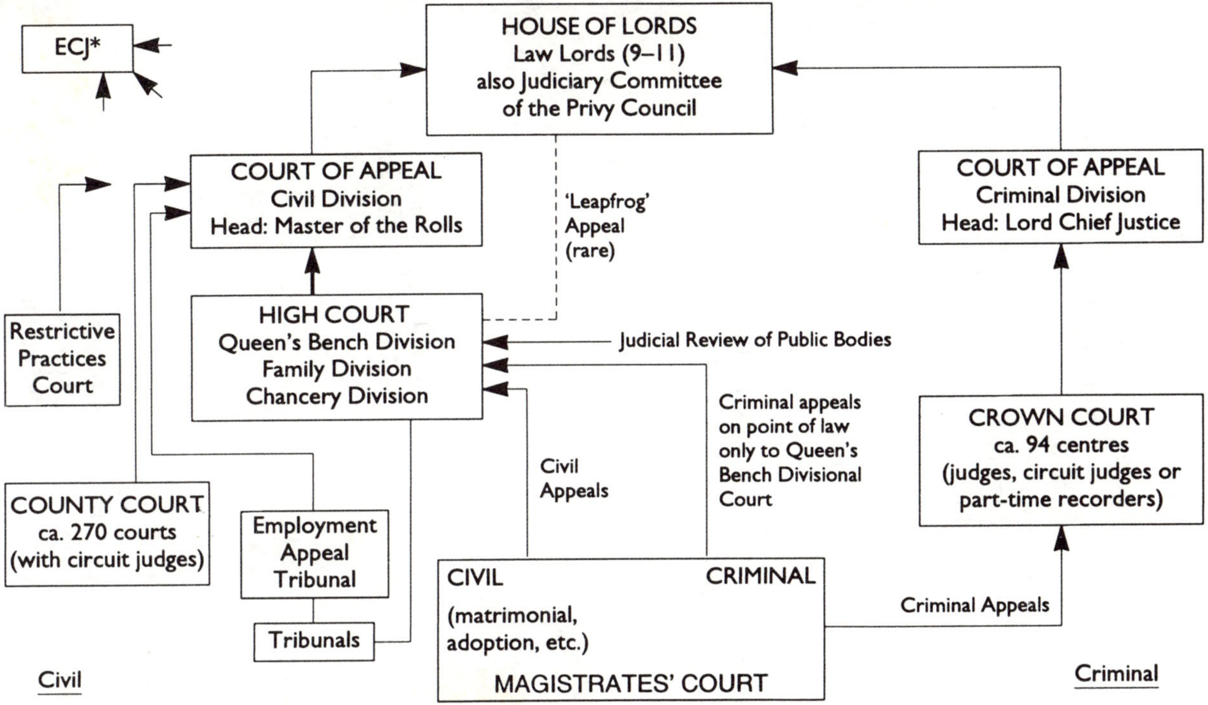

*ECJ: on a matter deemed to require clarification, any national court may, and the court of final appeal must, refer to the ECJ.

Figure 17.1 The courts of England and Wales: a simplified diagram

acknowledged origins have engendered some uncertainty about the status and jurisdiction of the courts, particularly in relation to the government. Is the Queen's government answerable to the Queen's courts? The uncertainty was demonstrated in the House of Lords in 1993 when lawyers acting for the former Home Secretary, Kenneth Baker, argued that no court had jurisdiction to make an order against a Minister of the Crown. They further argued that he could not be held in contempt of court. The Law Lords held this to be constitutionally incorrect, and ruled that a Minister of the Crown did not have the same immunities as the Crown, in the person of the sovereign (see *M.* v. *Home Office and Another*, Chapter 5).

The court system consists of two sets of courts, criminal and civil (see Figure 17.1). The final court of appeal for both criminal and civil cases is the House of Lords, that is, a court composed of the specially appointed Law Lords. The Lords also sit in a different capacity, as the Judicial Committee of the Privy Council. This used to be the final court of appeal for all Britain's overseas territories, but its role is now much reduced, as the former colonies acquired complete independence. However, the Privy Council still hears appeals from a few of the former colonies, most of which have legal systems based on the British model, and some of these may be concerned with constitutional interpretation. Thus, ironically, Britain does have a constitutional court, but it has no role in the home country.

The administration of the courts is the responsibility of the Lord Chancellor in England and Wales, and the Lord Advocate in Scotland. The Lord Chancellor is in effect a Minister of Justice, with the chief responsibility for appointing the judges, running the courts and reforming the law. In discharging these responsibilities he must accommodate his duty towards the Cabinet with his role as the senior member of the judiciary (see Chapter 6).

The civil courts

Civil cases are brought by one party against another without the participation of the state. Depending on the type and seriousness of the case, they are heard either in the County Court or in the High Court, usually by a single judge sitting without a jury. The High Court has three divisions – Queen's Bench, Family and Chancery –

the subject matter of the case determining which division hears the case (the Queen's Bench Division hears applications for judicial review against public bodies). Appeal in civil cases is to the Court of Appeal (civil division) and ultimately the House of Lords.

The criminal courts

The criminal courts hear cases brought by the Crown Prosecution Service on behalf of 'the Crown' (which here means the state). Less serious cases may be tried summarily (without a jury) in the Magistrates' Courts by two or more Justices of the Peace. The 30,000 unpaid JPs are not legally qualified but are advised on matters of law by the Clerk of the Court. They are appointed by the Lord Chancellor on the recommendation of local advisory committees. Frequently their names have been put forward by political parties although the booklet concerning the appointment and duties of Justices of the Peace, which is published on behalf of the Lord Chancellor, states that 'the Lord Chancellor . . . has regard to political affiliations only in order that he may ensure that no Bench becomes unduly overweighted in favour of any one political party'.

More serious criminal cases are tried by jury in the Crown Court, which sits in many locations. Northern Ireland is an exception: when the prosecution concerns a serious terrorist charge, the case is tried without a jury, because of the possibility of intimidation. The Crown Court also hears some appeals from the Magistrates' Courts, although appeals on questions of law go to the Divisional Court of the Queen's Bench. Appeals from the Crown Court go to the Court of Appeal (criminal division) and then, if appropriate, to the House of Lords.

The European courts

There are two European courts to which British citizens have access: the European Court of Justice, in Luxembourg, and the European Court of Human Rights at Strasbourg. The European Court of Justice is the court of the European Union and as such hears references from the British courts on matters of European Community law. It is not an appeal court; cases are in fact referred by a judge, and its jurisdiction is limited (see Chapter 3).

British citizens may also petition the Commission of the European Convention of Human Rights, on the grounds that the Convention has been infringed, with a view to bringing the case before the European Court of Human Rights. The ECHR is more like an appeal court in that the case can be brought before it by the individual concerned. However, the decisions of the Court are not binding on the British courts and a successful applicant therefore depends upon government action to give effect to the decision (see Chapter 15).

The legal system

The United Kingdom has three legal systems: for England and Wales, and for Scotland and Northern Ireland. Scotland's legal system has its own historic identity, though it is not so different that a Scottish lawyer like Lord Mackay cannot be Lord Chancellor in the British government. The system in Northern Ireland has peculiar features arising from the condition of continuing civil war in the province. However, the House of Lords in London is the final court of appeal for the United Kingdom, and the precedents it creates have a general application. Moreover, all law emanates from the same source: the Parliament at Westminster.

The legal system in England and Wales is based on common law. This gives the judges a greater role in the development of law than they have in a civil law system, such as that in France and Germany, where the law is laid down in codes. Procedure in the courts is adversarial, not inquisitorial; truth and justice arise from the open contest of the parties in court. Thus, so it is argued, justice is not only done but seen to be done. Evidence is given orally, witnesses are cross-examined in public, and lawyers, acting as rival advocates, play a prominent part in the proceedings.

The system may be criticised for being time-consuming and costly, archaic and theatrical, unduly technical and mystifying, and generally unsuited to dealing with both simple and highly technical evidence (for example, cases involving children, and cases of fraud). There is concern that the system in England and Wales has led to clear miscarriages of justice (mainly in cases concerned with terrorism, although a report by Sir John May, published in 1994 absolved the system from blame). There are also occasions when the outcome seems to have more to do with the performance of the participating lawyers than with the discovery of truth. This is confirmed by the general acceptance, not least within the legal profession, that the more expensive the lawyer, the better your chances of winning your case. Given the decline in the funding of legal aid, the courts now serve only the wealthy and the poor.

The judiciary

Appointment and accountability

The judicial system is the responsibility of the Lord Chancellor in England and Wales and the Lord Advocate in Scotland (see Chapter 6). Judicial appointments are made by the Lord Chancellor, either directly or, in the case of the most senior judges, indirectly through advice to the Prime Minister. The criteria used by the Lord Chancellor are obscure. In 1986 the Lord Chancellor's Department produced a pamphlet setting out the policy on judicial appointments. It stated:

> The Lord Chancellor's policy is to appoint to every judicial post the candidate who appears to him to be best qualified to fill and perform its duties, regardless of party, sex, religion or ethnic origin. Professional ability, experience, standing and integrity alone are the criteria, with the requirements that the candidate must be physically capable of carrying out the duties, and not disqualified by any personal unsuitability. (*Judicial Appointments*, pp. (iv), 2–3)

The statement tells us very little, perhaps inevitably: what information is used to decide who is 'best qualified' and what characteristics would make a person unsuitable? The whole selection process is carried out in secret. Officials in the Lord Chancellor's Office gather information on possible candidates from a variety of sources, especially comments by judges. However, this information is privileged and an individual may never know why he or she has not been appointed to the bench or why he or she has been passed over for promotion. The suspicion remains that the unacknowledged criterion (as in many such apparently rational and judicial procedures) is conformity to a traditional model, 'like choosing like' – in this case a model of high judicial office dominated by the views of the existing legal establishment. In an attempt to allay this suspicion, the appointment procedure was modified in 1994. Junior judicial positions are now openly advertised with applications invited from suitably qualified lawyers and short-listed candidates are interviewed by a selection panel, one member of whom is a lay person. However, the reform is only partial as the panel only makes recommendations. The final decision is still made in secret by the Lord Chancellor's department. Doubt therefore remains over the extent to which those who do not conform to the 'establishment model' will be appointed.

Once appointed, judges are not easy to remove from office. Circuit judges and magistrates may be dismissed by the Lord Chancellor, but a High Court or more senior judge can only be dismissed on an Address presented to the Queen by both Houses of Parliament – a rare event. Security of tenure is seen as necessary to ensure that the constitutional requirement of judicial independence is maintained (see Chapter 6). However, this means there is no effective sanction against a judge who seems ill-suited for the bench. Moreover, although occasionally the Lord Chancellor publicly admonishes a judge for a decision or comments he has made, generally there is no public accountability for the vast amount of power wielded by judges. Indeed, it is only recently that the Lord Chancellor has had a junior minister in the House of Commons to answer for him and thus provide a minimal answerability to the House.

The lack of accountability of officials charged with such broad powers and responsibilities is a matter of some concern. The traditional response is that judges should not be assessed like other officials: they are, like priests, above performance review. In effect they personify the law. Thus a distinguished former Master of the Rolls, Lord Denning, saw no need for any kind of judicial accountability: 'Some one must be trusted: let it be the judges' (1982, p. 330). A more rational version of this case is that the judges are indeed constrained by the law itself, have little discretion, and, undeniably, have to operate in open court.

Others do not share such simple certainties, believe that judges exercise a good deal of discretion in their interpretation of the law, are little troubled by publicity, and do in fact often contribute to the creation of the law. Hence there is scope for serious concern about judicial accountability and the composition and nature of the judiciary.

Composition and judicial culture

The composition of the judiciary has been criticised, most notably by J. A. G. Griffith in his book *The Politics of the Judiciary*, first published in 1977. Griffith argues that judges are naturally biased towards the establishment and have a conservative outlook on life, which affects the way in which they dispense justice. He suggests that conservative attitudes arise from the nature of the job, which is largely concerned with upholding public order and established law, and the narrow background and isolated and privileged position of the judiciary. He sees the judges as members of a middle-class, privately educated, male and white élite:

> [F]our out of five full-time professional judges are products of public schools, and of Oxford or Cambridge. . . . In March 1991, of the judges from the Law Lords to the Circuit bench (some 550 in all) only one was black. Two Lords Justice, two High Court judges and nineteen Circuit judges were women. (1991, pp. 34–5)

Given this background, Griffith suggests that it is not surprising that the judges often seem to be out of touch with the ordinary man or woman, and to appear less sympathetic to certain groups of people, such as the unemployed, the homeless, student protesters and trade unionists. This is a judicial version of a familiar argument, which applies to all the élite professions, including the civil service. In Britain, society, economy and polity are dominated by interlocking élites, forming an 'establishment'; and the judiciary is part of that establishment.

The argument cannot be fully reviewed here, but it is undeniable that the élites exist and have been influential in the recent past. All that is in doubt is the extent of influence, whether it is generally malign or beneficent, and whether there is change, an opening up of the élites to new classes of people.

Lord Taylor, the Lord Chief Justice, addressed the issues raised by Professor Griffith in his 1992 Richard Dimbleby Lecture on 'The Judiciary in the Nineties'. He accepted that 'until recently, the Bar and therefore the Bench tended to be drawn from the middle class upwards and may not always have related easily to the problems of the less fortunate.' However, he considered that this was no longer the case: 'more judges now are drawn from modest backgrounds', and they 'do now understand the problems of the poor, of the homeless and of the handicapped'. Similarly, whilst

Lord Taylor recognised 'the present imbalance between male and female, white and black in the judiciary', he had 'no doubt that the balance [would] be redressed in the next few years'.

This suggests that the need for change is at least recognised and steps are being taken to remedy imbalances, both in the composition of the judiciary and in the outlook of judges. Already some senior judges have been more open than ever before, both in expressing their opinions and beliefs and in contributing to legal debate. There has also been a widening of the base from which judges are drawn to include solicitors and even one academic barrister, as well as practising barristers; and an examination of selection procedures and assessment practices within the professions to ensure that ethnic minorities are not disadvantaged.

In addition, senior judges have lent their support to the incorporation into British law of the European Convention of Human Rights, or alternatively the enactment of a British Bill of Rights. These moves would fundamentally alter the role of the judges, requiring them to uphold the rights of citizens against parliamentary and executive infringement. But judicial involvement in such decisions about political and constitutional values raises again the question of accountability. Critics like Professor Griffith are not convinced the judges can be trusted with such broad constitutional powers.

The police

A ministerial commitment to 'law and order' carries with it, implicitly if not explicitly, an intention to 'crack down' on all crime and ensure that those responsible are punished, wherever possible by heavy prison sentences. Constitutional interest in 'law and order' concentrates upon the issue of 'public order' and on the powers of arrest and detention. This is because there is only a thin line between the preservation of public order, essential for the proper functioning of society, and the suppression of protest, dissent and free speech, all equally vital freedoms of the individual. Moreover, because there is no Bill of Rights in Britain, the rights of protest and freedom of assembly are legally unprotected and may be diminished either by design or as an unintentional consequence of legislation relating to crime and public order. Individual freedom is always more vulnerable than public order.

During the 1980s two major pieces of legislation, the Police and Criminal Evidence Act (PACE) 1984 and the Public Order Act 1986, increased substantially the powers of arrest of the police. However, neither removed the power of arrest without a warrant at common law, which may be used to prevent a breach of the peace. This continues to operate alongside the statutory powers.

Police powers and breach of peace

The police have a common law duty to uphold and enforce the law. In fulfilling this duty police officers may arrest, disperse or detain anyone for committing a breach of the peace or for being about to commit a breach. They may also take the persons concerned before a Magistrates' Court to be 'bound over'. This requires an acceptance by the persons concerned that should they breach the peace within a stipulated period (most commonly twelve months), then they are bound to pay a sum of money fixed by the court. A person who refuses to agree to be 'bound over' may be imprisoned for a period up to six months.

There are a number of problems associated with the powers of the police and magistrates as they relate to a breach of the peace, which is not itself a criminal offence. First, what constitutes a breach of the peace? The definition given by the Court of Appeal in *R.* v. *Howell* [1982] QB 416 is generally accepted as authoritative:

> [T]here is a breach of the peace whenever harm is actually done or is likely to be done to a person or in his presence to his property or a person is in fear of being harmed through an assault, an affray, a riot, unlawful assembly or other disturbance.

This covers a range of situations but the common thread is the element of violence or an implicit threat of violence. Thus peaceful, passive protest does not under this definition constitute a breach of the peace.

The second problem concerns the considerable discretion afforded the police, particularly regarding the prevention of a breach of the peace. Case law suggests that for the police to take action there must be 'a real possibility' or 'a real and imminent risk' of a breach of the peace. However, at times the police may seem to apply a lesser test, and their actions to prevent a breach of the peace may be considered extreme. During the Miners' Strike

(1984–5) the police in Nottinghamshire adopted an 'intercept policy' whereby striking miners were turned back some distance from the colliery they intended to picket. Any resistance from the miners resulted in their arrest for obstructing the police.

Such action, however justifiable in practice, would seem to be based on a wide interpretation of the requirement that an anticipated breach of the peace should be 'real and imminent', particularly when the policy was applied to Kent miners who were two hundred miles from their destination. However, an application for an interim injunction to prevent the police from taking this action was refused (see Thornton, 1987, p. 97), and the actions of the police were supported in Parliament by the Attorney-General:

> If a constable reasonably comes to the conclusion that persons are travelling for the purpose of taking part in a picket in circumstances where there is likely to be a breach of the peace, he has the power at common law to call upon them not to continue their journey. (HC Deb., vol. 56, Written Answers, col. 279)

This suggests that the police have an alarmingly wide power which interferes with the freedom to travel and could be used to prevent many types of political protest.

The third concern relates to the power to detain in police custody and the power of magistrates to commit someone to prison if they refuse to be bound over. Detention can be for as long as is necessary in the circumstances. The exercise of such a power may seem appropriate where it is used as a 'cooling off' period to prevent the resumption of a fight, but is more questionable when used, for example, to prevent individuals from taking part in a demonstration or sabotaging a fox hunt. In the latter cases detention might be seen as interfering with freedom of expression. Similarly, committing someone to prison for refusing to be bound over may also be seen as an interference with the right of an individual to engage in lawful protest. Hence civil libertarians have expressed concern over the imprisonment of hunt saboteurs who had committed no criminal offence but refused to be bound over.

The Public Order Act 1986

There is a need to balance the right of individuals to demonstrate and protest against the right of others not to be injured, inconvenienced or otherwise damaged in their interests. Often there may be conflict between these rights. Indeed, it may be argued that a demonstration which brought no inconvenience would be unnoticed and thus ineffective. The question is therefore where the balance is to be struck.

A number of occurrences during the 1970s and 1980s, such as the confrontation in Red Lion Square between rival processions of National Front and anti-fascist demonstrators, the mass picketing at Wapping and Warrington by print workers, and picketing during the Miners' Strike, suggested that the balance favoured the protesters, for there was no doubt at all that serious inconvenience had arisen, and some room for doubt about the ability of the police to keep order.

It was against this background that the Public Order Act of 1986 was passed. The Act increased the ability of the police to control processions and public meetings by giving them power to impose conditions. Such conditions can include altering the route or forbidding a procession to enter a particular area, and they can be imposed either before or during the procession. Conditions may be imposed if a senior police officer 'reasonably believes' the procession

(a) may result in serious public disorder, serious damage to property or serious disruption to the life of the community, or
(b) the purpose of the persons organising it is the intimidation of others. (s. 12)

This gives the police wide discretionary powers, particularly in relation to what constitutes 'serious disruption to the life of the community'. In the White Paper preceding the Bill, the Home Office suggested that a march through a shopping centre on a Saturday constituted a 'serious disruption to the life of the community'. Such an example indicates the breadth of the power.

In addition, if the police consider that the imposition of conditions will not be sufficient, they have the power to make an application to the relevant local authority for a ban on processions in a particular area for a period of up to three months (s.13). This power was used in 1989 to prevent 'New Age Travellers' approaching within four miles of Stonehenge.

The police have been given similar powers in relation to public meetings of more than twenty people. Directions can be given which stipulate the place of assembly, its duration, and the number who can attend. These powers were aimed at mass picketing but a wider application could interfere with the expression of political views in the forum of a public meeting.

The powers granted to the police under the Public Order Act suggest that the balance between the right to demonstrate and the need to keep public order and prevent inconvenience to the public has shifted in favour of the latter. The bias is reinforced by the fact that there is no appeal from any conditions imposed upon processions or meetings. The only challenge is by way of judicial review, which can only be concerned with the lawfulness of the decision and not its merits.

Offences under the Public Order Act

Failure to comply with conditions imposed upon processions and meetings constitutes an offence under the Public Order Act. In addition, the Act created an extended range of statutory public order offences, including riot, violent disorder, affray, threatening behaviour and disorderly conduct. All these are criminal offences with prescribed maximum penalties attached. The consequences are therefore very different for an individual arrested for an offence under the Public Order Act rather than for a breach of the peace.

Riot is the most serious of the offences, and carries a maximum penalty of ten years' imprisonment. It is aimed at the mob situation, where the use or threat of violence is for a 'common purpose'. The charge of riot was brought against miners in Nottinghamshire and South Yorkshire during the Miners' Strike, but there were no convictions because of the problem of proving a 'common cause'.

Violent disorder, which carries a maximum penalty of five years' imprisonment, is also concerned with actual or threatened violence of a group nature, ranging from major incidents of public disorder to that associated with 'lager louts' or football hooligans. Affray, on the other hand, does not require this group element and can be used to prosecute an individual acting alone as well as one who is part of a group. It is also applicable where there is a fight. Riot, violent disorder and affray all require that conduct to be such that it would cause a person 'of reasonable firmness to fear for his personal safety'.

The other two offences contained within the Public Order Act are threatening behaviour and disorderly behaviour. Under section 4 it is an offence to use 'towards another person threatening, abusive or insulting words or behaviour', such that 'that person is likely to believe' that violence will be used or provoked. This offence is very similar to that contained in the earlier Public Order Act. However, the offence provided by section 5 is new. It is concerned with disorderly conduct and the use of 'threatening, abusive or insulting words or behaviour' which is 'likely' to cause 'harassment, alarm or distress'.

In the White Paper, prior to the introduction of the Public Order Bill, the government declared that the purpose of the section was to provide some protection, particularly for the elderly and vulnerable, against groups of youths, who used abusive language or who rampaged through housing estates, banging on doors, knocking over dustbins and so on. Such behaviour under the Act is now a criminal offence. Moreover, there does not have to be a victim – someone who will stand up in court and state that he or she was alarmed or harassed. It is sufficient for a police officer to give evidence that the conduct was such that it was 'likely' to have this effect. It has also been held that it can be the police themselves who are likely to be harassed, alarmed or distressed.

The breadth and vagueness of section 5 has made it controversial. First, it would seem to be applicable to peaceful protest, for example a group of boisterous students waving banners outside the Department for Education, feminists demonstrating outside the (all-male) pavilion at Lord's cricket ground, and many others, all causing alarm and so harassment. Secondly, the section may be used to 'criminalize the unusual':

> Rowdy and boisterous Cambridge undergraduates may not be disorderly; but are Rastafarians or punks in exactly the same situation? Individuality and flair, the 'shock of the new', are more alarming than dull conventionality. In Section 5, we now have a mechanism for punishing non-violent nonconformity for the crime of being itself. (Ewing and Gearty, 1990, p. 123)

Of course we all in our personal and social lives make judgements of this kind about other people, reacting to appearance, dress, noise, style and so on. But while we may feel disapproval and turn away, the police officer has responsibilities for public order (peace and tranquillity) and carries legal powers to intervene.

The Criminal Justice and Public Order Act 1994 went further in extending criminality in relation to 'travellers', 'squatters', 'ravers', hunt saboteurs and other disruptive demonstrators. Again, all of these activities are unconventional, and fit awkwardly into the rules and customs of a society based on conformity, property rights and 'respectability'. It is difficult to draw a line between the unconventional nuisance, the mildly or seriously offensive and the properly criminal; nor is it evident that the criminal law is always an effective instrument of social control.

Peaceful protest is also unconventional behaviour, especially when it takes the form of passive resistance, in which the line between violence and non-violence is easily blurred. The 'right' of peaceful protest is a serious issue for liberal constitutionalists. Most of us do not engage in any form of public protest, and disapprove of demonstrations and disorder, including marching and picketing. The political culture is peaceable and passive, and it is easy to condemn any form of protest going beyond a letter to a Member of Parliament or a newspaper. Nevertheless, in the interests of freedom of expression it is necessary to make legal space for unconventional protest. This requirement of democracy poses a special problem for the police officer, whose quick judgement of the nature of a protest or demonstration and the threat of harassment and disorder carries legal consequences.

Police powers of arrest

The Public Order Act provides the police with the power of arrest for offences contained within the Act, as do other statutes which create particular offences. The police also have a common law power of arrest for breach of the peace. However, the most significant piece of legislation concerning police powers of arrest and detention is the Police and Criminal Evidence Act (PACE) 1984. As well as providing for arrest without warrant for serious offences, the Act extended the powers of the police to arrest without warrant and detain for any offence, or suspected offence, however trivial, in situations where it appears to a police constable that the 'service of a summons is impracticable or inappropriate'. Such situations include those where the name of the person is not known or cannot be found out, or where there are 'reasonable grounds for doubting' that the name is genuine, or where a 'satisfactory address' is not provided, or the constable has 'reasonable grounds' for doubting that the address is satisfactory.

The concern of civil libertarians is that the Act allows the police to arrest when they feel it is convenient to do so, and that it discriminates against the socially disadvantaged, particularly the homeless, who cannot provide a 'satisfactory address'. It may also enable the police to arrest for insolent behaviour. Moreover, other parts of the Act, which concern the detention of a person, seem to encourage arrest as part of the investigative process, rather than as the result of an investigation.

PACE also provides the police with stop and search powers, where there is a 'reasonable suspicion' that a stolen or prohibited article will be found, and with powers of entry to property. The Act lays down conditions concerning the exercise of all police powers. However, the requirements are sufficiently vague or flexible to allow the police considerable discretion; also, the courts may be reluctant to question the way in which this discretion is exercised for fear of undermining the agents of law and order.

This indulgence towards the police is also reflected in the attitude of the judges to the Code of Practice that accompanies PACE. The Code is not a legal document, but an outline of best practice to which the police are expected to adhere. It is intended to safeguard the interests of persons in police custody, but it is rare for the courts to disallow evidence or confessions on the grounds that the Code was not followed. However, as a consequence of a series of miscarriages of justice, changes have been made with regard to the admissibility of unsupported confessional evidence.

The powers of the police are increased by the Criminal Justice and Public Order Act 1994, which creates the offence of 'criminal trespass'. This is aimed at hunt saboteurs, travellers and squatters who can be arrested simply for being on private land. But it also has implications for any form of protest, imposing further restrictions upon its location, no matter how peaceful it might be. In addition, the Act provides the police with wider powers of stop and search. These, it is argued, are essential to combat the massive growth in crime. However, the wider the powers, the greater the consequences for personal liberty, and the more vigilant the courts need to be in ensuring that police powers do not unduly restrain the freedom to protest.

This again is a reflection of the absence of constitutional 'rights' within Britain, and the uncertain position of the courts in holding a balance between the prevention of crime and the liberty of the individual. The relationship between citizen and police is seldom seen in constitutional terms, yet the police are acting as agents of the state and have considerable power to encroach upon personal liberty.

Police accountability

There is a problem about police accountability. The police wield massive powers, including the coercive power of the state, and have a responsibility for the maintenance of public order. No other body has such powers to intervene in our private lives. It seems reasonable that the police should be accountable for all their actions, both for specific acts against individual citizens and their general policy and conduct. But, if so, then accountability must encompass political, managerial and legal considerations – a formidable agenda.

In the past accountability depended on a triangle: locally based Police Authorities, the police themselves (in particular the Chief Constable) and the national government (in effect the Home Office). Each arm of the triangle was supported by traditional arguments: local control for democracy and efficiency; autonomy to strengthen professional drives and disciplines and avoid contamination of the police function by party politics; and national control for democracy and efficiency, meeting nationwide needs, linking control to funding and avoiding the dangers of local party democracy or police autocracy. The structure of the police was based on the triangle, but the arms were never equal. The local arm always had an ambition to grow, but was in practice outgrown by the police (the Chief Constable), and the national arm has now outgrown them both.

The old structure of police government was based on forty-one Police Authorities (counties or amalgamated counties) plus the two London police forces. Two-thirds of members of the Authorities were drawn from elected councillors, one third from the local, nominated Justices of the Peace. The Chief Constable, once appointed by the Authority (subject to the approval of the Home Secretary), had substantial autonomy in the direction and control of the police. He was dependent on the Authority for funding but it was difficult for the Authority to claim a say in the direction and control of the police, which lay between the Chief Constable and the Home Office. The Home Office was never less than very influential, through its hold on funding, on appointments, its stream of advice and guidance, and increasingly detailed formal inspections. The Home Office was, moreover, the police authority for London's Metropolitan Police.

In this structure accountability lay through the local authorities and through Parliament. In addition PACE provided for consultation of the local 'community' – a response to the racial unrest of the early 1980s and a sensible recognition of the inadequacies of representation through local government. The new Police Complaints Authority established in 1984, though not independent of the police, proved comparatively active, even vigorous, in supervising the investigation of complaints. Further, the Audit Commission monitored the police service, took an interest in accountability procedures, and indeed reported in 1990 that the balance of power was 'tilted so far towards the centre that the role of the local police authorities . . . has been significantly diminished' and 'accountability is blurred'.

Thus Britain, exceptionally among modern states, managed without a national police force, and contrived an incoherent structure of police government, which achieved some of the virtues and vices of local government, professional autonomy, and the mix of ministerial responsibility and bureaucratic command to be found in the Home Office. The Home Office possessed powerful but blunt weapons; a Chief Constable with experience, a 'thick skin' and little ambition left enjoyed substantial autonomy. At its best the structure may well have contrived to place a square of accountability around the circle of professional autonomy; but there is little doubt that the role of the local police authorities was uneven and generally weak.

The weakness of the local police authorities lay especially in funding (central government provided about two-thirds of the costs of policing) and in operational control (the broadly defined sphere of the Chief Constable). The Chief Constables and the

Home Office together demonstrated during the Miners' Strike (1984–5) their capacity to move beyond local control by the organisation of national policing of the strike through the Association of Chief Police Officers and a 'National Reporting Centre'. In the *Northumbria Police Authority* case (1988 – see Chapter 5) the Home Secretary established the right to provide plastic bullets and CS gas at the request of a Chief Constable, despite the disapproval of the Police Authority.

The local Police Authority was a structure that could not survive the 1980s. Expenditure on the police increased, but crime rose even faster. Local government went out of fashion, especially in police matters when a few radical metropolitan Police Authorities tried to interfere with the policing of strikes. The control of local funding was tightened, and new standards of managerial efficiency were imposed. By the end of that radical decade aspirations to local democracy and to professional autonomy in the public services had been replaced by central control and sharp managerial accountancy. The police service was still locally based, but the outlines of a national police force emerged through the growing practice of co-ordination through the Home Office and the Association of Chief Police Officers (ACPO).

The central tilt of the new structure was formalised by the reforms incorporated in the Police and Magistrates' Courts Act of 1994. This Act was part of the Conservative government's new emphasis on tough 'law and order' policies. There was some evidence of disquiet among officials in the Home Office about the hasty abandonment of policies based on research, and carefully worked out over a number of years, in favour of measures which were politically attractive but demonstrably ineffective.

In the new structure only one half of the members of the Police Authorities are drawn from local elected politicians; the other half comprises three magistrates and five persons appointed by the Home Secretary. The original Bill provided for the Chairman to be no longer elected by the members but appointed by the Home Secretary; in face of sharp criticism in the House of Lords, notably from former Home Secretaries, this provision was withdrawn. Under the new structure the Chief Constable works under a short-term contract to specified performance targets. Under the original proposal both Chairman and Chief Constable would have depended on the Home Secretary for their continued employment.

A reform of this kind may improve accountability by imposing a new managerial structure including tight accountancy, prescribed targets and performance review – the managerial rhetoric of the 1980s, now applied to all public services except the law and the Cabinet. Such accountability may be enhanced by the application of 'market disciplines' to the service, by conversion of the Police Authority to a purchaser of the services provided by the force (competition might even be introduced).

This is not 'democratic accountability' as understood by constitutionalists, but it may provide the kind of responsiveness to users of the service which the customer in Marks and Spencer appreciates. Further, the new structure provides accountability to the central government department and, via ministerial responsibility, to Parliament. On the other hand, the reformed structure of police government conspicuously and deliberately weakens local accountability, which, it might be thought, was the best way of relating the police service to the people served. Nor does it strengthen the culture of accountability in the police force or among politicians.

Altogether the problems of arranging accountability in the police service show how elusive it is. There is a national interest in the police service, and it is absurd to argue that an element of national control leads to a 'police state'. Yet ministerial responsibility to Parliament appears to be an inadequate form of accountability. There is also a strong local and popular dimension to much of the work of the police; but local political control does not guarantee either democracy or efficiency. Election is better for accountability than appointment but is unlikely to be effective without a renaissance in local political culture and a transformation in the professional culture of the police. Thus the problems of accountability of the police reflect the problems of securing the accountability of any complex and expensive economic and social service funded by the state, not amenable to simple market solutions, and complicated by misunderstandings about its purposes.

The military and the security services

The military

The keeping of public order generally falls to the police. However, there are reserve powers which enable the government to provide the police with military assistance should this be deemed necessary. The disposition and use of armed forces is a prerogative power, although the extent to which the army may be used to maintain internal security is uncertain. Some statutory powers are available to the government, most notably those contained in the Emergency Powers Acts of 1920 and 1964, which provide for the declaration of a state of emergency. States of emergency were proclaimed three times during the 1920s as a consequence of the General Strike and the subsequent Miners' Strike. Since 1945 there have been eight states of emergency, five in the early 1970s during Edward Heath's period in office. These arose from strikes or other industrial action by dockers, power workers and miners.

The proclamation of a state of emergency enables the government to make regulations to ensure the supply and distribution of essential goods and services and for keeping the peace. This may involve using the armed forces for supportive services such as transport and fire-fighting. The Acts provide the executive, and hence the armed forces and police, with extensive powers, subject to the safeguard against abuse that regulations made by the government have to be approved by affirmative resolutions of both Houses of Parliament within seven days.

The Emergency Powers Acts are not the only statutes that provide additional powers in emergency or extreme situations. Northern Ireland is governed by the Northern Ireland (Emergency Provisions) Act 1987, which enables the troops to assist in security matters within the province. Local authorities also have the power under the Civil Protection in Peacetime Act 1986 to use civil defence resources in an emergency or disaster, where there is danger to life or property.

The security services

The role of the security services in the preservation of 'law and order' is more problematic for constitutionalists. First the security services are concerned for an objective, the general security of the state or defence of the realm, much broader than 'law and order' as it might be understood by the ordinary citizen, and involving secret surveillance. Secondly, the services are by their nature secret, and (not an inevitable consequence) largely unaccountable.

The security services include the domestic and foreign spying agencies known as MI5 and MI6 and the massive Government Communication Headquarters (GCHQ) at Cheltenham, the police Special Branch (a part of the Metropolitan Police, but operating nation-wide), and the intelligence branches of the three armed services. Intelligence reports are communicated through the Joint Intelligence Committee and its Secretariat, headed by the Cabinet Secretary. This is at the very heart of government, and confers a high importance on the intelligence function.

Until recently the existence of these organisations was not publicised. This is no longer the case. The Security Services Act 1989 placed MI5 on a statutory basis, and in 1993 the heads of MI5 and MI6 were introduced to the media and the government announced that it would accept the establishment of a special parliamentary committee to examine the workings of the security services.

This may be reassuring, but the claim of the security services to remain secret is regarded as legitimate, and there is little reliable information about them. In 1986 the Home Secretary, James Callaghan, told the Treasury and Civil Service Select Committee (TCSSC) that he did not know about the accountability of the security services:

> I am not sure what its accountability is to Parliament; I am not sure about Ministers. I find it a difficult question to answer, I really do. . . . I do not know. . . . I am very, very mixed up about this. (TCSSC, 12 February 1986)

Such an admission in a minister of immense experience in three great offices of state may suggest evasion as much as ignorance.

Expenditure is for the most part hidden, but amounts to about £1 billion, of which GCHQ takes more than one half. Whether the information gathered is useful, useable and good value for money is impossible to say. The intelligence function is often romanticised, and tends in practice to produce too much indiscriminately. The record of intelligence, for example in the Falklands and Iraq, is not impressive, and the security services' modes of recruitment have in the past led to spectacular disasters.

There is more to concern the constitutionalist than the possible waste of public money, compounded by secrecy and lack of accountability. The security services are concerned with the surveillance of persons suspected of being 'subversive of the State' (the phrase used in the Maxwell-Fyfe Directive of 1952). In a comparatively narrow definition, as proposed by Lord Denning, in his report on the Profumo Affair (1963), that would mean someone who 'would contemplate the overthrow of government by *unlawful* means'.

The Security Services Act 1989 provides a broader and more elastic definition: it lays down the function of the internal security service (MI5) as protecting national security, guarding against espionage, terrorism, sabotage and actions 'intended to overthrow or undermine parliamentary democracy by political, industrial or violent means' and 'to safeguard the economic well-being of the United Kingdom' against actions by foreigners (s. 1 (2) and (3)).

In the past the security services have been concerned about membership or recent membership of, or even known sympathy with, communist or fascist organisations and subversive groups 'acknowledged to be such by the Minister'. There are plainly grounds for concern about such broad definitions of threats to parliamentary democracy. It would be generally accepted that terrorist organisations and those involved in organised crime fall within this category, but there would not be full agreement on the inclusion among the proper targets of the security services of trade union leaders, members of CND, Greenpeace or legal if 'extreme' political parties. However, it seems that these have in the past been subjected to surveillance, including telephone taps to secure information on their activities (see Chapter 15).

In the 1970s some sections of the security services seem to have decided that the Labour Party and its leader, Harold Wilson, were engaged in 'subversion', and some efforts were made to 'destabilise' the party by the spreading of false rumours. (Peter Wright's book, *Spycatcher*, lent some colour and even substance to these extraordinary allegations; the evidence for an MI5 'plot' is carefully reviewed in Pimlott, 1992.) The allegation was denied, but there is no doubt that Wilson, when Prime Minister, and some of his Cabinet colleagues were worried by the affair.

Another senior Labour politician and Secretary of State for Employment, Barbara Castle, expressed surprise in her diary that she was receiving so much intelligence material on trade union leaders, such as Hugh Scanlon and Jack Jones, much of it obvious and useless. Edward Heath, the Conservative leader and Prime Minister (1970–4) said some people in the security services 'talked the most ridiculous nonsense' (quoted in Hollingsworth and Norton Taylor, 1988, p. 128). It does not appear that ministers or Prime Ministers ever thought to rein back the excesses of the security services; and, indeed, at other times ministers made use of security surveillance (for example, Harold Wilson in order to resist a dock strike, Michael Heseltine to combat CND).

Accountability: law, order and liberty

The control of the coercive power of the military and the security services lies with the executive, that is, the government, which in Britain is the repository and chief operator of the massive coercive power of the modern state. The government monopolises the supply of laws and funds, and thus exercises the major influence on the police and almost full control of the military and security services.

However, in all three cases there is an element of independent power. In part this is no more – but no less – than the power of any well-founded corporate bureaucracy (like the civil service or the Health Service) to develop its own momentum and priorities. But in the case of the services concerned with public order and security, and so dealing in coercive power, any element of independence is a matter of concern. The power of the forces of order and security may thus be doubly unaccountable: either hoarded and shielded by the government, or escaping even from the control of government. If some part of this analysis is true, then there are grounds for concern about the coercive power of this secret state.

The case of the police was discussed above. Britain is plainly a long way from the feared 'police state', which is the libertarian's nightmare. There is still only a shadowy national police structure, subject mostly to the scrutiny of a judiciary for the most part watchful for the abuse of power. Similarly, the military are unlikely to attempt to take over civil government, except in conditions of disaster on a nuclear scale. In conditions of industrial turmoil in the 1970s and 1980s, going far beyond those of the General Strike of 1926, the troops stayed in their barracks.

This is not to say that the military are not an influential force in British politics, but their influence is not applied outside their chief professional concerns. They enjoy popular support and gratitude for remembered victories (statues, museums, public ceremonies), high prestige among élites (the favoured profession for royals) and a privileged place in the structure of government, represented at the highest levels, with special access to the Prime Minister, and ready access to the media. Closing down a regiment still causes more trouble for the government than closing down a coalmine.

Indeed, one of the reasons the military do not intervene openly in politics is that they do not need to: they get much of their way already. Their occasional forays into open politicking (as when serious cuts in defence expenditure are threatened, or the Labour Party proposes to abandon nuclear weapons) confirm the validity of their assumption that their interests and the national interests coincide. Thus the influence of the military is directed quite narrowly at their own professional interests and concerns. The military are a built-in bias to the governing of Britain, not a threat to the constitution.

The security services cost less than the military and are much less influential. On the other hand, their work is almost entirely secret, and restricts the liberty of the individual. There is obviously a serious problem here for a constitutional democracy, properly concerned for order and security but at the same time aiming to maximise freedom under the rule of law. It is reasonable to believe that in Britain the political culture provides some protection for the liberties of the citizen, and imposes some restraints on governments. Faced with the excesses of less democratic regimes elsewhere, we are inclined to say complacently, if with some justification, 'it could not happen here'.

However, such informal and customary constraints on governments work best in good times, when governments are not anxious about order and security; and they are least effective when they are most needed, that is, when order and security are threatened, some citizens move near to the line dividing awkwardness and protest from 'subversion', and governments persuade themselves that security comes before liberty. Hence, there is a case for a constitution or a Bill of Rights, or at the least the writing down of rules, the definition and limitation of powers, and provision for effective scrutiny and accountability. In countries with established constitutions the balance between national security and individual freedom is protected to some extent by the provisions of the constitution. In Britain there is no such reference point and the balance depends more than it should on the self-restraint of the powerful. This is not a form of restraint that constitutionalists – and historians – are inclined to trust.

These considerations bring us back to the role of the courts and the judiciary. The judges enjoy immense prestige and political influence. They are drawn from a profession strongly represented in both Houses of Parliament, and with a leading member in the Cabinet. They are well-connected and strategically positioned to shape legislation, as well as to defend the privileges of their profession. The evidence of their influence, particularly in defence of their profession, is plain.

In liberal tradition the judges act as the guardians of the liberties of the citizen against an oppressive state; they are potentially the best protection the citizen has. But in Britain this role is not constitutionally available to the courts. They act more often as a support of state power and defender of public order. There is no constitutional support for a role of defender of our liberties, and without such support the judges are bound by the laws they apply, and perhaps by their own predispositions, to defend the integrity of state power. Insofar as that is true, the courts take their place, in this chapter as in the political structure, alongside the police, the military and the security services, as upholders of law and order.

PART IV

CONCLUSION

18

REDISCOVERING THE CONSTITUTION

There is a British constitution

It is apparent from the foregoing chapters that if a constitution can only be defined in terms of a written document, which is interpreted and upheld by the courts and which has the status of a higher law, Britain does not have a constitution. The courts cannot strike down legislation or executive action on the grounds that it is unconstitutional. Such a term does not belong to British legal vocabulary, nor is it a word in general usage, for one of the consequences of having no constitutional document is the lack of a constitutional culture. There is no constitution grounded in the people, to which appeals can be made or from which educators can extract principles of citizenship. Indeed, despite the promotion of Citizen's Charters, the concept of citizenship in terms of rights and obligations is absent; also missing is any concept of the state as the embodiment of 'the people' from which the government derives its power and to which it owes a duty of service.

The lack of a constitutional document and the constitutional framework this provides places Britain apart from other countries, and results in the need to express the constitutional arrangements in terms of 'theories' or 'principles'. However, one consequence arising from the writing of a book on the British constitution is the destruction of the idea that Britain is constitutionless, or that what is called 'the constitution' is simply a description of British government.

Certainly Britain's constitutional arrangements arise more from political practice than is generally the case. However, there are rules which prescribe how power is allocated and controlled and how the institutions of government should relate to each other. Moreover, some of these rules have the status of law and others which do not are still recognised by the courts. Thus the judges play a role in determining constitutional issues. They may not make rulings of 'unconstitutionality', but they frequently engage in discussion about the constitution; and the House of Lords, in its role as the highest court of appeal, is well aware of the constitutional impact of some of its decisions.

Generally, constitutional considerations are marginal in political discourse in Britain, but politics can never be entirely separated from constitutional structures and rules. A number of issues not far from the centre of politics are plainly constitutional: the relationship with Europe, the status of Northern Ireland, the persistent, if not quite so pressing, question of Scotland's position in the Union; the much-talked-about reform of the electoral system and the never-quite-dismissed device of the referendum, the whole area of Not-Quite-Government, and the concerns arising from long-term one-party government, or (for those who do not worry about that) the threat of a hung Parliament or a Labour government like that of the 1970s, which first gave rise to the cry of elective dictatorship. Plainly, constitutional concerns are inseparable from the practice of politics. Moreover, at times the lawyers are called upon to advise on the legal position relating to a constitutional issue, as was evident during the process of ratification of the Maastricht Treaty.

The rules of the constitution

The nature of the British constitution was considered in general terms in Chapters 1 and 2, and in some detail in the rest of the book. The unsystematic and heterogeneous quality of its architecture was apparent; it is a house with many mansions and some sheds and outhouses. Architectural analogies run to pillars and flying buttresses, and shadows and penumbras. These seem more appropriate than engineering analogies – the constitution is more like a building than a machine; but it is a structure which characteristically provides the rules under which its residents must live.

The British constitution includes many kinds of rules, both implicit and explicit, general and specific, mandatory and persuasive:

1. the political facts or conditions of the constitution;
2. institutions and their interrelationships;
3. conventions;
4. rules of procedure;
5. statute and common law;
6. judicial precepts of good government;
7. EC/EU laws;
8. precepts and understandings derived from culture or tradition.

Examples of these kinds of rules are to be found in every chapter of the book. They make up a substantial, complex and subtle rule-book, which defies instant summary and simplification, and perhaps too easy reformation.

Breaking the rules

The first test of the existence and validity of a rule of the constitution is to inquire whether a breach could reasonably be called 'unconstitutional'; the test is the acceptability of that term and its critical implication. Claims of 'unconstitutionality' are most frequently made when a proposal or action offends politically. In a sense this devalues the constitution and it is a claim that can never be tested in a court. However, it is also an acceptance or recognition that there is something above the political process which commands a greater respect and which engenders certain values.

Under a narrow interpretation any action of a government which is legal cannot be unconstitutional. This is easy and, on the narrow definition adopted, incontrovertible; but it does not help in the understanding of the constitution as a more extensive and useable concept. In the broadest interpretation of the appropriate meaning of a constitution, an act of government might be regarded as unconstitutional not because it was illegal, but because it was insensitive to the spirit of a tacit understanding of the constitution. Perhaps this is an excessive extension of the notion of constitutionality. Tacit understandings are important in the British constitution, but the line between constitutionality and unconstitutionality ought perhaps to be drawn a little above 'insensitivity', at the point at which not conforming to the rule damages or diminishes the rule and frustrates the purposes for which it was developed.

The second test of the constitutional is positive: does the rule uphold or contribute to the purposes of the constitution? It is time to address that question.

The purposes of a constitution and the test of constitutionality

The purpose of a constitution is to empower and to limit power, to allocate the power to govern and prescribe the relations between the power-holders, and to provide for the limitation of power and the rights of those upon whom it is exercised. In achieving these general purposes a democratic constitution has one overriding objective: to ensure government by consent of the governed. To achieve this it follows three subsidiary purposes:

1. to give to the governed a decisive role in the making and unmaking of governments (dismissability);
2. to make government continuously accountable to the governed (transparency and accountability);
3. to take fully into account the competing interests of the governed and to deal fairly with them (fairness – of procedure, if not of outcome).

The last may appear to be novel, fanciful and impractical; but it sets out roughly what the barons were seeking in Magna Carta, and the Whig grandees in the Bill of Rights.

These considerations offer grounds for assessing accusations of unconstitutionality made against recent governments. No government has offended against the first rule, dismissabiity; all have offended against the rules of accountability and fairness. The most obvious examples are the replacement of locally elected authorities by unaccountable public bodies governed by ministerial appointees; the persistent secrecy of much goverment decision-making and activity; the continuing subordination of Parliament to the purposes of the executive; the attempt to protect legislation from judicial review. (No government in this century is innnocent of at least the second and third of these offences.)

On the other hand, the poll tax was not unconstitutional; nor was the concentration of power in 10 Downing Street under Margaret Thatcher; nor the privatisation of the nationalised industries and the public utilities (though there remains a doubt about the fairness of the distribution of the proceeds of the sale). The reformation of local government may be defended as not only legal, but also concerned precisely with the rules of accountability and fairness. The House of Lords has not behaved unconstitutionally in refusing to pass government legislation, except insofar as it is in itself a standing contradiction of the three rules of constitutionality.

The case for constitutional reform

Constitutional reform is not a popular cause in Britain, yet there have been movements in favour of reform in each of the last three decades, and continuing though fragmented attempts at institutional reformation. In the 1960s nationalist discontent in Scotland and Wales led to the establishment of a Royal Commission on the Constitution. This confined its deliberations almost entirely to the problems of the 'peripheral nations' and proposed schemes of devolution (see Chapter 12).

While the Labour government was pursuing these rather half-hearted attempts at reform, a more general criticism of the power of central government developed. This was encapsulated in Lord Hailsham's forceful denunciation of 'elective dictatorship': once elected, Hailsham (1976, 1978) argued, a government in Britain was constrained neither by Parliament nor by the courts, and its power amounted to dictatorship. This critique was compatible with the notion of government 'overload'. It sat less easily with the alleged condition of 'ungovernablity', but that related mostly to trade union militancy, which Margaret Thatcher's government was soon to conquer.

Lord Hailsham's argument was not pursued by him when he joined the new Conservative government and so became part of the elective dictatorship. The specifically Conservative theory of elective dictatorship was, it seems, grounded in the threat of a permanent Labour government, and lapsed when that threat collapsed. But the theory was taken up by others: old-style liberal constitutionalists, the new Liberal Democrats and eventually and gingerly by Neil Kinnock's Labour Party. Meanwhile, the Conservatives, while not inclined to regard themselves as constitutional reformers, set about radical institutional reforms concerned with the diminution of the scope of goverment activity, if not of power. In this way, unexpectedly, the Conservatives became the party of constitutional reform, though the reformation was not of a kind espoused by the liberal constitutionalists; nor was it accompanied by any public debate on the constitutional implications and in particular the consequences for accountability.

These two strands of reforming doctrines were derived from differing historical analyses as well as sharply opposed political values. The liberal constitutionalists believed that a largely Victorian constitution based on small government and an influential Parliament was no longer suitable to an age of big government and a dominant executive supported by a party machine. The Conservatives seemed more concerned to diminish the scope of government (at least in economic matters), leaving the executive to dominate other areas with little constraint. The Conservative constitution aimed to provide for 'a free economy and strong state'.

A third strand of reformist thought was concerned with the party system, in particular the failure of the non-Conservative centre and left to develop a serious challenge to the hegemony of the Conservative Party in the twentieth century, and the apparent decline of the alternation of parties which underlay the democratic functioning of the Westminster model. The solution to the electoral weakness of the centre and left, and to the constitutional problem, was a coalition between the Labour and Liberal parties; that was the accepted logic of the ballot system – but not an acceptable development within the party system, which plays by its own rules, or political imperatives.

An indirect approach to the same solution lay in reform of the ballot system. There were of course other fundamental arguments for a more proportionally representative system (see Chapter 11), but the crucial point was its effect on the party system, on the probability of alternation in government, party instability or, the most likely outcome, coalition government. There is no doubt that the replacement of majority government by coalition government as the norm would have a radical effect on the working of the

Westminster model, in particular on the role of Parliament. Hence, proportional representation is the most fundamental constitutional reform currently under serious discussion.

Reform proposals and programmes

Thus in the 1990s there are three main strands of argument about constitutional reform: anti-statist, liberal constitutionalist and electoral reformist. The first of these is being put into practice by the Conservative government, which in the 1992 election stressed its commitment to the Union ('The United Kingdom is far greater than the sum of its parts'), and the Citizen's Charter. The other two strands are part of the liberal constitutionalist package of reforms, promoted by 'Charter 88' and the Liberal Democrats. The latter included a substantial section on electoral and constitutional reform in their 1992 election manifesto. The Labour Party also included a section on 'A Modern Democracy', with rather more limited commitments to a Scottish Parliament, eventual reform of the House of Lords and a debate on the electoral system.

The nature of Conservative constitutional reform has been indicated above and, insofar as it is concerned with local government, in Chapter 13; also in Chapter 16 on the redress of grievances. The basic principles of the reform are those of private enterprise and managerial accountancy. The freedom, rights and choices of the citizen are best protected by the replacement of government as far as possible by private 'enterprise' serving customers in a competitive market. Where government is unable to divest itself of its responsibilities, it must be subjected to rigorous accounting and efficiency audits, again to ensure the proper service of the people. In addition the aim of the Citizen's Charters is to ensure a high quality of service to the public by the publication of standards and provision for complaint and in some cases compensation.

These reforms have not been presented by the government as specifically constitutional reform, but at a time of some constitutional concern this is all that is on offer. The reforms are plainly attractive, and potentially effective in some areas. However, there are some evident defects: for example, the replacement of elected local governments by nominated bodies; the assumption by the central government of substantial new powers over education and the police; the conversion of public monopolies into private monopolies; the inadequacy in some cases of regulatory bodies. There are problems, too, about the constitutional theory, which amounts to the claim that privatisation and the market can adequately meet the needs of the people, and that the customer/client in the market has freedoms and rights not available to the citizen in the government office or polling booth. The 'empowerment' of the citizen by these reforms is achieved rather patchily. The wealthier the citizen, the greater the freedom; but that has always been the case, and a major aim of modern government has been to enlarge the freedom of those who could not afford to buy it.

The liberal constitutionalist prescription amounts to a substantial package of reforms, all directed to the institutions and procedures of government. These include the following:

1. reform of the House of Lords, replacing hereditary rights and Prime Ministerial patronage with some form of regional representation;
2. devolution to the nations and regions, and the strengthening of local government;
3. 'open government' and a Freedom of Information Act;
4. a Bill of Rights;
5. reform of the electoral system to achieve a more proportional representation.

Most of these proposals have been discussed at appropriate points in the text. The reform of the electoral system is, as indicated above, the most radical, but a Bill of Rights is in a sense the flagship of the liberal constitutionalists. This is because a Bill of Rights is wide-ranging, represents the traditional lawyer's approach to constitutional reform, has a place in all the best constitutions, and, of course, has a famous precedent in English history.

A Bill of Rights for Britain?

The importance of a Bill of Rights is that it provides the individual with positive rights and with a means of redress if these rights are infringed by legislative enactment or executive action. The enactment of such a Bill in Britain would end the reliance on common law freedoms and alter the balance between government and the governed. A Bill of Rights tends to sound better in rhetoric than in practical detail. A right is after all only a claim deemed so natural or fundamental or simply desirable that it should not be denied, and so should be guaranteed by the state. But rights are not easy to define, may conflict with each other (for example, the right to life and the right to liberty) and can rarely be established in absolute form. However, the importance of a Bill of Rights is partly in the rhetoric and in the changed constitutional culture it engenders.

In practice a Bill of Rights is an expression of general principles applied to specific cases. The application depends on the circumstances of the case, the political climate of the time, and the interpretation of the Bill of Rights by the courts. The usual model for a Bill of Rights in Britain is the European Convention of Human Rights, drawn up in 1950. It was ratified by Britain in 1951 but has never been incorporated into British law. British citizens have the right to petition the Commission of Human Rights to take the case to the European Court of Human Rights in Strasbourg.

However, this is costly in time and money. Applicants have to have exhausted all legal remedies in Britain and bringing a case before the European Court of Human Rights can take up to six years. Nevertheless there have been a significant number of cases brought against the British government. Indeed, since 1965 twice as many cases concerning Britain have come before the Court than any other country, probably a reflection of the inability of British citizens to secure redress for the infringements of rights at home. The British government has usually voluntarily complied with adverse judgments of the Court.

The European Convention includes the following provisions:

1. a right to life;
2. a right to liberty and security of person;
3. a right to a fair and public hearing, and safeguarding of the rights of the accused;
4. respect for private and family life, home and correspondence;
5. freedom of thought, conscience and religion, expression, assembly and association;
6. a right to education, in conformity with religious and philosophical convictions;
7. rights to be protected by effective remedies.

Some of these rights are subject to exceptions, and these are expressed in terms which are as abstract as the rights they concern. Thus Article 8, which declares that everyone has a right to respect for his or her private and family life, home and correspondence, allows an exception for measures 'necessary in a democratic society in the interests of national security, public safety or the economic well-being of the country' or 'necessary for the protection of health or morals'.

The breadth of the exceptions arises from the fact that the European Convention of Human Rights is a compromise document, which had to accommodate different legal traditions and systems as well as political requirements. If the Convention were to be incorporated into British law, it is possible that British judges would feel bound to interpret such exceptions in a way that allowed the government to evade its responsibilities. However, given the interest and power of government, it seems unlikely that agreement could be reached on a British Bill of Rights drafted more tightly.

It has often been argued that Britain cannot have a Bill of Rights since the doctrine of parliamentary sovereignty prevents entrenchment. However, the argument has diminishing force since the passing of the European Communities Act 1972; for there is nothing to prevent a Bill containing similar wording to the Act and no reason to suppose the courts would not accept the Bill in the same way, even to the extent of holding subsequent legislation void if it conflicted with the Bill.

In addition, the European experience suggests that the courts might be prepared to move away from the rigidity that parliamentary sovereignty has historically imposed and recognise the requirement for a special procedure before amendment or repeal. They might be particularly amenable to a referendum as a representation of the democratic will. During the 1990s senior judges have made clear their support for a Bill of Rights, which suggests they see no problem in the mechanics of its operation. In any case, even if such a Bill were not legally entrenched, it would be politically difficult, if not impossible, for a government to take away the rights guaranteed by the Bill.

A further argument against a Bill of Rights is that it submits issues concerned with rights to judges who are alleged to be conservative and disposed to favour the executive over the citizen. Their legal tradition, born out of the doctrine of parliamentary sovereignty, favours a narrow and literal interpretation of legislation rather than the liberal, purposive approach that is required where a Bill of Rights is concerned. This view may underrate the readiness of the judges, increasingly concerned about their own role in what may seem to be an executive-dominated single-party system, to take up a new constitutional position. It also fails to recognise the effect of Europe upon the judges. When charged with the responsibility of applying a Bill of Rights, judges may well adopt the purposive construction necessary for the protection of rights.

Towards a constitutional culture

A constitution supports and is supported by a constitutional culture or public philosophy. Britain needs a revitalised constitutional culture before it needs constitutional reform; indeed, the philosophy necessarily precedes the reform. A new constitutional culture should be based on a more sophisticated understanding of the purposes and workings of constitutions, the nature of politics and the lessons of history.

In particular, the constitutional culture needs to absorb a new understanding of constitutions, and some changes in constitutional discourse. The new understanding includes the following:

1. An acceptance of the duality of constitutions, the combination of rules and the constitutional conditions arising from political facts, hence the existence of a British constitution.
2. A recognition that constitutions, and particularly Bills of Rights, are aspirational. They are a reflection not of what is, but of what ought to be. Once this is recognised, then many concerns about their interpretation disappear.
3. The replacement of confidence in the mantra of parliamentary sovereignty with some understanding of the checks and balances implied by separation of powers and federalism, and an appreciation of the constitutional value for Britain of notions of the sharing, balancing and restraint of power.

The changes in constitutional discourse follow on from these understandings:

1. the replacement of the term 'the government', implying legitimised omnipotence, by 'the executive', implying some division of governmental functions.
2. the enhancement of the status of the citizen as a component of political discourse. The term 'citizen' sounds a little archaic and un-English, as indeed it is, but it can carry economically much of the burden of democratic values in a modern constitution. Since the British people are all now citizens of Europe with rights associated with freedom of movement and voting, it seems proper that they also see themselves as citizens of a nation-state.

Further, it would be helpful if there were a more widespread understanding of the few great and indubitable lessons of history – the corruptions of power, eternal vigilance as the price of liberty, and the need, where government is concerned, for 'Light, more light!' That was Professor Finer's cry at the end of his account of the 'Anonymous Empire' of the lobby (1958), and after forty years it is still freshly relevant to all areas of government.

Leaving well alone?

There is always a plausible case for leaving well alone. But the fact is that the constitution is not standing still: reformation is taking place mainly under the direction and in the interests of the executive (but with some influence by the judges), and as a consequence of Britain's membership of the European Union. So the issue is not reform or not, but reform by whom and in whose interests?

GLOSSARY OF LEGAL TERMS

case law – body of law made by judges, comprising application of the common law and the interpretation of statutes

certiorari – an order which quashes or nullifies an action or decision

civil or **private** law – law concerning disputes between individuals or an individual and a company

common law – judge-made law based on doctrine of precedent

declaration – a remedy which declares the rights of the parties and the state of the law

delegated legislation – legislative acts, e.g. regulations, made by minister, local authority, etc., as authorised by, and in accordance with, a particular statute

entrenchment – the requirement that special procedures be followed before a constitutional provision is amended or repealed

ex parte – on behalf of (thus *R.* v. *Secretary of State for Social Services ex parte Stitt* indicates that the case has been brought by the Crown against the Secretary of State on behalf of Stitt)

habeas corpus – a writ or summons to bring before a court or release from prison (literally 'in that you have the body of . . .'). Important in the seventeenth-century struggle against illegal detention

implied repeal – the doctrine whereby conflict between two Acts of Parliament is resolved by accepting the latest statute as the law. The earlier statute is repealed by implication

injunction – an order made by the court which forbids or, less commonly, orders a specific action; *interim or interlocutory injunction* – an order which operates until the case comes before the court for a full hearing

judicial review – the process by which the High Court exercises its supervisory function over public bodies and those wielding public power

jurisdiction – the power to decide

justiciability – suitability of a matter for judicial determination

locus standi or **standing** – the requirement that an applicant in a judicial review case has sufficient interest in the matter to which the application relates

mandamus – an order which requires the carrying out of a public duty which has been imposed by law (usually a statutory duty)

obiter dicta – comments made by judges which are not necessary to decide the case; have persuasive authority

precedent – doctrine which requires judges to follow decisions made in previous cases; there is a *hierachy of precedent* which binds the lower courts to follow decisions of higher courts

prerogative (royal or Crown) – the residual powers, immunities and privileges belonging to the Crown which have not been abrogated by statute

primary legislation – Acts of Parliament (Britain); law deriving from the treaties, amendments, etc. (EU)

prohibition – an order preventing the making of an unlawful decision or doing an unlawful act

ratio decidendi - that part of the legal reasoning essential for the decision in the case; provides the *precedent*

relator proceedings – legal proceedings brought by an individual in the Attorney-General's name. The Attorney-General may consent to such proceedings where an individual does not have the necessary *standing* to bring an action by him- or herself

secondary legislation – in British context, another term for *delegated legislation*; in European Union context, directives, regulations and decisions

statutory instrument – form in which most delegated legislation is passed

stay – similar to an *interlocutory injunction* but application more limited. Holds everything as it is until case comes to court

sub judice – under judicial consideration

tort – a civil wrong (e.g. negligence)

ultra vires – i.e. beyond the powers conferred by law

REFERENCES

Allan, T. R. S. (1993) *Law, Liberty and Justice*, Clarendon Press: Oxford.

Bagehot, W. (1963) *The English Constitution*, Collins/Fontana: London. (Originally published 1867.)

Baker, K. (1993) *The Turbulent Years*, Faber & Faber: London.

Bogdanor, V. (1979) *Devolution*, Clarendon Press: Oxford.

Bogdanor, V. (1983) *Multi-Party Politics and the Constitution*, Cambridge University Press: Cambridge.

Bogdanor, V. (1988) 'Britain, the political constitution', in V. Bogdanor (ed.), *Constitutions in Democratic Politics*, Gower: Aldershot.

Brazier, R. (1990) *Constitutional Texts*, Clarendon Press: Oxford.

Calvert, H. (1985) *British Constitutional Law*, Blackstone Press: London.

Clark, G. N. (1934) *The Later Stuarts, 1660–1714*, Clarendon Press: Oxford.

Daintith, T. (1989) 'The executive power today: bargaining and economic control', in J. Jowell and D. Oliver (eds), *The Changing Constitution*, Clarendon Press: Oxford.

Denning, Lord (1982) *What Next in the Law?*, Butterworths: London.

de Smith, S. and Brazier, R. (1989) *Constitutional and Administrative Law* (6th edn), Penguin Books: Harmondsworth.

Dicey, A. V. (1959) *An Introduction to the Study of the Law of the Constitution* (10th edn), Macmillan: Basingstoke and London. (Originally published 1885.)

Erskine May (1989) *Parliamentary Practice: Treatise on the law, privileges, proceedings and usage of Parliament* (21st edn), Butterworths: London.

Ewing, K. (1987) *The Funding of Political Parties in Britain*, Cambridge University Press: Cambridge.

Ewing, K. and Gearty, G. (1990) *Freedom under Thatcher*, Clarendon Press: Oxford.

Finer, S. (1958) *Anonymous Empire*, Pall Mall: London.

Graham, C. and Prosser, T. (1991) *Privatizing Public Enterprise*, Clarendon Press: Oxford.
Griffith, J. A. G. (1991) *The Politics of the Judiciary* (4th edn), Harper Collins/Fontana: London.
Griffith, J. A. G. and Ryle, M. (1989) *Parliament: Functions, practice and procedure*, Sweet and Maxwell: London.
Hailsham, Lord (1976) *Elective Dictatorship*, BBC: London.
Hailsham, Lord (1978) *The Dilemma of Democracy*, Collins: London.
Hansard Society (1981) *Paying for Politics*, Hansard Society: London.
Healey, D. (1989) *The Time of My Life*, Michael Joseph: London.
Hennessy, P. (1986) *Cabinet*, Basil Blackwell: Oxford.
Heuston, R. (1964) *Essays in Constitutional Law* (2nd edn), Stevens: London.
Hewart, Lord (1929) *The New Despotism*, Ernest Benn: London.
Hollingsworth, M. and Norton Taylor, R. (1988) *Blacklist: The inside story of political vetting*, Hogarth: London.
Jennings, I. (1959) *The Law and the Constitution* (5th edn), Cambridge University Press: Cambridge. (Originally published 1933.)
Johnson, N. (1977) *In Search of the Constitution*, Methuen: London.
Johnson, N. (1978) 'The public corporation: an ambiguous species' in D. Butler and A. Halsey (eds) *Policy and Politics*, Macmillan: Basingstoke and London, pp. 132–9.
Keir, D. L. (1966) *The Constitutional History of Modern Britain*, A. and C. Black: London.
Kellas, J. (1990) 'The constitutional options for Scotland', *Parliamentary Affairs*, 43, 4, pp. 426–34.
Lawson, N. (1992) *The View from No. 11*, Bantam Press: London.
Loughlin, M. (1986) *Local Government in the Modern State*, Sweet and Maxwell: London.
Marshall, G. and Moodie, G. (1971) *Some Problems of the Constitution*, Hutchinson: London.
Moran, M. (1980) 'Parliamentary control of the Bank of England', *Parliamentary Affairs*, 33, 1, pp. 67–78.
Mount, F. (1992) *The British Constitution Now*, Heinemann: London.
Norton, P. (1993) *Does Parliament Matter?*, Harvester Wheatsheaf: Hemel Hempstead.
Pimlott, B. (1992) *Harold Wilson*, HarperCollins: London.
Pliatzky, L. (1989) *The Treasury under Mrs Thatcher*, Basil Blackwell: Oxford.
Plowden, W. (1994) *Ministers and Mandarins*, IPPR: London.
Pollard, D. and Hughes, D. (1990) *Constitutional and Administrative Law*, Butterworths: London.
Rawlings, H. F. (1988) *Law and the Electoral Process*, Sweet and Maxwell: London.
Ridley, F. (1988) 'There is no constitution: a dangerous case of the Emperor's clothes', *Parliamentary Affairs*, 41, 3, pp. 340–61.
Ridley, F. (1991) 'Defining constitutional law in Britain', *Anglo-American Law Review*, 20, 2, pp. 101–15.

Robertson, G. (1993) *Freedom, the Individual and the Law*, Penguin Books: Harmondsworth.
Taylor, Lord (1992) *The Judiciary in the Nineties* (The Richard Dimbleby Lecture, 30 November), transcript.
Thornton, P. (1987) *Public Order Law*, Financial Training: London.
Turpin, C. (1990) *British Government and the Constitution* (2nd edn), Weidenfeld and Nicolson: London.
Wade, H. W. R. (1955) 'The basis of legal sovereignty', *Cambridge Law Journal*.
Wade, H. W. R. (1980) *Constitutional Fundamentals*, Stevens: London, pp. 172–97.
Watson, J. Steven (1960) *The Reign of George III, 1760–1815*, Clarendon Press: Oxford.
Woodward, E. L. (1938) *The Age of Reform, 1815–1870*, Clarendon Press: Oxford.
Wright, P. (1987) *Spycatcher: The candid autobiography of a senior intelligence officer*, Viking: New York.

Official reports and papers

In chronological order (published by HMSO except where indicated)

Northcote–Trevelyan Report (1854) printed as Appendix B of Fulton Report, Vol. I, 1968 – see below.
Report of the Committee on Ministers' Powers (Donoughmore Committee, 1932), Cmd 4060.
Report of the Committee on Administrative Tribunals (Franks, 1957), Cmnd 218.
Report on the Profumo Affair (Denning, 1963), Cmnd 2152; also published by Pimlico, 1992: London.
Report of the Committee on the Civil Service (Fulton, 1968), Cmnd 3638.
Report of the Royal Commission on the Constitution (Kilbrandon, 1973), 2 vols, Cmnd 5460.
Report of the Select Committee on Members' Interests (Declaration) (1974–5) HC 102.
Report of the Committee of Inquiry on Financial Aid to Political Parties (Houghton, 1976), Cmnd 6601.
Report of the Committee on Ministerial Memoirs (Radcliffe, 1976), Cmnd 6386.
Report of the Committee on Local Government Finance (Layfield, 1976), Cmnd 6453.
Eleventh Report from the Expenditure Committee, 1976–7, Vol. II, Part II, 535 II.
Fifth Report from the Select Committee on Nationalized Industries (1977–8), HC238.
Report on the Supply of Petroleum and Petroleum Products to Rhodesia (Bingham, 1978), FCO, September.

Third Report from the Defence Committee: The D-Notice system (1979–80), HC773.

Third Report from the Foreign Affairs Committee (1979–80), HC553.

Cabinet Office (1980) *Select Committees: Memorandum of guidance for officials* (The Osmotherly Rules).

Annual Report of the Parliamentary Commissioner for Administration (1983), HC322.

Report of a Committee of Privy Councillors: The Falkland Island Review (Franks, 1983), Cmnd 8787.

Armstrong, Sir Robert, *The Duties and Responsibilities of Civil Servants in Relation to Ministers: A note by the head of the home civil service* (The Armstrong Memorandum, 1985), TCS (1985–6) HC 92, II, pp. 7–9, also reprinted (revised) in HC Deb. 123 (1987–8) cols 572–5, Written Answers, 2 December 1987.

Fourth Report from the Defence Committee: Westland PLC: The government's decision-making (1985–6), HC519.

Second Report from the Trade and Industry Committee: The Tin Crisis (1985–6), HC305–I.

Seventh Report from the Treasury and Civil Service Select committee: Civil Servants and Ministers: Duties and responsibilities (1985–6), HC92.

Judicial Appointments (1986), Lord Chancellor's Department.

Report of the Committee of Inquiry into the Conduct of Local Authority Business (Widdicombe, 1986), Cmnd 997.

The Government's Responses to the First Report from the Treasury and Civil Service Committee (HC 62) and to the First Report from the Liaison Committee (HC 100) 1986–7, Cmnd 78.

Report to the Prime Minister by the Efficiency Unit: Improving Management in Government: The next steps (1988).

First Report from the Agriculture Committee: Salmonella in eggs (1988–9), HC108–I and II.

First Report from the Defence Committee (1988–9), HC68.

Report of the Parliamentary Commissioner for Administration: The Barlow Clowes affair (1989), HC76.

Second Report from the Select Committee on Procedure: The workings of the select committee system (1989–90), HC19.

Annual Report of the Council on Tribunals (1989–90), HC64.

Annual Report of the Parliamentary Commissioner for Administration (1990), HC299.

Report of the Audit Commission: Footing the Bill: Financing provincial police forces (1990), Audit Commission.

Questions of Procedure for Ministers (1992), Cabinet Office.

FURTHER READING

In addition to the books listed in the References, the following are useful sources.

Brazier, R. (1988) *Constitutional Practice*, Clarendon Press: Oxford.
Cane, P. (1993) *An Introduction to Administrative Law*, Clarendon Press: Oxford.
Chapman, R. A. and Hunt, M. (eds) (1987) *Open Government*, Croom Helm: London.
Feldman, D. (1993) *Civil Liberties and Human Rights in England and Wales*, Clarendon Press: Oxford.
Finer, S. (ed.) (1975) *Adversary Politics and Electoral Reform*, Anthony Wigram: London.
Hartley, T. C. (1994) *The Foundations of European Community Law*, Clarendon Press: Oxford.
Holme, R. and Elliott, M. (eds) (1988) *1688–1988: Time for a New Constitution*, Macmillan: Basingstoke and London.
Jowell, J. and Oliver, D. (1989) *The Changing Constitution* (2nd edn), Clarendon Press: Oxford.
Lee, S. (1988) *Judging Judges*, Faber and Faber.
Marshall, G. (1986) *Constitutional Conventions*, Clarendon Press: Oxford.
Munro, C. (1987) *Studies in Constitutional Law*, Butterworths: London.
Oliver, D. (1991) *Government in the United Kingdom: The Search for Accountability, Effectiveness and Citizenship*, Open University Press: Milton Keynes.
Waldron, J. (1990) *The Law*, Routledge: London.
Woodhouse, D. (1994) *Ministers and Parliament: Accountability in Theory and Practice*, Clarendon Press: Oxford.

INDEX

Readers should refer also to the Contents and the lists of cases and statutes (pp iii–xii).